SPEAKING
ILL *of the*
DEAD

SPEAKING ILL *of the* DEAD

Jerks in Montana History

Edited by Dave Walter

Contributing Authors

Jon Axline

Salina Davis

Jodie Foley

Lyndel Meikle

Anne Sturdevant

Dave Walter

TWODOT®

GUILFORD, CONNECTICUT
HELENA, MONTANA
AN IMPRINT OF THE GLOBE PEQUOT PRESS

A · **TWODOT**® · **BOOK**

Copyright © 2000 Morris Book Publishing, LLC
Previously published by Falcon Publishing, Inc.

Library of Congress Cataloging-in-Publication Data
Speaking ill of the dead: jerks in Montana history / Jon Axline... [et al.].
    p.cm.
    ISBN-13: 978-1-58592-032-7

1. Montana—History—Anecdotes. 2. Montana—Biography—
Anecdotes. 3. Rogues and vagabonds—Montana—Biography—
Anecdotes.
4. Criminals—Montana—Biography—Anecdotes. I. Axline, Jon.

F731.6 .S65 2000
978.6--dc21   00-044310

Manufactured in the USA
First Edition/Seventh Printing

Contents

Introduction
Speaking Ill of the Dead: Jerks in Montana History
by Dave Walter

jerk *(n.)*, *slang*—a person regarded as fatuous, offensive,
undesirable, or eccentric; a numbskull, a creep, a loser, or
a contemptible fool (*etymology uncertain*).

In April 1996, Federal Bureau of Investigation agents captured
Ted Kaczynski—"the Unabomber"—in a cabin outside Lincoln,
Montana. As a result, the state received a wheelbarrow full of
unwanted publicity. Some of the reaction played off those catchy
slogans created by the state's tourism bureau, Travel Montana:

"Montana: The Last Best Place—to Hide!"
"Montana: Bigoted Sky Country"
"Montana: Crazies in Every Gulch"

All this furor might have died a slow, quiet death, had
Kaczynski's capture not been followed by a series of bellicose
activities perpetrated by the ultraconservative "Montana Militia."
Then the "Militia's" antics were succeeded by an eighty-one-day
standoff between Montana's dissident "Freemen" and FBI agents
near Jordan, in Garfield County.

Next—Montana's self-image still reeling—Rusty Weston, Jr.,
followed the "Freemen." Sometime-Helena resident Weston, in the
summer of 1998, rampaged through the Capitol in Washington,
D.C., and fatally shot two Capitol policemen. By this time, the fact
that Montana had run for several years *without any daytime speed
limit* on its highways (including the Interstate segments!) seemed
incidental.

One state wag commented, "It is long past time to replace Montana's
public relations firm." Two staff writers for the *Washington* (D.C.) *Post*
penned a column (July 28, 1999): "Montana: Land of the Loony Loners?"
Most Montanans simply drew deep breaths and hunkered down to
weather the public ridicule. For this is an old story here.

Montana, through the years, indeed has assembled a splendid gallery of historical misfits and "jerks." British nimrod Sir St. George Gore performed some of his best "game hog" escapades in eastern Montana; Mary Gleim terrorized Missoula's "red light district" for more than two decades; hooded Ku Klux Klansmen burned crosses all over the state in the 1920s; nudist Congressman Jacob Thorkelson became a "fellow traveler" of Adolf Hitler as World War II approached.

The state's setting remains conducive to the propagation of social and ideological whackos. With a population still less than 900,000—spread over 145,000 square miles—Montana offers lots of open space. It always has allowed its "jerks" plenty of room and has matched that spaciousness with a genuine tolerance of idiosyncrasies. It is more than coincidence that Bob Fletcher—who wrote the verse that became Cole Porter's classic "Don't Fence Me In"—was a Montanan.

Then, sometimes, that thin line between "rugged individualism" and bizarre behavior fades to obscurity, and Montana produces another "jerk." Thus the state will continue to draw its share of public criticism for the actions of extremists like Kaczynski, the "Freemen," and Rusty Weston. And yet, one should not panic. The current crop of misfits just needs to be seen in historical context. Hence the volume *Speaking Ill of the Dead: Jerks in Montana History.*

⤳

This idea of looking at "jerks" in the American West evolved as an antidote to Montana's statehood centennial celebration in 1989. Since that time, it has become an extremely popular session at the annual Montana History Conference, a talk delivered statewide for the Montana Committee for the Humanities' Speakers Bureau, and—finally—this volume.

In 1989 I was working on the reference desk at the Montana Historical Society Library in Helena. This position fields all kinds of incoming Montana-history inquiries—by phone, by mail, from walk-in patrons, and from the staff. Early in the year, requests for Montana information escalated sharply. National publicity for the state's centennial obviously had prompted historians, genealogists, and researchers to learn more about their Montana ancestors. The typical inquiry ran:

I have wondered about my great grandfather for a long time, and I hope you can help. Ezra Boxhalter rode from Ohio to

Montana Territory with a wagon train in the 1870s. What happened to him once he got there, though, I don't know. I think that he ended up as the Governor [or U.S. Senator, or Congressman, or judge]. . . .

Or the query said:

Congratulations on your state centennial. It reminds me that our aunt Bertha (Mrs. Fred) Windlass moved to Butte with her husband in 1906. I am looking for copies of obituaries for both Bertha and her husband. Fred started out working in the copper mines, but then he became a "Copper King" [or bank president, or lumber mogul, or cattle baron]. . . .

The perspective here is obvious. *Everyone's* ancestor had been an illustrious person, a citizen of real significance, a Montanan who mattered. *No one's* grandfather had ever spent his life as a clerk in a drug store, or as a sheepherder, or as a railroad worker, or as a sugar-beet farmer. Further, *no one* ever contemplated himself the descendant of a scoundrel, a misfit, or a criminal.

The conclusion here is equally obvious: when looking back, particularly at our ancestors, we tend to emphasize only the greatest aspects, only the most admirable characteristics, only the most wonderful things about our past. Conversely we tend to minimize, conveniently to ignore, or even to bury historical information that is uncomplimentary or distasteful.

The trouble with this selective approach to history is that it is wholly one-sided. It sanitizes our history. It strips the humor from our history. It becomes simple "hero worship." Worst of all, the "smiley face" analysis of history portrays a past that never was. The *real* past included *real* people—like us—people who were a combination of strengths and weaknesses, a mixture of admirable and inferior characteristics. They were *human*. And, for all of the honorable folks in the real past, there are some equally damnable characters.

⌒

Admittedly, an approach to Western history that celebrates its "jerks" has drawn some detractors. These critics honestly feel that it is founded on disrespect, that it panders to sensationalism, that it

3

amorally "speaks ill of the dead." I would counter that the past deserves an honest, objective look—or it is not history. It is simply panegyric, eulogy.

In addition, if the story of a "jerk" prompts the reader to investigate some aspect of Western history, that is sufficient justification for me. For, finally, a foray into the world of Montana "jerks" can encourage us to reevaluate our beliefs, to reassess our smugness, and to revise our approach to the past.

This volume also legitimately falls within a strong Montana tradition of looking with irreverence at our predecessors. As noted Montana historian K. Ross Toole once remarked, "Historians just dearly love rascals." The most stirring example of this genre is Dorothy M. Johnson and Robert T. Turner's *Bedside Book of Bastards* (New York: McGraw-Hill, 1973). This little-known work is a collaboration between a noted Western writer and a longtime University of Montana history professor, respectively. Their scope proved broad: from Parysatis in the fourth century B.C. to Liver-Eating Johnson in the nineteenth century A.D. Yet their focus remained "a bastard . . . as an obnoxious or nasty person. . . . Villains, murderers, plotters, stinkers, knaves, and assorted rascals"—in short, "jerks."

The *Bedside Book of Bastards* serves best when it reminds us not to take any historical interpretation too seriously. Because what Johnson and Turner—and the authors of this volume—are doing is using present-day standards to judge past people and past behavior. This mechanism constitutes an absolute travesty among historians! The professional historian argues that "we should strive to judge people and their actions in the context of their own times and their own situations."

The fledgling graduate student, on his first day in a big-university history department, is assembled with his associates. A full professor admonishes the group of neophytes *never* to judge past people and events by today's standards. As a group, the wanna-be historians swear that they *never* will stoop to such unethical depths. And they stick to that pledge . . . right up to the point at which they select thesis topics. Then they do what we all do—historians and nonhistorians alike: they earnestly interpret the past from a present-day perspective, relying on present-day criteria. It is extremely difficult to do otherwise.

By using current standards of judgment, in the case of a "jerk," we might find his behavior unusual, or unacceptable, or loathsome, or illegal, or—if we are really lucky—truly detestable! Frequently the "jerk's" contemporaries viewed him that way. Yet, sometimes only we—steeped in historical hindsight—carry the perception. Thus our look at "jerks in Montana history" remains an exercise in administering an ill-defined set of judgmental standards.

At the beginning, in 1989, no guidelines specified who qualified for the "Montana Hall of Shame." As a result, both men and women proposed their spouses; parents offered up their children, often as a group selection; everyone nominated his boss. Finally, for the sake of familial tranquility, we instituted one rule: the nominee must be dead. This requirement also has proven helpful in defending against the inevitable libel suits.

∽

In 1968 Democrat presidential candidate Bobby Kennedy was campaigning in a housing project on the south side of Chicago. Here aides introduced him to a ten-year-old Black girl. The young lady had been dressed and coiffed elegantly by her mother—a bright new dress, shiny patent-leather shoes, and her pigtails in ribbons.

In front of the snapping cameras, Kennedy posed a question to the young lady that he had used previously on the campaign trail. He asked, "If all good people were the color white, and all bad people were the color black, what would you be?" And, without a moment's hesitation, the girl looked the politician right in the eye and replied, "I'd be striped."

Montana has been the home of some reprehensible people, who were involved in some abhorrent activities—and they deserve "equal time!" The mission of this volume is to tell the stories of several of these nefarious Montanans—as well as some out-of-staters who "earned their stripes" here.

In fact, this is a book about striped Montanans. Like us, most of these subjects are a combination of the honorable and the dishonorable. Additional nominees are welcome. After all, if a Montanan knows anything, he knows that the supply of "jerks" is endless.

∽

Each of this volume's authors owes sincere gratitude to a bevy of friends and family who have inspired, assisted, reviewed, and advised him/her in the pursuit of these stories of Montana "jerks." However, all of the authors hold a common debt of gratitude to a single institution: the Montana Historical Society in Helena. As a repository of information, images, and material culture concerning the Montana past, the Society holds no equal. The "Sources" note concluding each chapter indicates just how seminal the Society's collections and staff have been to each and every one of us. Our collective thanks is immense.

In addition, for a decade, the Montana Historical Society has provided the authors with a forum to develop "jerk" tales. Beginning in 1989, the annual Montana History Conference has offered a "Jerks in Montana History" session—which has become a favorite among conference-goers. Again, our collective appreciation to the Society for its willingness to experiment with conference programming is immeasurable.

Finally, these authors are historians, not commercial writers. Rather than flounder in the market place and produce regrets to last our lifetimes, we enlisted the assistance of Ms. Marilyn Grant. This former associate editor of *Montana, The Magazine of Western History* has served as our "literary agent," and for this kindness we all are most indebted to her. Thank you so much, Marilyn.

The Unsaintly Sir St. George Gore
Slob Hunter Extraordinaire
by Dave Walter

Some "jerks" in this volume are homegrown. Others come to Montana from afar to perform their nefarious acts. None comes farther—or performs his reprehensible antics with greater excess—than Sir St. George Gore, the epitome of the "slob hunter."

Outfitted to the hilt for a "gentleman's safari" on the American Great Plains (1854-1857), the British "sportsman" slaughtered more than 4,000 bison, 1,500 elk, 2,000 deer, 1,500 antelope, 500 bear, and hundreds of assorted smaller animals and birds. Gore massacred half of those creatures in Montana's Yellowstone Valley during a ten-month period (1855-1856)—most frequently leaving their carcasses to rot.

In the end, however, the "nobleman" paid a severe price for his arrogance and his waste of natural resources. Ah, sweet retribution.

Each fall thousands of out-of-state hunters invade Montana. They pay dearly in license fees for the privilege of stalking Montana's game. The State Department of commerce estimates that each visiting hunter spends an average of $1,600 while here. And every fall the media carries stories of hunters who wound their guides, marksmen who drop a rancher's pet cow near the barn, and game hogs who unconscionably slaughter wildlife.

Yet all of these miscreants compare poorly with that paragon of the foreign nimrod: the Englishman Sir St. George Gore. On an 1854-1857 expedition that cost an estimated $250,000, Gore hunted lands now located in Colorado, Wyoming, Montana, and the Dakotas. He hunted in a style and to an extreme *never* duplicated on the Great Plains. In fact, Sir St. George Gore funded the largest private expedition into the Rocky Mountain West, either before or since.

The Gore family controlled vast estates in northwest Ireland, concentrated around Manor Gore, near Sligo. The family also held a long lineage in English aristocracy. The title "Baronet of Manor Gore," established in 1621, was one of the oldest baronetcies (a rank between knight and baron) in Ireland. George was born into this line of the landed gentry in 1811. He was educated at Winchester School and at Oriel College, Oxford. At the age of thirty-one, he received the title of "the Eighth Baronet of Manor Gore."

Soon George established his residence in the family's Victorian mansion. This manor house was located on fashionable Brunswick Square, in the seaside resort of Brighton, East Sussex, about fifty miles south of London. George's annual income exceeded $200,000, primarily from the family's substantial Irish land holdings—although he seldom visited the manor.

The Eighth Baronet was a stocky, hearty bachelor who was prematurely balding. A contemporary described him as "a fine built, stout, light haired, and resolute-looking man." Fully bearded, Gore sported "straw-colored Dundreary whiskers."

The Irish baronet meshed an appreciation of classical literature, music, and art with a real love of the outdoors. He was a member of England's elite Turf Club, and he earned a reputation as a skilled horseman, marksman, and fisherman. Sir St. George Gore epitomized the Victorian sportsman, scholar, and gentleman. He also proved an excellent judge of Irish whiskey, and he gained notoriety for his fiery temper. Indeed, George was the Victorian aristocrat to the hilt.

Gore followed another hunter, Sir William Drummond Stewart, the seventh baronet of Murthly, into the American West. A Scotsman, Stewart had toured the West from 1833 to 1838; he returned in 1843, again to hunt the Great Plains. Stewart and Gore had met in European hunting circles and become friends. Stewart recommended the American West to Gore as a bountiful hunting ground, replete with an infinite supply of wildlife.

On Stewart's recommendation, Sir St. George Gore arranged his Great Plains tour through the London office of the American Fur Company (AFC). This corporation operated home offices in New York and St. Louis, as well as trading posts throughout the American West, most notably in the Missouri River Valley.

Gore contracted the American Fur Company to provide him with the most current maps of the Rocky Mountain West and to use its St. Louis office to hire experienced frontiersmen to comprise his entourage. The company also agreed to supply the Gore expedition from its posts throughout the West and to exchange U.S. currency at any AFC office or post for drafts on Gore's Baring Brothers' London bank account.

The Irish baronet would be accompanied on the first leg of his American hunt by another well-heeled English sportsman, Sir William Thomas Spencer Wentworth-Fitzwilliam, the sixth earl of Fitzwilliam. Usually addressed as "Lord Fitzwilliam," Gore's companion was thirty-nine years old, married, a barrister, and a member of the English Parliament. His father was considered the richest man in the British nobility.

In January, 1854, the Gore party sailed from Southampton, England, for America: the forty-three-year-old Gore; his personal valet; his dog-handler and fifty hunting hounds; the eager Lord Fitzwilliam; huge amounts of crated supplies and equipment; Gore's personal carriage. At dockside, the group most resembled a safari embarking for the plains of Africa!

Gore's party arrived in New York in February, passed through Pittsburgh in early March, and reached St. Louis on March 12, 1854. Here the baronet outfitted for the two-year expedition through the American Fur Company office, as arranged. In addition to topping off his cache of supplies and purchasing some "Indian trade goods," Gore's AFC agents hired forty experienced frontiersmen—the very best—to comprise his retinue. Besides general laborers, he enlisted cooks, camp tenders, interpreters, hunters, teamsters, bullwhackers, and such specialists as wheelwrights and blacksmiths.

The company's hiring coups included Great Plains hunter and guide Henry Chatillon. In 1846 mountain man Chatillon had piloted the historian Francis Parkman's tour from St. Louis, along the Oregon Trail to Fort Laramie, and into the Rocky Mountains. Subsequently Parkman immortalized Chatillon in his classic *The California and Oregon Trail*, published first in 1849:

> Mounted on a hardy gray Wyandot pony, [Chatillon] wore a white blanket-coat, a broad hat of felt, mocassons [sic], and trousers of deer-skin, ornamented along the seams with rows of long fringes. His knife was stuck in his belt; his bullet-pouch and powder-horn hung at his side, and his rifle lay before him, resting against the high pommel of his saddle, which like all his equipments, had seen hard service, and was much the worse for wear.

In preparation for his tour, Gore had read Parkman. So, given the opportunity to employ the legendary Chatillon, he was eager to contract him at the top-guide price of five dollars per day.

The AFC then surpassed this coup by engaging fifty-year-old Jim Bridger ("Old Gabe"), already a living legend in the Trans-Mississippi West. Bridger had covered the Rocky Mountains for thirty years; he had discovered the Great Salt Lake in 1823; he had led fur expeditions all through the West; he had established Fort Bridger on the Oregon Trail in 1843.

Gore likewise paid Bridger the prime five-dollars-per-day wage— to serve as his personal driver and companion on the two-year trek. Somewhat surprisingly, Gore and Bridger would become fast friends, despite their real differences of background, education, and experience.

Once Gore had supervised the branding of his stock and the painting of his vehicles, the expedition was ready. From the federal Superintendent of Indian Affairs, Colonel Alfred Cumming, the baronet had received a passport to travel in "Indian country" to the west. The party left Westport (Kansas City), Missouri, in mid-June 1854, traveling west on the Oregon Trail, "in quest of anything that walked, bawled, flew, or swam." The caravan was unlike *anything* before seen in the West. In addition to the forty experienced frontiersmen, it included about 115 horses, 20 yoke of oxen, and 50 hunting dogs.

Experienced guide Henry Chatillon pointed the procession. The lead vehicle was Gore's two-horse carriage—the one he had freighted over from England. Bridger sat on the leather-cushioned driver's bench, while Gore and Lord Fitzwilliam lounged under the canvas sunshade on padded seats. The specially-made carriage converted into a sleeping compartment by cranking up its fitted top from the carriage bed. It had been repainted a bright yellow, and its chassis incorporated a series of coil springs to soften the ride for the aristocrat.

Strung out behind the carriage, in increasingly thick clouds of trail dust, were twenty-one modified Red River carts. These two-wheel, single-horse, Metis vehicles (*charrettes*) had been painted a shocking red. Their loads were covered with white canvas. Sixteen of the carts carried Gore's personal baggage; five carts contained the gear of the forty hired men and some "Indian trade goods."

Four large Conestoga wagons trailed the Red River carts. Six-horse-draft hitches pulled each of these vehicles. They packed all manner of foodstuffs and a full set of carpentry tools. Because vehicle breakdowns could delay travel, the Conestogas also carried a complete blacksmith shop and an extensive array of wheelwright's equipment, for on-the-spot repairs.

Deep in the choking dust rolled the last two vehicles: commercial freight wagons, hitched in tandem and hauled by eight yoke of oxen. Each wagon carried ten tons of bulk supplies. Horsemen herded the expedition's stock herd behind the procession. The seventy-five-head bunch contained extra horses, extra oxen, and several milk cows—the suppliers of milk for Gore's breakfast porridge.

And everywhere skittered Gore's fifty hunting hounds—sniffing, exploring, digging, chasing birds and small animals alike. The pack included eighteen purebred English foxhounds (trained for tracking) and thirty-two greyhounds (bred for the chase). An admiring reporter who saw these animals working the prairie outside Westport described them as "the most magnificent pack of dogs that were ever seen in this country."

Gore's personal arsenal filled one entire Red River cart. In addition to huge amounts of ammunition, kegs of gunpowder, and the materials to fabricate all types of shells and cartridges, it included more than one hundred custom-made pistols, rifles, and shotguns. An observer to whom Gore displayed his arms, noted the names of such celebrated English gunsmiths as James Purdey, Westley Richards, and Joseph Manton.

The Englishman's fishing equipment filled another Red River cart. Before leaving St. Louis, Gore had added to his retinue a skilled fly-tier. Upon reaching a stream that he wished to fish, Gore would detail the man to check the hatch on the water and then to fashion feathered lures to match. On occasion, Gore and Fitzwilliam caught hundreds of fish—enough to feed the entire camp at day's end.

Other travelers that season on the Oregon Trail included Mormons on their way to the Great Salt Lake, families headed for the lush valleys of Oregon, and little bands of men traveling to various placer-gold strikes in the Rocky Mountains. They all must have stood dumb, in absolute disbelief, as Gore's cavalcade passed—looking most like a medieval procession on its way to a shrine. Their bewilderment increased when they learned that Gore had traveled so very far from home simply to chase and hunt game.

The same amazement engulfed any Oregon Trail traveler who witnessed the pitching of Gore's camp. For the Celtic baronet had spared no creature comforts when planning his tour on the prairies. An observant journalist described the "unexampled camp luxuries."

The hired men first erected a sixteen-foot by twenty-foot, green-and-white striped, canvas wall tent. Within, they laid a full, fitted India-rubber pad and covered it with thick French carpets. Workers then hauled from the freight wagons, and erected, the tent's furnishings:

two wood-burning heater stoves; an oval, steel bathtub with the Gore family crest embossed on both sides; a portable iron table and a matching washstand; an ornamental brass bedstead and a feather bed; two lounge chairs; an oak dining table and single oak chair; dinnerware of the finest English pewter; heavy trunks containing the baronet's extensive wardrobe and his large collection of leather-bound classics; a fur-seated commode with removable pot.

Sir St. George Gore in his tent.

Jack Roberts Artist. Painting owned by The Lord Gore Restaurant at Manor Vail Lodge.
Originally printed in *The Amazing Adventures of Lord Gore* by Jack Roberts
(Silverton, Colo: Sundance Publications, 1977).

Ever the aristocrat, Sir St. George Gore ate alone—rather than with the hired help. A personal cook prepared Gore's meals, which were served by three frontiersmen who doubled as waiters. The menu combined fresh game, fish, and the high-quality staples he had brought along. The meals were complemented by fine French wines, English gins and brandies, and Irish whiskeys.

Gore frequently stayed up until midnight, reading by the several Camphene lamps burning in his tent and sipping his imported liquors. Although most of the hired help struck camp and hit the Oregon Trail by 5 A.M., their leader usually slept until 10 A.M., then bathed and ate a leisurely breakfast before beginning the day's hunt. While he and Fitzwilliam chased bison, coyotes, timber wolves, deer, antelope, and birds across the plains, his immediate party pushed to overtake the main procession.

The grand Gore cavalcade reached Fort Laramie, on the North Platte River, in mid-July 1854. The Englishman stored some of his supplies at the American Fur Company's nearby Gratiot's Houses and then established a temporary camp two miles up the Laramie River from the fort.

Within a week, Gore had mounted a full-retinue hunting trip into the nearby Medicine Bow Mountains and the high mountain parks of Colorado. After this three-month foray—punctuated by buffalo chases, confrontations with grizzly and black bears, the shooting of trophy elk bulls, and incredible trout fishing—Gore's caravan returned to Fort Laramie in mid-October.

The aristocrat then discharged most of his employees, paying their wages. He included healthy bonuses, to entice them to return in the spring. Gore retained only a half dozen men to tend the livestock herd through the winter. Chatillon and Bridger led many of the frontiersmen back to St. Louis for the winter. Lord Fitzwilliam accompanied this group and continued his travels to England, to sit in Parliament that winter. Gore took up winter quarters at Gratiot's Houses, from which he conducted several winter buffalo hunts.

In the middle of May 1855, the English sportsman rehired most of his men and embarked on the next leg of the expedition—into the Crow and Sioux strongholds of the Yellowstone River Valley. Jim Bridger would serve as Gore's scout, guide, carriage driver, and companion for the next seventeen months. After crossing the North Platte, the caravan pushed north, passed the ruins of the Portuguese Fort on the headwaters of the Powder River, and trailed down that drainage toward the Yellowstone.

Bridger's "tall tales" proved correct: The baronet could chase and kill scores of bison, elk, deer, antelope, wolves, grizzlies, black bear, bighorn sheep, and birds every day. Gore hunted most frequently from his favorite horse "Steel Trap"—a big, gray Kentucky thoroughbred that he had purchased in St. Louis and trained himself. In early summer, the Powder River Valley was a veritable hunter's paradise. However, unless the quarry were exceptional—of trophy quality—the baronet left the carcass to rot where it dropped on the prairie.

Although isolated in a vast prairie wilderness, this consummate hunter always maintained his elegant Victorian lifestyle. In addition to the medieval tent, daily bath, and luxurious furnishings, Gore surrounded himself with fine food, quality liquor, and good books— "unexampled camp luxuries." Aside from his valet and servants, only Jim Bridger was allowed in the aristocrat's green-and-white striped tent.

Frequently in the evening, following a sumptuous dinner, Gore would summon Bridger to his tent. Here they would drink Irish whiskey or English brandy into the night, while the nimrod read Shakespeare, Charles Dickens, and Robert Burns's poetry to the frontiersman. In return, Bridger—by all accounts a spellbinding storyteller—would relate tales of the American West, many of which he had lived!

When the hunting party reached the Yellowstone River, Bridger headed the procession upstream to the mouth of the Tongue River (the current site of Miles City, Montana). He then pushed up the Tongue about ten miles to the mouth of Pumpkin Creek, where he located a site for their new quarters: the 100- by 120-foot stockade to be known as "Fort Gore."

The baronet supervised the beginning of construction and then began hunting sweeps through the Yellowstone Valley—upstream as far as present-day Forsyth and downstream to the current town of Terry. In the course of these travels, he met and traded with local Crow bands. But he remained focused on the hunt. During the summer and fall of 1855, the Englishman devastated local herds, and flocks, and individual trophy beasts.

Through the winter of 1855-1856, Gore continued to hunt, almost daily. He broke his aristocratic pattern of separation only at Christmas, when he ate dinner with the men. And an incredible menu it was: roasted prairie chicken, broiled elk steaks, candied sweet potatoes, creamed corn, hot cinnamon buns, molasses, plum pudding, mincemeat pies, strong coffee, fine French wines, and Irish whiskey.

During that winter, one of Gore's men—a Spaniard known as Uno—died of natural causes. When the men wished to bury their companion in the fur-trade tradition (i.e., wrapped in blankets and laid in a shallow grave), their leader refused. He insisted that Uno receive a proper Christian burial and ordered one of the Red River carts dismantled to provide cut lumber for the coffin. He further detailed a squad to dig a grave six feet deep—no small chore in the frozen prairie sod.

To the party assembled around the grave, Sir St. George Gore read the Twenty-third Psalm from his King James Bible. He then returned to his quarters in respect, while the men filled the grave. Once again, the aristocrat simply could not relinquish his heritage, not even in the face of wilderness expediency.

Also during that winter, a raiding band of Piegans stole about forty horses from the company's herd. Gore's men pursued the thieves north for several days, but lost them in a blizzard. In response, the baronet doubled his night guard, and the party suffered no additional losses. Gore would replenish the herd in the spring by trading with local Crow bands in the Rosebud Valley.

The Irish baronet and his men lived at Fort Gore from July 1855 until May 1856. During this ten-month period, watchful Crows estimated that his hunting tally included 105 bear; more than 2,000 bison, and 1,600 elk and deer. Crow leaders complained about the devastation of their meat supply to the American Fur Company's factor at Fort Union, located near the confluence of the Yellowstone and the Missouri Rivers.

Factor James Kipp forwarded those charges to federal authorities in St. Louis. Although Superintendent of Indian Affairs Alfred Cumming became angered, he could do little to curtail the foreigner's activities—since he was removed almost two thousand miles from Fort Gore. However, Cumming contemplated a hot reception for the nimrod when he finally returned to St. Louis.

In the spring, Gore ordered his men to build two flatboats, each ten feet by twenty-four feet, to transport his trophy heads, animal hides, antler sets, and bison robes down the Tongue and Yellowstone Rivers to Fort Union. He and Bridger would lead the rest of the grand caravan to the fort, following the Yellowstone and hunting all the way.

Gore's plan, when he reached Fort Union, involved paying off about two dozen of his men, selling his surplus goods, livestock, and vehicles to the American Fur Company "at a fair price," and floating down the Missouri River with the remainder of his retinue to St. Louis—hunting all the way. For the Victorian had a date in October 1856 to join his aristocrat friends to hunt stag in the Scottish Highlands.

Gore's men torched Fort Gore in late May, but his cavalcade did not reach the Fort Union area until the end of June, because of his many side trips to hunt. The fish, birds, and game in the lower Yellowstone Valley were extremely rich, and the baronet followed his usual pattern of slaughter. When the overland vehicles finally reached the mouth of the Yellowstone, they had trophy heads and hides tied to the sides of all the Red River carts. The Celtic baronet established his camp on the south side of the Missouri River, almost directly opposite Fort Union.

Bison slaughtered on the Montana plains.
COURTESY MONTANA HISTORICAL SOCIETY, L. A. HUFFMAN PHOTOGRAPHER

The story of Sir St. George Gore's Great Plains expedition very well could have concluded at this point. By this time, the sportsman had survived on the Great Plains for two years—including two winters. And the purveyor of "unexampled camp luxuries" never once lowered his standards of Victorian elegance—or deviated from his "slob hunter" behavior.

The baronet lived for the chase, for the thrill of the kill, for the trophy heads. His prairie hunting behavior proved so extreme that it offended *both* local native bands and many of the frontiersman whom he had hired for the expedition. These Great Plains residents never fancied "sport hunting," particularly when it depleted their immediate food supply. So, upon arriving at Fort Union, Gore received a cool welcome.

In the mid-1850s, Fort Union served as the kingpin of the American Fur Company's trade network in the upper Missouri River Valley. The company's regional supervision belonged to longtime frontier capitalist Alexander Culbertson, but the experienced, seventy-year-old James Kipp ran the daily activities at the fort.

To honor the Gore-AFC agreement, Factor Kipp was prepared to provide the Irish baronet with U.S. currency to pay off some of his men and to purchase Gore's surplus goods, livestock, and vehicles "at a fair price." He also agreed to build two mackinaw boats—sixty-feet long, with twenty-foot beams—to transport the remainder of the party, its residual goods, and its trophies downriver to St. Louis.

Kipp performed these tasks with little enthusiasm, since he had fielded the "slob hunter" complaints from Crow and Piegan leaders that winter. And these tribes were vital to the AFC's upriver trade. However, Kipp was also a solid "company man," so he performed his prescribed duties. By coincidence, both Kipp's AFC superior, Alexander Culbertson, and the federal Indian agent for the upper Missouri, Alfred Vaughn, were visitors at the fort. They too treated the English sportsman with extreme reservation.

Kipp estimated that it would take his men five weeks to construct the two sixty-foot mackinaws. Gore received this news with pleasure, for he had hunted little around the confluence of the Yellowstone and Missouri Rivers. The baronet paid off twenty-seven of his men—providing sizeable bonuses—and the party's remaining sixteen members maintained the camp across the river from the fort. Gore split his time between hunting or fishing with Jim Bridger and separating his goods for sale to Kipp.

With some difficulty, the nimrod's men moved their camp and wagons and livestock herd to the north side of the Missouri. Here Gore stockpiled those supplies and equipment that he wished to reserve for his return trip to St. Louis. His men stacked the "surplus goods" on the prairie, within fifty feet of the fort's front gate. They pulled the extra wagons and Red River carts—even his bright-yellow carriage— to a spot nearby, and drove the livestock herd close to the fort. Gore spent the midday drinking whiskey, and he then informed Kipp that he was ready to negotiate.

But these talks went badly. Kipp seemingly believed that the foreigner was asking too much for the European staples; Gore apparently thought that the factor was taking advantage of him, because of his isolated circumstances. The two men argued. One of Gore's hired men observed:

> There was a misunderstanding as to the terms of the bargain, and [Gore] fancied that, in his remoteness from man, the Company was seeking to speculate upon his necessities. He [Gore] seems to have been mercurial, wrathful, effervescent, and reckless, and, heedless of the consequences, he would not stand for the terms [that Kipp] prescribed.

Kipp retreated through the fort gates. The intoxicated Englishman returned to his camp in a rage and fumed for several hours, punctuating his rantings with generous draughts of Irish whiskey.

By late afternoon, Gore's anger had produced a plan. He ordered a few of his men to drive the expedition's livestock a ways from the fort. Others he detailed to pull the twenty Red River carts, the four Conestoga wagons, and the two freight wagons in concentric circles around his bright-yellow, imported carriage, parked right in front of the fort's main gate.

Gore himself climbed into the one-of-a-kind carriage, poured lamp oil over the seats, and touched it off. Soon flames were licking at all the carts and wagons, and a huge plume of smoke was rising into the blue prairie sky. The baronet's intent was clear: he would destroy these valuable vehicles, rather than sell them to the duplicitous American Fur Company, at *any* price.

As the fire grew, the Irish baronet's anger rekindled. He ordered his men to pull items from the nearby stacks of "surplus goods" and pitch them into the conflagration. Crazed, he soon decided to burn *everything.* On his command, Gore's men heaved boxes and bales and chests into the crackling, super-hot pile.

The aristocrat sacrificed everything to his anger—the green-and-white striped tent, the brass bedstead and feather bed, the trunks of clothing and leather-bound books, the India-rubber pad and French carpets, the full set of pewterware, the sextants and chronometers and barometers, all of the fishing equipment, kegs of gunpowder, casks of fine liquor—even the oval bathtub, with the Gore family crest embossed on both sides.

Perhaps most irrationally, a frenzied Gore rushed toward the blaze and heaved in his leather satchel—containing his Baring Brothers' London bank drafts, his U.S. passport to travel in "Indian country," his letters of introduction, his expedition maps, and even his personal journal of the expedition—everything! With the fire roaring, he then tapped his casks of fine liquor and invited all non-AFC men to an all-night drunk.

Having exhausted his fuel supply, a fuming Gore stomped back to his camp and prepared a buffalo-robe bed beside the hired men's campfire. The blowout flourished on Gore's private liquor stock, and the men then graduated to the trade whiskey. The fire raged all night, and it still smoldered the next morning.

After dawn, Gore returned to the bonfire circle and observed that intense heat from the blaze had scorched the gates of the venerable fort. Unrepentant and spiteful, he ordered his men to rake the ashes to recover any scrap of metal and to hurl those fragments as far as possible into the Missouri's muddy waters, so no one from the American Fur Company could reuse them.

In the upper Missouri wilderness, removed by hundreds of miles from factories and supply warehouses, the wanton destruction of such precious goods and equipment was absolutely unforgivable. Not surprisingly, the contractual ties between Sir St. George Gore and the American Fur Company disintegrated in the flames of the baronet's pyre.

Now the Englishman had to reassess his situation. Without bank drafts, he could not purchase the two mackinaw boats from Kipp. So he decided to send his trophies downriver to St. Louis on his two Yellowstone River flatboats. Led by Bridger, he and the remaining men would ride horseback the well-traveled Missouri River trail, 1,760 miles to St. Louis. At least he could hunt the river corridor all the way downstream.

As with the aristocrat's arrival at Fort Union, the Gore hunting saga also could end here. However, to believers in retribution—for the "sportsman's" hunting excesses, for his fit of temper that destroyed valuable goods in the wilderness, and for his wanton arrogance—this tale will deliver retribution. In fact, the Gore story contains elements of Greek tragedy: the mighty protagonist first holds sway and then plunges to the depths because of a character flaw or a personal indiscretion.

Shortly after the bonfire episode, Jim Bridger rode downriver to Fort William, run by an "opposition" competitor of the American Fur Company. Here he obtained an area map, which he and the baronet studied carefully. The map contained a mountain range to the south of Fort Union, labeled "unexplored." Despite his circumstances, the huntsman in Gore could not be suppressed. He proposed to Bridger a side trip to investigate and hunt this intriguing "unexplored territory" (the Black Hills) and then to exit east, following the Cheyenne River to its confluence with the Missouri. The legendary guide agreed.

Gore detailed his two flatboats downriver, the 580 miles to the mouth of the Cheyenne, near Fort Pierre. There the expedition would reunite early in October. The Celtic baronet planned then to buy passage on a steamboat to St. Louis. In the meantime, the nimrod would convert his predicament into a special adventure.

So, in August 1856, the reconstituted Gore procession began its ascent of the Little Missouri River Valley—this time without carriage, or Red River carts packed with supplies, or Conestoga or freight wagons carrying "unexampled camp luxuries." Rather, the party consisted of Sir St. George Gore, Jim Bridger, eleven hired men, sixty-five saddle and pack horses, and the fifty hunting dogs.

After the pack string passed through a "bad lands" section, game in the Little Missouri Valley proved bountiful. The baronet reverted to his hunting pattern of chasing and shooting bison, elk, deer, antelope, grizzlies, and black bear at will. Although he had reduced his amenities (Gore now ate with the hired men, slept on the ground, and took a regular turn on night guard duty), meat and other staples remained plentiful.

Nevertheless—despite advice from the experienced traders at Fort William—the headstrong nimrod had penetrated deep into the heart of Teton Sioux country. After almost three weeks on the trail, the hunting party had moved three hundred miles off the Missouri and was approaching the mysterious Black Hills. More important, they were violating lands long held sacred by regional Sioux bands.

As they approached the distinctive Inyan Kara Mountain

(southwest of current Sundance, Wyoming), the 13-man party suddenly was surrounded by a war party of 135 Teton Sioux, led by Bear's Rib. This warrior's usual practice, when he found whites in the sacred Black Hills, was simply to kill them.

However, possibly fearing retaliation by the U.S. Army, Bear's Rib issued Gore an ultimatum. The party either could stand and fight, at the obvious ten-to-one odds. Or the men could abandon their weapons, their equipment, their horses, their clothing, and their food stuffs—and just walk away by the route they had entered the "unexplored" Black Hills.

Well, Gore may have been an arrogant aristocrat, but he was no fool. He fully understood the situation, so he chose to surrender and walk out. All the men hoped that Bear's Rib would not subsequently pursue such a vulnerable quarry. For the Irish baronet now *really* had been reduced to the basics of wilderness life.

For the next five weeks, Gore's band of thirteen naked men and their dogs struggled back down the Little Missouri drainage: living on roots, berries, lizards, insects, birds' eggs, and small game; cutting their feet on prickly pear cactus; both toasted and chilled by the September weather. Left defenseless with the loss of their weapons, the party traveled at night to avoid detection by hostiles. For the same reason, the men lived without warming or cooking fires.

After almost three hundred miles of excruciating overland travel, Gore, Bridger, and the hired men stumbled into a hunting band of friendly Hidatsa tribesmen near the mouth of the Little Missouri River. The natives fed the survivors and led them to their camp near Fort Berthold on the Missouri. It was the end of October 1856, and the English gentry was assembling to hunt stag in the Scottish Highlands—this year *without* Sir St. George Gore.

Reclothed, the Celtic baronet bought passage for Jim Bridger and the men on an "opposition" fur-company mackinaw, bound for St. Louis in mid-November. For the fare, he improvised a voucher to an "opposition" fur company in St. Louis. Bridger would instruct the crews on the two flatboats—still waiting at the mouth of the Cheyenne River—to proceed to St. Louis, and he would supervise the storage of Gore's spoils.

Then Gore, his valet and his dog-handler, and three other members of the original party settled into one of the Hidatsa earthen lodges in the Like-A-Fishhook village of Crow's Breast, near Fort Berthold. So the Gore tale does mete out some justice, some retribution:

during the winter of 1856 1857, the erudite aristocrat lived like a Hidatsa native, without lavish resources, without the amenities of European life, without any of his "unexampled camp luxuries."

In July 1857, the sportsman and his two servants boarded the "opposition" steamboat *Twilight* at Fort Berthold for St. Louis. Upon arrival, the baronet established himself in the exquisite Planter's House and spent two months socializing. Finally, from a warehouse, he recovered the substantial trophies and curiosities produced from his Great Plains safari. In late summer, the Gore party (including the pack of hunting dogs) traveled to New York City and then returned to England—in time for the 1857 Scottish stag hunt.

The baronet never did marry. He never did return to the American West—although he spent a portion of 1876 in the Florida Everglades. He died in 1878 at Inverness, Scotland, at the age of 67.

This sporting foray of Sir St. George Gore into the North American heartland—and specifically into Montana—is one of the first lavishly supplied and organized expeditions mounted solely to hunt and fish. The three-year trip cost an estimated $250,000—in mid-nineteenth-century dollars. However, cost was never a factor for Gore. What was important was the chase, the hunt, the kill, and one's ability to maintain his lifestyle, even in the wilderness.

Sir St. George Gore has earned full "jerk" status: for his wanton waste of precious supplies; for his demonstrable arrogance; for his hunting excesses. Historians estimate that Gore killed, over the course of the three-year expedition: 4,000 bison; 1,500 elk; 2,000 deer; 1,500 antelope; 500 bear, at least 100 of them grizzlies; scores of other assorted animals and birds.

Those figures alone—the baronet's personality aside—earn Sir St. George Gore the title of consummate "Jerk in Montana History." No question.

~

Sources

Two accounts, covering limited aspects of the Gore Expedition appear in the ten-volume series *Contributions to the Historical Society of Montana*: F. George Heldt, "Sir George Gore's Expedition," Vol. I (Helena, Mont.: Rocky Mountain Publishing Company, 1876), 128-131; James H. Bradley, "Sir George Gore's Expedition, 1854–1856," Vol. IX (Missoula, Mont.: Missoulian Publishers, 1923), 245-251.

Some of the principals in the story—e.g., Jim Bridger, Henry Chatillon, James Kipp, Alexander Culbertson—are the subjects of biographical sketches in the ten-volume set: LeRoy R. Hafen, ed., *The Mountain Men and the Fur Trade in the Far West* (Glendale, Calif.: Arthur H. Clark, 1968). The standard work on Bridger remains J. Cecil Alter, *James Bridger: Trapper, Frontiersman, Scout, and Guide* (Salt Lake City: Shepard Book Company, 1925), often found in its numerous, subsequent editions.

Although the work contains some erroneous information, the Gore tale is addressed in: John I. Merritt, *Baronets and Buffalo: The British Sportsman in the American West, 1833-1881* (Missoula, Mont.: Mountain Press, 1985). Somewhat marred by similar inaccuracies, see also: Clark C. Spence, "A Celtic Nimrod in the Old West," *Montana, The Magazine of Western History*, Vol. IX, #2 (Spring 1959), 56-66.

The very best source is the excellent work by Jack Roberts: *The Amazing Adventures of Lord Gore* (Silverton, Colo.: Sundance Publications, 1977). Based on some imaginative, thorough research, this account is rich in context, reasonable in its attribution of motives, and replete with maps, photographs, and illustrations. Where other authors have fumbled or fabricated or exaggerated the events of the expedition, Roberts tells a measured tale with verve and expertise.

No Paper Trail
Crooked Agents on the
Crow Reservation, 1874–1878
by Lyndel Meikle

Among the least forgivable Montana "jerks" are those who cheated and robbed their fellow man. Duplicitous Indian agents assigned to the Crow Reservation in the mid-1870s seized their appointments as opportunities to "get rich quick." They used many ploys to augment their government salaries. All of these schemes relied on the collusion of private-sector merchants who held federal supply contracts for the agent's Native American charges. A more sordid partnership could not have been forged in hell.

In 1876, when Lieutenant Colonel George Armstrong Custer fought and died at the Battle of the Little Big Horn—on the Crow Reservation—these Indian agents were betraying their trust to the very natives who had allied themselves with the U.S. military. Unfortunately this tale of government corruption, while set in the nineteenth century, remains timeless.

–Dave Walter

WHEN A HISTORIAN EMBARKS ON A WORK-RELATED RESEARCH PROJECT, she follows standard guidelines. She sets goals and objectives. She selects her subject on the basis of her need to determine particular facts about a relevant topic. However, when that historian is just poking around in old records on her own time, her philosophy can best be compared to picking out the cashews in a bowl of mixed nuts. She is very liable to pursue any tangent that appeals to her.

Among the more than 1,400 business letters in the archival collection at Grant-Kohrs Ranch National Historic Site in Deer Lodge is one written in 1892 by Montana cattle baron Conrad Kohrs. The letter is directed to L. H. Hershfield, the president of the Merchants Bank in Helena. In it, Kohrs emphatically states that his hired hands had nothing to do with the tarring and feathering of the agent on the Crow Reservation!

This intriguing statement offered a tangent worth following.

Perhaps the records at the Montana Historical Society in Helena could be used to investigate this incident? But it was not that simple. Over a matter of weeks, and then months, the quest led to printed reports dating back to the 1860s, through reels of microfilm and volumes of brittle newspapers, into the offices of the *Washington Post* in Washington, D.C., and eventually to the Crow Reservation in southeastern Montana.

A definitive answer to the Kohrs-Hershfield lead still has not been found. However, this historian now knows what an Indian agent was and why this one probably needed to be tarred and feathered.

From 1789 until 1824, the Office of the Secretary of War administered Indian affairs in the United States. In 1824 the government created a separate agency—the Office of Indian Affairs—within the War Department. In 1849 Congress transferred the Office of Indian Affairs to the Department of the Interior, and in 1947 it assumed the new name of the Bureau of Indian Affairs (BIA).

During the nineteenth century, two main types of jurisdictions existed within the Office of Indian Affairs: superintendencies and agencies. Superintendents assumed general responsibility for Indian affairs in a specific geographical area. Agents usually exercised responsibility for the affairs of one tribe or one reservation.

In 1869 the Office of Indian Affairs established the Crow Agency in southeastern Montana—where the tarring and feathering allegedly occurred—as part of the Montana Superintendency. Originally responsible for the Mountain Crows, the agency soon also supervised the River Crows. Although authorities abolished the Montana Superintendency in 1873, the Crow Agency continued to operate, as did four other Montana agencies: Fort Peck, Fort Belknap, Blackfeet, and Flathead.

My investigation of Montana-agency activities during the 1870s and 1880s reveals the agents to be well-qualified for full-blown "jerk" status. This discovery is neither new nor shocking to historians of Indian-white relations. Still, my investigation of old reports exposed an annoying pattern. Although the dishonesty of the agents is legendary and accusations of criminal activity are numerous, pinning their crimes on them from a late-twentieth-century perspective is difficult. Rarely does a "paper trail" exist.

Two factors produce this lack of documentation: The federal government did not always record its misdeeds or failures, sometimes for political reasons; and much tribal history exists only in the oral tradition, a realm frequently inaccessible to the white researcher. Nevertheless, though the complete picture may be impossible to draw, enough material exists to produce a revealing rough sketch. So, this examination focuses on Montana's Crow Agency from 1873 to 1878, and on three specific agents: Dr. James Wright (1873-1874); Dexter E. Clapp (1874-1876); George W. Frost (1877-1878).

In Major James Sanks Brisbin's incisive report of Indian frauds, submitted to General Philip Sheridan in December 1878, some very revealing observations appear:

> In 1873 . . . the old Crow Agency on the Yellowstone [River] had become too near the settlements. . . .

(This statement is just a subtle way of saying that white settlements gradually were encroaching on Crow Reservation boundaries.)

> . . . And it was desired to move the Indians into a more remote location where the opportunities for frauds would be greater and the liability to detection less.

(This latter statement honestly portrays the situation.)

The government moved the agency, and it appointed Dr. James Wright the Crow agent. His administration pleased few. Robert Cross, a trader associated with pioneer cattleman Nelson Story, had expected to make substantial profits from the new agency. The Brisbin report notes:

> He [Cross] said it was hard to get the Agent, old Dr. Wright, to help them make money out of the Indians, as Wright was a Methodist minister and had always been a good and honest man, until he got into the Indian Department. Dr. Wright's wife . . . was anxious to make money. She wanted to make enough out of the Indian business so she and the Doctor could go back to their home in the East and live comfortably the rest of their days.

It is likely that Wright finally capitulated, however, because Brisbin notes that Cross told Yellowstone Valley stockman Horace Countryman that "he had entered into an arrangement with Wright for making money at the Agency, and they were to share the profits equally between them." Official government policy assigned each agency to a religious body and then employed ministers as Indian agents. Some historians question, however, whether the employees thus obtained were religious men turned agents, or agents who conveniently became religious.

General James S. Brisbin.

"Making money from the Indians" developed as the theme of this historical investigation. Although Brisbin's report does not detail Dr. Wright's tenure, it is explicit about the activities of his successor, Dexter Clapp. Clapp's term as agent proved much more controversial, and many charges were brought against him.

So how did one "make money from the Indians?" The accusations against Agent Clapp are most revealing.

In 1878 the Commissioner of Indian Affairs in Washington, D.C., detailed Captain Edward Ball, of the Second U.S. Cavalry, to investigate charges of corruption at the Crow Agency. In his subsequent report to the commissioner, Captain Ball alleged open fraud. Of fifty-seven barrels of pork delivered to the Crow Agency in 1876 by contractor Nelson Story of Bozeman, Ball found them to contain not "mess pork," as required by the government contract, but the entire hog, ham and feet excluded. Ball continued:

> That portion of the pork belonging to "mess pork" was of good quality and would have passed the inspection had it been packed separately. But the entire head, shoulders, backbone, and tail, with all the trimmings from the hams, were also packed.

Ball rejected the shipment and added,

> I would further state that . . . while at the Agency and previous to my inspection of this pork, Mr. Nelson Story, contractor, made two propositions to me to defraud the Government and cheat the Indians out of their supplies. In each of these propositions it was evident to me that the agent Mr. Dexter E. Clapp was a party to the proposed fraud.

The initial fraud allegedly suggested by Story to Ball required the captain to accept the pork shipments at 450 pounds to the barrel, when the barrels actually averaged about 250 pounds. For his cooperation, Ball would receive $1,000.

The second alleged proposition made by Story to Ball directed the officer to certify the receipt of approximately three hundred thousand pounds of flour—flour that, in reality, had not been delivered. Story noted that "they would make a good thing of it," if Ball would cooperate. When the captain suggested that Agent Clapp

Nelson Story.

might not agree to the scheme, Story was alleged to have replied, "Yes, he will. That is all right with the agent."

Captain Ball then asked Story on what the poor Indians would subsist if they perpetrated this flour fraud. According to Ball's report, Story replied that, "There were plenty of buffalo, and they could live on buffalo meat, as it was good enough for them." Ironically, another charge against Story was that he had stolen cases of cartridges—which the Crow surely would need if they were to subsist on buffalo, as he suggested.

Captain Ball proceeded to Agent Clapp's store, where two thousand sacks of new flour reportedly awaited his inspection. When he arrived, he found the new flour stacked with flour received the preceding year. He then separated the shipments and counted the new flour sacks. They numbered only 1,197 sacks, or 803 sacks short of the order. Ball suspected that Clapp expected him blindly to add the old sacks of flour to this total. At least, Ball conceded, the new shipment was of excellent quality.

Agent Clapp and contractor Story appeared to have tried to cover their bets—just in case Captain Ball refused to take a bribe and proved wise enough to notice the old flour sacks mixed in with the new shipment. According to agency procedure, the inspecting authority (in this case Captain Ball) would insert a probe into each sack, inspect the flour, and brand the sack with paint if he accepted it.

Contractor Story, in this particular case, had requested the miller who processed the flour to package it in double sacks. That is, the flour was sacked, the sack sewn shut, and then the entire sack was placed inside a second sack that was sewn shut. With the flour in double sacks, it would be possible to strip off the outer sack once it had been branded and then present the flour for a second inspection. In this way the contractor could double the apparent number of flour sacks in his inventory.

Fortunately, the miller had informed Captain Ball of the contractor's request to sack the flour in this unusual way, so he understood the ruse. Otherwise, Ball probably would have branded only the outer sack upon acceptance.

Captain Ball had encountered the two most common types of agency fraud: providing inferior goods, and receiving payment for goods never delivered. The open-range character of the Crow Reservation also created an opportunity for another, typically Western type of theft—cattle rustling.

The U.S. Army believed that, if the buffalo could be eradicated, the job of taming the Great Plains natives would be relatively simple. To this end, the population of bison in this country was reduced from an estimated 60 million when Lewis and Clark made their historic journey (1804–1806) to fewer than 500 animals in the wild by the mid-1880s. The War Department fervently endorsed this slaughter.

In return for this eradication, the military undertook to provide beef to the Indians. William Carr of Bozeman accused Nelson Story, the Crow Agency contractor, of taking forty head of cattle from the agency, placing them in his ox train, and sending them to the Missouri River country. Captain Ball noted that the matter of cattle thefts normally did not fall under his jurisdiction. However, he had received so many such reports that he considered it his duty "as an officer of the Government to lay them before the Department for its consideration." Ball strongly recommended an investigation of these reports.

The Department of the Interior investigated the charges against Agent Clapp. Then it added new charges:
—white cattlemen had been allowed to run their cattle on reservation land;
—the Department brand (ID) had been altered on some reservation stock;
—when a shipment of cattle arrived at the Agency, only the heaviest ones were weighed, and this figure then was accepted as the "average" weight of the entire shipment.

Other charges arose against both the agent and the contractor. They included the sale of annuity goods—staples that should have been distributed to the Crows without charge—to Indian and white

Indian Agents on the Crow Agency, Montana Territory, 1869-1878

Agent	Date of Appointment
Capt. Erskine M. Camp	June 2, 1869
Fellows D. Pease	September 9, 1870
Dr. James Wright	July 17, 1873
Dexter E. Clapp	October 7, 1874
Lewis H. Carpenter	August 15, 1876
George W. Frost	April 26, 1877
David Kern	Appointed August 2, 1878, but did not serve
Augustus R. Keller	November 4, 1878

alike. However, the Crows might not have benefitted *even if* the goods had been distributed. An affidavit from Captain George Leslie Browning, which appears in Brisbin's report, claims that many of the goods were simply unfit for use. These included thousands of dollars of such merchandise as,

> ... overcoats with velvet collars, cashmere pants and vests, all of a material too light and fine to be of use to the Indians, and not one tenth part of which were ever used by them, they being traded off almost immediately to squaw men and other whites at the agency and elsewhere.

Additional allegations appeared that Agent Clapp had hired some of his cronies, at high wages, to perform work for which there had been lower bidders. Page after page of charges from more than one dozen witnesses built a very convincing case against the agent. Finally federal prosecutors also brought charges against Nelson Story, the contractor. At this point, however, the "paper trail" disappears.

A jury acquitted the contractor. A bitter Captain Ball learned that Story had bragged that his acquittal cost him $10,000. This amounts to a considerable sum of money in any age. If this claim was true, the bribe gives a clear indication of "the wealth to be made from the Indians." Complicating the issue was the fact that many of the witnesses against the contractor were men who had hoped to make money from the agency themselves, so they could hardly be considered disinterested parties.

So what became of the Reverend Dexter Clapp? He simply . . . left—as did his predecessor Dr. Wright, and as would his successor, the Reverend George W. Frost. The accusations against Frost were numerous, and his alleged crimes made a mockery of the Indian-agency system. He paid for goods not delivered; he did not pay for goods that were delivered. He paid wages to nonexistent employees; he failed to pay real employees. In time he was suspended and replaced by Agent A. R. Keller. Further research is required to discover whether Keller followed in the footsteps of Wright and Clapp and Frost.

The absence of a "paper trail" is remarkable. None of these dealings on the Crow Agency is mentioned in the annual reports of the Superintendent of Indian Affairs. While contemporary newspaper accounts list accusations, they report no clear outcome of the investigations. Crow oral histories are very selective, are not easily accessed by traditional white historians, and do not provide what a law-enforcement officer would consider "probable cause."

That lack of a "paper trail" is even evident in modern times. Official government documents recently written present the three Crow agents as nothing more than civil servants. The National Park Service has produced such a document within the last twenty years. It gives the reader the impression that Agents Wright, Clapp, and Frost fulfilled their duties as expected, and that no controversy surrounded their administrations.

The author of that document, when recently asked why his narrative fails to mention these accusations against the agents, stated:

> The study was basically an historical overview of the area, and the question of agents was not really relevant to the projected interpretive themes as proposed by the enabling legislation, and. . . .

Should then the Park Service consider reviewing this portion of the study, to provide a fuller, more accurate picture of the agency's operation—particularly in view of the many interpretive changes made in Native American studies during the last twenty years? To this inquiry the author responded,

> No. If someone were to become personally interested, that is the only way I see it being done. As I said, it is not really relevant to the interpretive themes, and. . . .

The public historian knows better! If the *truth* about those agents is "not really relevant," surely it is at least inappropriate to perpetuate *lies* about them. The maxim observes: "Those who cannot learn from the past are condemned to repeat it." Yet, if the recorded history is a lie, what does it teach?

With unlimited time and resources, one could probably find sufficient documentation to build a solid case against these agents, but that would not be an easy task. The federal-government record system has evolved into an unwieldy mass of incomplete cross-references, widely scattered documents, and discreet omissions.

Certainly no one today is interested in protecting the reputations of these long-dead agents. However, the system that allowed these men to resign and quietly slip away—leaving little or no documentation—remains as active and useful today as it was 125 years ago. A few comparisons will suffice.

During the 1800s, federal nepotism ran rampant. As the Commissioner of Indian Affairs explained in his annual report for 1877, it was possible for an Indian agent to employ his son as a clerk for $1,000 per year, his daughter as a teacher at $600 a year, and his brother as a farmer for $900 per year. With federal laws currently in place to prevent this type of nepotism, it remains common for special-interest groups to hire the spouses of political appointees and of elected officials to serve as "consultants."

Officials at the highest levels may display sticky fingers. Charles N. Hoffman, appointed subagent for the Crows and Assiniboines in 1867, stopped by the office of the Secretary of the Board of Indian Commissioners in 1873. He was curious because, between 1867 and 1869, the tribes for which he held responsibility should have received $120,000 in annuity goods. They had received about 15 percent of that amount.

Government records showed that all the allocated money had been spent. Hoffman never could determine where the funds had been diverted, but the "mistake" clearly occurred in Washington, D.C. In comparison, in 1984, the Chief of Staff of the federal Health and Human Services (HHS) agency was indicted for diverting more than $33,000 in funds (earmarked for a foundation working under an HHS grant) to his personal credit-union account.

The *Bozeman Times* ran several editorials in 1876 accusing Agent Clapp of favoring a particular contractor. And, in 1982 the Deputy Assistant Secretary of the Department of Housing and Urban Development (HUD) resigned after the Inspector General released a report alleging that the deputy had received financial compensation in return for the favorable treatment of private developers.

The similarities between the activities of the early Indian agents and the abuses reported today extend beyond the types of crimes for which these government employees are accused. Today, as 125 years ago, very frequently "no paper trail" remains. The accused often are allowed simply to resign. Because no conviction exists, often no documentation exists—or it is scattered, sporadic.

In conclusion, one possible solution to the historical problem of crooked agents can be offered. The Sioux leader Red Cloud made the suggestion. He said,

I don't see why the Government changes our Agents. When one Agent gets rich at his trade of looking after us and has about all he wants, he may stop his stealing and leave us the property which belongs to us, if he keeps his place.

Perhaps Red Cloud's solution would have worked in Montana Territory during the 1870s and 1880s. Or was there no limit to the greed of people like Dr. Wright, Dexter Clapp, and George Frost—federal employees who saw public service as a shortcut to private wealth?

~

Sources

The basic official source for following activities on the Crow Reservation during the 1870s and 1880s is the series of *Annual Reports of the Commissioner of Indian Affairs to the Secretary of the Interior* (Washington, D.C.: Government Printing Office, 1861-1902). In these serial set volumes, the researcher can track the annual reports of the respective Crow agents.

Major James Sanks Brisbin's 1878 report to General Phillip Sheridan on Indian-agency frauds can be found in the archival holdings of the Montana Historical Society in Helena: Manuscript Collection 39: the James Sanks Brisbin Papers, Box 1, folders 11-28. Captain Edward Ball's 1878 submission exists as Appendix N to Brisbin's report: MC 39, folder 22.

An additional, equally fertile source for researching fraud on Montana Indian reservations during this period is the general correspondence preserved between individual agents and their superintendents. See particularly the microfilm holdings of the Montana Historical Society Library/Archives: Microfilm #293: Crow Indian Agency Records, 1877-1894; Microfilm #358: U.S. Bureau of Indian Affairs, Montana Superintendency Records, 1870-1873; Microfilm #389 (reels 79-86): Indian Census Rolls, Crow Reservation, 1891-1940; Microfilm #389a (reels 1-3): Records of the Montana Superintendency of Indian Affairs, 1867-1873; Microfilm #389b (reels 2-3, 8-9, 12, 14-16, 26, 53): Reports of Inspection of the Field Jurisdictions of the Office of Indian Affairs, Montana, 1873-1900.

The Red Cloud quotation, regarding Indian agents, appears in: Ruth A. Gallaher, "The Indian Agent in the United States since 1850," *Iowa Journal of History and Politics*, Vol. 14, #2 (April 1916), 189.

A thematic study of the Crow, in the context of relations with the federal government, is the National Park Service publication: Edwin C. Bearss, *Bighorn Canyon National Recreation Area: Montana-Wyoming Basic Data Study*, 2 vols. (Washington, D.C.: NPS Office of History and Historic Architecture, Eastern Service Center, February, 1970).

The best available works on Crow history include: Rodney Frey, *The World of the Crow Indians: As Driftwood Lodges* (Norman: University of Oklahoma, 1987);

Frederick E. Hoxie, *Parading through History: The Making of the Crow Nation in America, 1805-1935* (Cambridge, England: Cambridge University Press, 1995); Robert H. Lowie, *The Crow Indians* (New York: Holt, Rinehart and Winston, 1935; and Lincoln: University of Nebraska, 1983); Joe Medicine Crow and Charles Bradley, Jr., *The Crow Indians: 100 Years of Acculturation* (Wyola, Mont.: Wyola Bilingual Project, 1976); Peter Nobokov, *Two Leggings: The Making of a Crow Warrior* (New York: Crowell, 1967; and Lincoln: University of Nebraska, 1982).

⌁

Although I had gained some oral-history interviewing experience prior to tackling the topic of Crow Indian agents, this research provided my first opportunity to work in the oral-history *tradition*. While archival material provided much pertinent information, my wanderings around the Crow Reservation, graciously guided by Mickey Old Coyote, created the greatest fascination.

In the end, I learned nothing on the reservation about the alleged 1892 tarring-and-feathering or about Agent Dexter Clapp's tenure there. To the Crows, Clapp had become just another agent who came, robbed everyone, and left. He existed as no part of the Crow culture, and he seems to hold no place in Crow history. While this is perfectly understandable, it is frustrating! On the other hand, I did learn how to cure nightmares and insomnia, and I did find out where meadowlarks go in the winter, and I did learn a lot of Crow history and philosophy.

The incident that remains most impressive to me has little to do with Indian agents, except as it relates to the descendants of Fellows D. Pease, who served as the Crow agent before James Wright. I was sitting outside the home of tribal-council member Bill Pease, drinking coffee and learning about some of the contemporary issues on the Crow Reservation. Other tribal members arrived to discuss some business matters, and in the course of the conversation, a woman called "Grandma Beans" was mentioned.

She was related somehow to the Crows who recently had arrived. But "beans" and "peas" exist as the same word in the Crow language. And it suddenly occurred to one of the new arrivals that "Grandma Beans" was really a descendant of Agent Pease. Thus *they* were related to *Bill Pease*. I quickly lost track of who was whom as the speakers explored the relationship. But I was delighted to watch family connections emerge on the basis of something so simple as a translated word.

If understanding one word can bring people together, think how powerful a full understanding of each other's culture could be!

Fell Deeds
Unconscionable Timber Depredations on Montana Public Lands
by Lyndel Meikle

Desecrating what belongs to all Montanans or all Americans—the public lands—earns a host of our forebears a spot in the "Montana Hall of Shame." Prime violators include the open-range stockmen who overgrazed the public domain in central and eastern Montana during the 1880s and the twentieth-century corporate polluters of Montana's air and water. Lumber companies that illegally cut timber off public-domain lands in the late nineteenth century also skulk into the "Hall."

Specifically, the Montana Improvement Company and the Bitter Root Development Company—in league with the Northern Pacific Railroad and the Anaconda Copper Mining Company—raped Montana's public forests for private profit. This protracted program of theft scrambled territorial politics and reached deep into the federal Department of the Interior.

In this chapter, we meet not only the villainous depredators, but three champions. Each hero, in his own way, became a savior of America's timber lands: John Muir, Gifford Pinchot, and Theodore Roosevelt. Montana's forests survive today because of their complementary work almost a century ago.

–Dave Walter

A SEARCH FOR "JERKS" ON THE WESTERN LANDSCAPE PRETTY QUICKLY turns up several groups of Euro-American entrepreneurs who exploited the nation's public domain for personal gain. From greedy fur trappers, to rapacious hydraulic miners, to avaricious open-range stockmen, to clueless dryland homesteaders, many of these "field entrepreneurs" served America's corporate profiteers. All of them, however, sought "something for nothing" from the West's vast public lands.

Clearly none of these groups has earned greater opprobrium than those capitalists who stole billions of board feet of timber from Western forests—all under the guise of progress, laissez-faire economics, and "taming the frontier."

The practice of reforestation began in Germany more than six hundred years ago. This system subsequently spread through much of Europe. However, when colonists reached the shores of the New World, they encountered endless forests, stretching as far to the north, and to the south, and to the west as white explorers could travel. So, without restriction, the immigrants cut timber for homes, barns, businesses, ships, and manufactured goods. They also burned off valuable timber simply to clear land for the plow—"slash-and-burn" techniques.

Then, by the time the colonies became a fledgling nation, some farseeing Americans worried that such wholesale destruction of forests might leave the new nation with insufficient timber to build ships. So, in 1799, Congress authorized the President to purchase land on which grew timber suitable for naval uses.

Meanwhile, out West, the government rarely interfered directly with native bands using a few lodgepole pines for tipi poles. For the indigenous peoples used the trees—like the bison and the camas root—in reasonable quantities, with respect.

The first sawmill in what would become Montana Territory was located at St. Mary's Mission (Stevensville) in the Bitterroot Valley in the 1840s. Both missions and trading posts made inroads into the stands of timber along Montana river bottoms. Still, these were essentially domestic uses. Missions, trading posts, homes, barns, and line fences hardly threatened the vast forests that covered the mountains and foothills of the western one-third of Montana.

Then, in 1862, Montana's placer-gold rush began. Miners cut more and more timber as they built flumes, stamp mills, tramways, trestles, and underground shafts. Montana timber made possible some amazing engineering feats in the early days of mining. However, it took the arrival of the railroad in the 1880s to combine timber, mining, and railroad interests in an extraordinary, symbiotic relationship that would lay waste to vast tracts of public land. The lumbermen needed saw logs and a market. The mines needed incredible amounts of timber, whereas the railroads needed both timber and financing. All three industries turned to the public lands for their raw materials.

Let it be said, *some timber was cut legally.* Under the Timber Culture Act of 1873, homesteaders could increase the size of their claims from 160 acres to 320 acres, *if* they would grow 40 acres of trees on the new acreage. However, claimants frequently undermined the legislative intent of this act. They simply selected a wooded plot of 160 acres, logged off 120 acres of timber, and retained 40 acres in trees.

Subsequent federal legislation also produced legal timber harvests. The Free Timber Act of 1878 was designed to allow timber to be removed from land which was valuable chiefly because of its mineral content. Under the Timber and Stone Act (1878), entrants could file on 160 acres of land that were not valuable for mining or agricultural purposes. Most often this proved to be wooded land, which could be logged—but only for domestic use, not for commercial purposes. Congress amended the Timber and Stone Act in 1892 to include Montana.

Railroad land grants also included forests. Federal land grants to railroads began in 1850. By 1860 Congress had dispensed 20 million acres of formerly public land to various rail companies to finance their construction projects. Eventually railroads would receive 116 million acres; they would *use* many more millions of acres. It was *those other* millions of acres—land that did not fall within land grants or under provisions of various congressional acts—that formed the basis of the government's charges of timber depredations.

In the 1860s, Western mining and railroad harvests of public timber began to cause controversy. The government hoped to be able to control timber use. However, by 1870, Commissioner of Mining Statistics R. W. Raymond stated that he did not believe that the entire United States Army could enforce timber-cutting regulations on public lands.

Through the 1870s, Secretary of the Interior Carl Schurz tried mightily to curtail illegal cutting. In 1882, though, Schurz was replaced by Henry M. Teller, a mine owner and former railroad company attorney. Suddenly the fox had been sent to guard the hens.

Meanwhile, America's first transcontinental railroad had been completed at Promontory Point, Utah, in 1869. By the 1880s, the Utah and Northern had connected Montana Territory with the Union Pacific line, the Northern Pacific Railroad had completed (1883) a transcontinental line through Montana, and the Great Northern Railway had built (1887) west along the Hi-Line to Great Falls, with connections to Butte.

The original Congressional land grant to the Northern Pacific Railroad comprised 47 million acres. Nearly 15 million of this acreage was in Montana—and 1.5 million acres of the Montana land was timbered. Fifteen million acres is one-and-one-half times the size of Switzerland! Timbered land in the amount of 1.5 million acres is the equivalent of three-quarters of Yellowstone National Park!

While still pushing to close the gap in its transcontinental line, the Northern Pacific had contracted with Eddy, Hammond, and Company of Missoula to supply the railroad with its construction materials—building lumber, ties, tunnel timbers, and trestle supports. This proved a very sizeable transaction.

Assured of continued railroad business, the lumber company incorporated in 1882, capitalizing at $2 million. Ironically, it took the name of the Montana *Improvement* Company (MIC). Of the $2 million capitalization, the Northern Pacific provided $1,000,100, a controlling interest.

The Montana Improvement Company operated under the guiding hand of Andrew B. Hammond. This entrepreneur eventually used money extracted from Montana timber harvests to finance his other enterprises in California and Oregon. Montana "Copper King" Marcus Daly also proved to be an incorporator and a major investor in the MIC.

While the Northern Pacific main line remained "under construction," the MIC (as the N. P.'s contractor) had federal permission to cut timber for construction purposes from lands "adjacent to" the railroad's land grant. MIC's rather liberal interpretation of this permission included cutting timber on the Flathead (Indian) Reserve— sometimes at points hundreds of miles from the mainline.

This federal permission supposedly terminated when the Northern Pacific no longer was "under construction" to the West Coast. With great ceremony, Henry Villard and other Northern Pacific officials attended the "Last Spike Ceremony," near Garrison, Montana Territory, in 1883. Yet, in 1884, the Secretary of the Interior received complaints that MIC had hired hundreds of men again to cut trees on the Flathead Reserve. Moreover, these MIC employees had threatened locals who attempted to cut firewood or fenceposts on reserve land.

Soon other Western lumbermen were complaining about the Montana corporation that had grown to dominate the industry, both by its size and by receiving favorable Northern Pacific freight rates. In 1884 the railroad charged MIC $23 to haul each carload of lumber. The N. P. charged all other lumbermen $47 per carload—more than twice the MIC rate!

The Department of the Interior did investigate these complaints. By arrangement, Special Timber Agent M. H. Haley would report his findings to General Land Office Commissioner William Andrew Jackson Sparks in Washington, D.C.

Northern Pacific officials clearly were concerned about the course of Haley's investigations. On June 2, 1885, N. P. Vice-President Thomas F. Oakes wrote to Montana Territorial Governor Samuel T. Hauser. Interestingly, Hauser was both a Helena banker and an area mine operator. He regularly used the Northern Pacific's Wickes branch line to supply his mines and to carry ore from these mines to his Helena stamp mill.

Oakes's salutation to the Territorial Governor Hauser was simply "S.T.H."

Read this over carefully and let me know if you intend to take this position in reference to our timber interests.

If we have no rights in this property [that] you will respect, I shall at once withdraw our deposits from your bank. I also will put the Wickes Branch on a strictly local basis. And in every other respect I will make things so hot for you, you will think the Devil is after you.

The Northern Pacific Company has not spent $70,000,000 to be bulldozed by you or anybody else.

Let me know exactly what your position is. The Northern Pacific Company has the right to demand of you the fullest support in every reasonable effort to protect its interests. It has never asked anything of you thus far. But it has done a great deal for you and your interests thus far, with very little return.

Oakes closed the missive simply "T.F.O."

Some wag has noted that, when a politician changes his position, it is sometimes difficult to tell whether he has seen the light or felt the heat. It is *not* difficult in this instance, however. The Northern Pacific applied the heat, and Governor Hauser soon was calling for changes in federal legislation addressing public timber.

In conjunction with Montana Congressional Delegate Joseph K. Toole, Hauser quickly submitted a petition to the Department of the Interior that had been signed by lumber dealers in the Helena area. The petition claimed that it was difficult to secure timber under the Free Timber Act of 1878 because the government had not identified all the sites where minerals existed.

The Toole/Hauser petition requested that the department's circular regulations on the Free Timber Act be rewritten to allow trees to be cut in any district where mines existed. This marked a departure from the existing requirement that the land in question must actually contain valuable minerals. Since prospectors already had swarmed all over western Montana in their quest for gold, most of the territory's timbered land would qualify under the Toole/Hauser proposal.

The petition then stretched further—requesting that, if insufficient timber existed in the immediate area of a mine, then timber in contiguous districts could be cut. And the petition continued. The existing Free Timber Act stipulated that such timber must be cut by individuals for their own use. Toole and Hauser asked that mill owners also be able to cut timber from mineral lands and sell it to the miners.

Vice-President Oakes must have been most pleased.

The intent of the Free Timber Act of 1878 was to allow settlers to supply their own needs, not to subsidize private enterprise. However, the Toole/Hauser liberalization of the law would have produced precisely the opposite effect. By allowing lumber companies to sell to other businesses, the companies could establish virtual monopolies in parts of western Montana—all on the basis of public-domain timber. At times, some of Montana's territorial entrepreneurs seemed unable to distinguish between their "need" and their "greed." Fortunately, the pleas of Toole and Hauser went largely unheard by the Department of the Interior.

In October 1885, Montana newspapers published the text of Special Timber Agent J. J. Haley's letter to General Land Office Commissioner Sparks. As quoted in the *Helena* (Montana) *Weekly Independent* (October 15, 1885), Haley accused MIC of illegally cutting from the public domain: 45,100,000 board feet of lumber and bridge timber; 84,744 railroad ties; 15,400,000 shingles; 20,000 cedar posts; 32,035 cords of wood.

Haley estimated that this unlawful cut was worth more than $600,000. On today's market, the total cost of the illegally harvested materials would exceed $20 million: cut lumber, $9,020,000; shingles, $10,730,000; posts, $300,000; cordwood, $192,210.

Another wag has noted that "politics is the conduct of public affairs for private advantage." Thus, like Oakes, A. B. Hammond—president of the Montana Improvement Company—and major MIC investors E. L. Bonner and Marcus Daly moved politically to defend their timber interests.

At issue in 1888 was a race between Democrat "Copper King"

William Andrews Clark and young, relatively unknown Republican Thomas H. Carter for the seat of territorial delegate to Congress. Although this was a nonvoting position, it constituted Montana's only Congressional voice. Hammond and Daly concluded that Clark, if elected, could never protect the MIC against anti timber reform forces within the Republican administration of President Benjamin Harrison. So they abandoned the Democrat Clark and threw their support to the Republican Carter.

When the ballots were counted in November 1888, Carter had beaten Clark by a whopping 5,000 votes! Obviously Hammond, Bonner, Daly, and the Northern Pacific Railroad had persuaded other Democratic leaders to desert Clark. This stunning defeat smashed the "Democrat Big Four" (Clark, Daly, Hauser, and Charles A. Broadwater), which had run Montana politics for more than a decade.

Some Montana historians also contend that the 1888 election constitutes the first battle in the eighteen-year "War of the Copper Kings," primarily pitting Daly against Clark. So, somewhat ironically, this colossal confrontation among mineral magnates began over timber.

Still under fire as a result of Haley's unfavorable report, the Montana Improvement Company appeared to "disincorporate." However, in reality, it simply ran its operations under different names (most notably the Big Blackfoot Milling Company) and with ostensibly different management. For years Andrew Hammond remained in control of this massive, economically powerful business.

Once the Northern Pacific had completed its transcontinental mainline, it turned to constructing branch lines and to transporting cut lumber by rail. The latter endeavor, in particular, proved to be big, profitable business. Carloads of Montana public-domain cut lumber—much of which Congress had made available for "domestic use" only—found its way east to Minnesota. And Montana's burgeoning copper mines became literally bottomless pits of timber consumption.

In the early days of smelting in Butte, processors used "heap roasting" to reduce the raw ore. In an area the size of a city block, workmen spread a foundation layer of timber. They placed a layer of raw ore atop the wood, then another layer of timber, then another layer of ore—until they had built a heap the height of a man. They then fired the pyre at several points, whereupon it burned for days, covering the entire city of Butte in a toxic haze.

Some residents thought that the impenetrable haze was an advantage: it mercifully hid the surrounding hills, denuded of all vegetation by wholesale lumbering and sulphur-dioxide air pollution. By 1888 the Anaconda Copper Company was using 40,000 board feet of lumber *per day*!—exclusive of its smelter operations.

In 1891 the Forest Reserve Act gave the President the power to establish forest reserves on public land. However, during the very next year, Congress undermined this progress. It crafted revisions to the 1878 Timber and Stone Act that brought *all public lands* under this earlier legislation.

In addition, amendments to the Timber and Stone Act allowed valuable timber land to be purchased by individuals for as little as $2.50 per acre. Lumber companies quickly executed a ploy used successfully under the Homestead Act: they hired dummy entrants to file on rich timber land and then transfer their land titles to the company. Under this legislation, 663,552 acres of Montana public-forest land passed into private hands, primarily to larger lumbering companies.

By this time, W. A. Clark's rival, Marcus Daly, had left the Montana Improvement Company and created his own lumber department,

Timber cut to fuel smelters in Butte and Anaconda.

associated with the Anaconda Company—the Bitter Root Development Company (BRDC). In time, this corporation would rival the MIC in the volume of timber removed from the public domain. In 1895 the U.S. General Land Office accused the BRDC of having cut 31,525,000 board feet of saw logs from public lands!

So, in the mid-1890s, prospects looked bleak for the preservation of virgin-forest timber in western Montana. However, all was not lost! These larger-than-life villains were about to run headlong into a gang of larger-than-life heroes.

Three champions appeared on stage at just the right time. Or perhaps *they made it* just the right time.

Naturalist John Muir spoke for the wilderness and carried its message to the nation—and to Theodore Roosevelt.

Forester Gifford Pinchot offered Roosevelt an alternative to the two extremes of either locking the nation's forests away forever or completely destroying them.

President Theodore Roosevelt possessed the drive and the know-how to ramrod desperately needed changes in forest policy.

John Muir was a naturalist who concluded, in the 1870s, that his supreme purpose in life must be "to entice people to look at Nature's loveliness." Had he not subsequently become a militant conservationist, his destiny might have been only "to entice" Americans to look with sorrow on the last stump of the last giant sequoia logged off in Yosemite National Park. Instead, he could take pride in the protection of Yosemite's "Big Trees," while devoting his last energies to a doomed effort similarly to protect California's Hetch Hetchy Valley.

In 1903 Muir had booked passage to Japan, Russia, and Manchuria, when he learned that President Roosevelt wished to visit the Sierra Nevada country with Muir. Muir immediately canceled his Asian trip, so he could "do *some* forest good in freely talking around the campfire."

As a result of this trip, Roosevelt concluded that California's sequoia groves should be preserved—simply because "it would be a shame to our civilization to let them disappear. They are monuments in themselves."

The President, however, still believed that *other* timber should be cut. He added,

I do not ask that lumbering be stopped, . . . only that the forests be so used that not only shall we here, this generation, get the benefit for the next few years, but that our children and our children's children shall get the benefit. . . . We are not building this country of ours for a day. It is to last through the ages.

Muir, the naturalist, could not provide Roosevelt with guidance in timber management, but Gifford Pinchot, the forester, could.

In 1891 Congress had empowered the President to exempt public-domain forested land from development. By the time he left office, Republican President Benjamin Harrison (1889-1893) had set aside millions of acres in forest reserves—lands completely excluded from use.

Harrison's successor, Democrat Grover Cleveland (1893-1897), added more than 21 million acres to the reserves in 1897. Particularly this Cleveland action infuriated Montana capitalists. The state had escaped the earlier forest-reserve process, but Cleveland's mandates removed 8 million acres of Montana saw logs from harvest! Then President William McKinley (1897-1901) protected an additional 7 million forested acres, all across the country.

With McKinley's assassination in September, 1901, Vice-President Theodore Roosevelt assumed the Presidency. A conservationist at heart, the new executive relied for much of his public-lands policy on Gifford Pinchot.

Where Muir had been poetic, Pinchot was pragmatic. Where Muir might have rhapsodized about the wonders of nature, Pinchot stated: "The first duty of the human race is to control the earth it lives upon."

Pinchot had studied forestry in Europe. He returned to America embracing the concepts of multiple-use and sustained-yields. In 1905, through his influence, 65 million acres of the Department of the Interior's Forest Reserves were transferred to the new Department of Agriculture as "national forests." Roosevelt then selected Pinchot to head the fledgling agency. As national forests, these wooded public lands could be logged, mined, and grazed. However, the department would control them and collect fees for these uses.

Two years later (1907), the Senate was considering an agricultural-appropriation bill. Senator Charles W. Fulton of Oregon secured an amendment to the bill. It provided that the president could set aside no additional national forests in the greater Northwest (Washington, Oregon, Idaho, Colorado, Wyoming, and Montana). Nevertheless the crafty Roosevelt, in his autobiography, gloated, "For four years the Forest Service had been gathering field notes as to what forests ought to be set aside in these States."

Roosevelt neither wanted to sign the legislation with Fulton's amendment attached, nor could he veto the entire bill. So he took advantage of the stipulation that allowed him ten days to sign the appropriation. He then ordered Pinchot to prepare the text for a series of executive orders that would create twenty-one new forest reserves. The President signed these orders a couple of days *prior to* the deadline for signing the appropriation bill.

The President reflected,

> When the friends of the special interests in the Senate got their amendment through and woke up, they discovered that sixteen millions acres of timber land had been saved for the people by putting them in the National Forests before the land-grabbers could get at them.

The timber monopolists had met their match in the triumvirate of Muir, Pinchot, and Roosevelt.

Meanwhile the federal government's prosecution of Montana's timber depredators dragged on. The initial accusations against the Montana Improvement Company had been made in Montana's territorial days (pre-1889). World War I (1917-1918) had ended before Andrew B. Hammond finally agreed to pay a court judgment in the amount of $7,066.66 to satisfy his timber violations on the public domain.

Marcus Daly's Bitter Root Development Company was accused of stealing $1,350,000 worth of timber from public lands, but the U.S. Supreme Court finally denied this charge on technical grounds. The government then tried to sue Daly's estate for $2 million for timber theft, but the courts decided against the plaintiff.

The frustration of federal attorneys at these losses was tempered somewhat by the knowledge that the national forests would provide a measure of protection against similar future depredations. However, it would be absurd to suggest that all controversy ended with the creation of the national forests. A few decades later, another Roosevelt—Franklin Delano—observed that "European countries . . . treat timber as a crop. We treat timber resources as if they were a mine."

Today, public-land debates remain hot topics: logging, mining, grazing, recreation, prescribed burns, clear-cutting, and controlled burns. Yet, in some ways, the national forests are to nature what the Bill of Rights is to U.S. citizens. Assailed from all directions and subject to ongoing interpretation, they still provide a framework of protection. National forests continue to demonstrate the nation's intention to protect the public's land.

A September 3, 1998, story in the *Missoulian* reported the conviction of timber depredators in the Troy area of northwestern Montana. These violators had moved boundary markers and clear-cut more than fifteen acres of national forest land. Paltry!!

The Montana Improvement Company and the Bitter Root Development Company were in a different class. And—thanks to the policies and laws crafted by Muir, Pinchot, and Roosevelt—it is a class that has been dismissed.

~

Sources

It is difficult to understand why anyone would wish to follow the dreary political scandals of today, when that same person can open a box of archival records and read the truly impressive scandals of an earlier era. I had found several references to Thomas Oakes's letter to Sam Hauser in secondary sources. However, it proved an extraordinary experience to lift *the actual document* from an archival box and hold, in my own hands, an angry, open threat against the Territorial Governor. That letter is contained in the archival holdings of the Montana Historical Society in Helena: Manuscript Collection 37: the Samuel Thomas Hauser Papers, Box 17, folders 7-13.

The following collections held by the Montana Historical Society Archives also provided background material for this piece: Manuscript Collection 55: the Thomas Charles Power Papers; Manuscript Collection 80: the Anton M. Holter Papers; Manuscript Collection 169: the Anaconda Copper Mining Company Records; Small Collection 1103: the George May and Company Records.

Background publications on Western forestry, the public domain, and Montana timber depredations include: John Ise, *The United States Forest Policy* (New Haven, Conn.: Yale University, 1920); Benjamin H. Hibbard, *The History of the Public Land Policies* (New York: Macmillan, 1924); Edward B. Butcher, "An Analysis of Timber Depredations in Montana to 1900," M.A. thesis, University of Montana, Missoula, 1967; Butcher, "Timber Depredations on the Montana Public Domain, 1885-1918," *Journal of the West*, Vol. 7, #3 (July 1968), 351-362.

For background on the Northern Pacific Railroad's role in this controversy, see: Louis T. Renz, *The History of the Northern Pacific Railroad* (Fairfield, Wash.: Ye Galleon Press, 1980); Thomas Clinch, "The Northern Pacific Railroad and Montana's Mineral Lands," *Pacific Historical Review*, Vol. 31 (August 1965), 323-335; Sig Mickelson, *The Northern Pacific Railroad and the Selling of the West* (Freeman, S. Dak.: Pine Hill Press, 1993).

The pertinent aspect of Montana's "War of the Copper Kings" is addressed in: K. Ross Toole, "The Genesis of the Clark-Daly Feud," *Montana, The Magazine of Western History*, Vol. 1, #2 (April 1951), 21-33; Michael P. Malone, Richard B. Roeder, and William L. Lang, *Montana: A History of Two Centuries*, rev. ed. (Seattle: University of Washington, 1991).

The best works on John Muir include: W. F. Bade, *The Life and Letters of John Muir* (New York: AMS Press, 1973); Stephen Fox, *John Muir and His Legacy: The American Conservation Movement* (Boston: Little, Brown, 1980); Herbert F. Smith, *John Muir* (New Haven, Conn.: College and University Press, 1965); Muir, *The Story of My Boyhood and Youth* (Boston: Houghton Mifflin, 1913).

An interest in Gifford Pinchot can be pursued in: Harold T. Pinkett, *Gifford Pinchot: Private and Public Forester* (Champaign-Urbana: University of Illinois, 1970); M. Nelson McGeary, *Gifford Pinchot: Forester-Politician* (Princeton, N.J.: Princeton University, 1960); Pinchot, *The Fight for Conservation* (Seattle: University of Washington, 1910).

Passages quoted from Teddy Roosevelt appear in: Roosevelt, *Theodore Roosevelt: An Autobiography* (New York: Charles Scribner's Sons, 1913). Other Roosevelt writings pertinent to the timber issue are: *American Ideals and Other Essays* (New York: G. P. Putnam's Sons, 1897); *The New Nationalism* (New York: Outlook Company, 1910); The *Works of Theodore Roosevelt*, National Edition, 26 vols. (New York: Charles Scribner's Sons, 1926), *passim.*

Finally, for biographical information on Roosevelt, see: Paul Russell Cutright, *Theodore Roosevelt: The Making of a Conservationist* (Urbana: University of Illinois, 1985); Lewis L. Gould, *The Presidency of Theodore Roosevelt* (Lawrence: Kansas State University, 1991); Edmund Morris, *The Rise of Theodore Roosevelt* (New York: Coward, McCann and Geoghegan, 1979).

Calamity Jane
The Wild Cat's Kitten?

by Jon Axline

The quick reader already has concluded that there are damned few "jerk women" in this volume. One wag has observed that a ratio of 6 to 1, bad men to bad women is, indeed, an accurate reflection of Montana and American society. Be that as it may, the historian struggles to assemble enough documentation to move a Western woman from the "unusual and colorful" category up to the disgusting "jerk" level. Then who walks in but Calamity Jane Canary.

Jane, wearing any number of hats, makes a strong bid to be enshrined. Calamity once said that she "always preferred the company of men to that of women." And her lifestyle followed that precept, emphasizing quantity to quality. To compound the historian's dilemma, Jane laid land mines of "tall-tale autobiography" throughout her life. So, what do we have here—a devil or an angel? The jury remains sequestered.

–Dave Walter

JUST WHO WAS "CALAMITY JANE?" THIS WOMAN, A TRUE FRONTIER icon, is remembered by many as a heroine of the plains—a female who almost single-handedly tamed the West. She has been characterized posthumously as an Indian fighter, a bullwhacker, a scout, and an "angel of mercy." Hollywood has carried on a love affair with Calamity Jane since 1916. However, not until the 1995 television adaptation of Larry McMurtry's *Buffalo Girls* were many Americans finally treated to a more accurate portrayal of this self-proclaimed "Queen of the Prairie."

Martha "Calamity Jane" Canary (ca. 1848-1903) was many things during her lifetime, but "heroine" was not one of them. Nineteenth-century newspapers most often portrayed her as an unattractive, manly, loud-mouthed, two-fisted boozer who was prone to sleeping around. She remained on a first-name basis with most of the jailers in South Dakota, Wyoming, and Montana. And she built a reputation as a "wild girl" and a "booze fighter," according to one man who knew her well.

One thing is certain about this "Belle of the Bull Trains": details about her life and "career" are contradictory, confusing, and just plain fantastic.

In 1958 Roberta Beed Sollid noted, in *Calamity Jane: A Study in Historical Criticism,* that "no career is so illusive to the historian as that of a loose woman." In Calamity Jane's case, however, this patently is not true! The real difficulty in assessing this phenomenon is separating the fact from the fiction.

Sollid's book—one of the first forays into public history in Montana—goes to great lengths to discount most of the nineteenth-century and posthumous accounts of Calamity. The author, however, was unable to paint Jane as anything more than a true frontier character whose loose morals, hard drinking, and colorful language earned the affection, if not the respect, of those people who knew her.

Tenderfeet paid their heroes in drinks to relate picturesque stories of the Wild West. Jane, an alcoholic with a vivid imagination, was more than willing to accommodate them. Sollid has not written the definitive biography of "the Beautiful White Devil of the Yellowstone," nor has she crafted an apologia for a less-than-savory character. Calamity Jane emerges from Sollid's treatment as a real person whose story is one of the most serio-comic in American history.

The life of the real Calamity Jane (nee Martha Jane Canary) began in Illinois, or in Missouri, either in 1844, or in 1848, or in 1852. She was reputedly the daughter of an abusive, failed farmer and an unreformed prostitute. In 1864 the Canary family left the comfort of wherever-they-were-from and headed west to the gold fields of southwestern Montana Territory.

After an arduous, five-month journey—during which Martha spent considerable time hunting game and generally enjoying herself with the men—the Canarys arrived in Nevada City, Montana. Here her father engaged in gambling; her mother worked as a prostitute, reputedly as "Madam Canary." Nevertheless, by December 1864, the family had fallen on hard times. Martha and her two sisters were forced to the streets of nearby Virginia City, seeking handouts to survive.

In 1865 or 1866, the family left Alder Gulch for the new mining camp of Blackfoot City, northeast of Deer Lodge. There Madam Canary—who was, according to one source, the proprietor of the "Bird Cage brothel"—died. The Canarys then departed for Utah where, before long, the father also died.

Left to their own devices, the children split up. By some accounts,

Martha then pursued the life of a prostitute. She allegedly followed the Union Pacific Railroad's construction gangs as they pushed their way west, across Utah Territory to Promontory Point.

Jane subsequently tried to throw a more romantic twist on this portion of her life. She maintained that she had spent her teenage years working in a saloon near an Army post just outside of Butte, Montana Territory (although no such post ever existed). From the saloon's bar, she "sang as a child to the soldiers, then she learned to drink and to swear and to play cards, until the men were afraid to compete with her. She learned to shoot and to ride with a recklessness which made the town wonder. She was afraid of nothing. . . ."

Martha likely received the sobriquet "Calamity Jane" during the early 1870s. How she acquired it, though, remains a point of conjecture. She claimed, in her 1896 autobiography, that it was bestowed upon her by Lieutenant James "Teddy" Egan when she rescued him from imminent death at the hands of a band of Lakota Sioux in 1873. This story Egan—himself a colorful liar—vigorously denied. He labeled her "a damned chippy" and said that he had thrown her off the Army post after she was caught living in the enlisted-men's barracks.

By other accounts (specifically those written by frontier humorist Bret Harte), she gained the name because of her predilection to cause trouble. She also may have received the sobriquet as a result of her profession. Nineteenth-century prostitutes frequently were referred to as "janes," and "calamity" was a slang term for venereal disease.

Physical descriptions of Calamity Jane are as abundant as the origins of her nickname. Photographs of Calamity, of course, provide the best testimonial to her looks. They show a rather mannish, stocky woman who dressed, at least in most of the photos, like a frontier scout. She appears packing a revolver, a large knife, and occasionally a rifle.

Some contemporaries described Jane as a "freak," someone whose figure resembled "a busted bale of hay." Her trademark buckskin clothes were worn, according to one drinking buddy, as a matter of convenience. He added, "The reason she got so much notoriety was partly because she was always doing some crazy thing, and partly because she wanted to be notorious."

Other late-nineteenth-century accounts, created primarily for dime-novel readers, describe her in much more romantic terms (*Helena Daily Herald*, June 20, 1877):

A correspondent tells of a Black Hills character known as

"Calamity Jane". . . . As she sits astride her horse, there is nothing in her attire to distinguish her sex, save her small, neat-fitting garters and sweeping raven locks. She wears buckskin clothes, gaily beaded and fringed, and a broad-brimmed Spanish hat. . . . She is still in early womanhood, and her rough and dissipated career has not altogether "swept away"the lines where beauty lingers.

By 1901 Calamity's legend already had overtaken the reality. The *Anaconda* (Montana) *Standard* reported that, since an early age, Jane had carried a six-shooter. The paper noted further that her body had "accumulated a considerable amount of lead in the shape of bullets that have been fired at her from time to time in the encounters with wild Indians." Although many writers eventually conceded that Martha was anything but beautiful, most were reluctant to abandon the legends that had become associated with Calamity Jane.

Calamity's fame as a scout, pony-express rider, and female gunfighter was confined primarily to connoisseurs of the popular dime novels. To these readers—many of whom were urban-dwellers, working for wages in the nation's steel mills, slaughterhouses, and garment factories—Calamity was the exemplification of the Wild West. Yet to people who knew her, or knew of her real lifestyle, she was nothing like the frontier heroine idolized in the East.

Prior to Jane's death, few newspaper accounts actually celebrated the woman. Instead, Western journals regularly reported the latest mayhem caused by Calamity Jane during her repeated drunken revels.

By the 1920s, however, a novice to the history of the Old West would think that she almost single-handedly had tamed the frontier. According to these popular-press authors (many of whom falsely claimed to have known her), Calamity was an Army scout, a mule skinner, a consort to Wild Bill Hickok, a midwife, a vigilante, a Robin Hood thief, a nurse, an Indian fighter, a lawman (or law person), a horse thief, a gambler, and a stagecoach driver.

While it is probable that Jane did work for a time as a mule skinner and a bullwhacker, her career as portrayed by these writers was greatly exaggerated. Not until the late 1950s did accounts begin to portray Calamity as a low-class prostitute and an "amoral braggart."

Through the decades, most stories concerning Calamity Jane focused on her "career" as an Army scout. According to her autobiography, she served with George Armstrong Custer and with

George Crook in their respective campaigns against the Apaches and the Lakota Sioux. In the former case, it has been proven conclusively that she was grossly mistaken: Custer never fought the Apaches! This exception, however, failed to keep her from claiming a close friendship with the "Son of the Morning Star."

Jane's claims regarding General George Crook are more plausible, although not in the way she intended. Much evidence exists that Calamity joined the Jenney Expedition to the Black Hills in 1875. She also accompanied Crook's forces in Wyoming and Montana in 1876—but as a "camp follower" rather than as an ace Army scout, as she claimed. She repeatedly had attempted to volunteer as a scout, under the name "Frank Marden." However, her sex always was discovered (usually through some indiscretion with the troops), and she was sent back to the originating Army post.

Given Jane's profession as a "loose woman," the most picturesque incident of this type involved skinny-dipping with some of Colonel R. I. Dodge's troops in a creek near Fort Laramie in 1875. The stories of her life as an Army scout were first presented to the reading public in Ned Buntline's dime novels. Yet her friend George Hoshier claimed (1906) that "she did come into the [Black] Hills with General Crook and wore men's clothes . . . but she was no more a scout than I was."

Calamity probably did work as a mule skinner and a bullwhacker from the 1870s into the early 1890s in the Dakotas, Wyoming, and Montana. Numerous sources have commented on her skillful use of profanity and obscenities. This skill would have recommended her as an effective mule skinner to most freighters in those days. Stories about Jane's tenderness and humanity in the Deadwood, Dakota Territory, smallpox epidemic of 1878 are legion. In this instance, she earned the nickname of the "Black Hills Florence Nightingale."

The literature also carries occasional references to her as a desperado and a small-time thief. This evidence would add credence to the stories that Calamity sometimes resorted to petty theft to survive. However, this type of theft would be inconsistent with "the Robin Hood who gave to the poor and indigent of the Black Hills," as she and some supporters have claimed.

It also is credible to imagine Calamity as a vigilante. Many vigilante actions originated in saloons among bored patrons. So Jane very well could have taken an active and vocal role in the lynching of other camp miscreants. Also prevalent are prevaricated stories of Calamity Jane saving the day by killing renegade Indians and outlaws.

These tales regularly attest to her dexterity with a gun and the numerous scars that decorated her body. Yet, how anyone could be aware of these scars without seeing the proof is unknown.

One subject that irritated Calamity was her marital status. At the time her autobiography was published (1896), she referred to herself as "Mrs. M. Burk." According to other stories that she disseminated, she was married at least twelve times, with all but one of her husbands meeting violent ends. Reliable sources state that she was married at least once, and probably twice. These would have been common-law unions.

Between 1885 and 1895, Jane professed to have settled into domestic bliss in Texas and Colorado as "Mrs. Martha Burk." This story, however, is also false. In 1887 the *Livingston* (Montana) *Enterprise* reported that Calamity was at "a ranch down in Wyoming trying to sober up after a thirty-years drunk."

In November 1888, Calamity was arrested in Livingston and charged with fornication. She apparently had consorted with a local ne'er-do-well named Charles Townley. Jane paid her fine and was released. Townley, however, blamed his troubles on a prostitute (Jane) who had hocked his painting supplies to buy whiskey, thereby sending him down the road to ruin. Many other contemporary accounts of Calamity Jane do mention a partner, usually a male of questionable reputation.

A number of additional reports exist of Calamity being seen in the company of a child or children. Considering her profession, it may be a foregone conclusion that she bore some children. Indeed, one of the hottest controversies in Montana and elsewhere in the 1940s revolved around a woman by the name of Jane Hickok McCormick, who claimed to be the daughter of Calamity Jane and Wild Bill Hickok. Although later proved a hoax, this dispute did raise the possibility that some of Calamity Jane's children were still alive.

The storied romance between Calamity and Bill Hickok also has proven a fabrication of the dime novelists, although many authors repeated the tale as gospel after her death. Calamity and Hickok did arrive in Deadwood together in late June or early July 1876. One local newspaper reported that they "rode the entire length of Main Street, mounted on good horses and clad completely in buckskin, every suit of which carried enough fringe to make a considerable buckskin rope."

Wild Bill was murdered in the Nuthall and Mann Saloon (a.k.a. "Saloon No. 10") just a few weeks after his arrival in Deadwood.

Reliable accounts say that Jane did follow Hickok around the mining camp during the days before his death. However, only after the killing did she broadcast her supposed romance with the gunfighter.

Before his death, Hickok (a renowned ladies' man) vehemently denied any romantic entanglement with Calamity. By the end of the nineteenth century, though, the love story had grown to such proportions that even Calamity believed it. She reportedly requested, on her deathbed, that she be buried next to Wild Bill. Nevertheless, other than their adjacent graves at the Mount Moriah Cemetery in Deadwood, no known partnership existed between these two legends of the Old West.

Although Calamity Jane worked as a mule skinner, bullwhacker, and professional public nuisance for the remainder of her life, she increasingly fell under the shadow of "Calamity the fictional heroine"—a figure who sparked the imagination of people throughout the country. As one author reflected: outside the Black Hills, Montana, and Wyoming, the real Calamity's life was totally unknown to most Americans. Indeed, shortly before her death, the *Great Falls* (Montana) *Tribune* printed a story about her (January 18, 1903) that concluded,

> She of today is old and poverty-stricken and wretched. The country has outgrown her and her occupation is gone. . . . It is the Calamity Jane of the old days, the Indian fighter, the scout, the mail carrier, the cow puncher, the man among men, who stands heroic. It is she whom the small boy reads about in the dime novel which he carries hidden beneath his coat. It is she who is to be found in the Army records at Washington, who is mentioned for bravery in many an officer's report.

Jane's twilight years were spent largely in a futile attempt to live up to the legend that had been manufactured about her. This proved a daunting task, in which she failed miserably.

In 1896 (the year she published her autobiography) Calamity embarked on a new career as a professional sideshow attraction in the Midwest. People, of course, paid to see the Calamity Jane of the popular press—the beautiful, rootin'-tootin', authentic female scout and Indian fighter who had fired the imaginations of young boys throughout the country. What they saw, however, was a broken-down old war horse, dressed in ill-fitting buckskin apparel, who hawked her autobiography to one and all for 25 cents a copy.

Calamity had been recruited by an agent of the Kohl and Middleton Museum to allow herself to "be placed before the public in such a manner as to give people of the eastern cities an opportunity of seeing the Woman Scout who was made so famous through her daring career in the West and the Black Hills countries." Within a year, however—and after only one engagement, at the Palace Museum in St. Paul, Minnesota—the contractor released Jane and she returned to Deadwood.

Yet interest in Calamity remained high. In 1901 the American News Company directed newspaper writer and novelist Josephine Brake to hire Calamity Jane as a midway exhibit for the Pan-American Exposition in Buffalo, New York. Brake and *Livingston Enterprise* editor Adelbert M. Alderson found Calamity in the aptly named coal camp of Horr, south of Livingston. She was "lying in a dirty bunk in a Negro house of ill-repute, sick and half-dead from a long drunk."

With promises of good money, a large home, and lots of publicity, Brake convinced Calamity to return east with her. One condition was that Jane at least *try* to limit her liquor consumption. Thus Calamity agreed to ask Brake's permission first, before taking a drink— something she did frequently during the trip east.

Within two weeks at Buffalo, however, Jane had magnificently fallen off the wagon. She proceeded to make life miserable for Brake and for all others with whom she dealt. Calamity reportedly assaulted a local policeman, after shooting up the exposition's midway.

Montana journalists chided Brake for making a "sensation out of a woman who has few of the instincts of the finer sex and whose removal from [Montana] will not cause anything like an aching void in the communities in which she has lived." These writers criticized Calamity for smoking cigars. They also jeered her for her attempt to wear "up-to-date feminine apparel" and make-up, including bright-blue shirtwaists and liberal amounts of face powder.

By September 1901, Calamity had been fired by Brake's newspaper chain and sent packing for home. Jane had to borrow money from Buffalo Bill Cody to reach Chicago. From there she worked her way back to Montana by exhibiting herself in dime museums and by selling copies of her autobiography.

Once home in Livingston, she told a newspaper reporter that she had left Brake's employ because of a dispute over the royalties on her

Calamity Jane in Livingston, Montana.

Courtesy Montana Historical Society, C. E. Finn photographer

sale of the autobiography. In truth, Calamity was fired because she had repeatedly sought solace in booze to relieve the loneliness she experienced in the East.

During 1902 Calamity wandered through Montana, panhandling drinks in saloons and periodically checking herself into county poorhouses. She sequentially listed her "place of residence" as Livingston, Bozeman, Billings, Great Falls, Butte, Miles City, and a run-down shack in Gardiner.

In Butte, the city's businessmen took up a collection to provide support for her. They stipulated that the money be dispensed by a guardian, so she could not spend it on whiskey. Among the subscribers to Calamity's fund were rumored to be some of the most prominent men in Montana.

Also in 1902, Calamity stepped off the Great Northern Railway train in Glasgow with a four-year-old girl in tow. She was not welcomed. County Clerk Robert Crossett and County Commissioner Dan Kyle labeled her "a window smasher of the most virulent type" and refused her pleas to enter the county poorhouse as an inmate. Instead, they firmly placed her on the next train for Great Falls, which she then was calling her home.

While Calamity Jane occupied a place of affection in many Montana hearts, others believed that she was responsible for her own condition. Most agreed that she was a true frontier character, but that her time had passed. The *Lewistown* (Montana) *Democrat* observed (July 11, 1902):

> The proposition that the government should make "Calamity Jane," the obstreperous and somewhat wild-and-wooly noted female character, the beneficiary of a pension allowance is not being received with hilarious approval by the public at large.... It is true that Calamity Jane is a pioneer of the Western country, but it would appear that, in the natural order of things, she has had about all that was coming to her. She has been given unbounded freedom in her exploitation of those peculiar gifts which distinguish her from the average woman. She has been feted and wined and dined by those who looked upon her as a Wild West heroine. She has been lionized and made famous by the effete journals of the East. She has been exhibited throughout the country as a dazzling product of the great West. And yea, verily, what

more can she ask.... If Calamity Jane is not contented with
these honors, she must indeed be hard to satisfy.

Apparently Jane also spent considerable time in jail. In one 1902
case, Judge Frank L. Mann sentenced her to sixty days in the Yellowstone
County jail to recover from a particularly nasty drunken jag in Billings.

By early 1903, Calamity had relocated to South Dakota, dividing
her time between Pierre and Deadwood. As a young girl in Pierre, Mrs.
I. N. Walker knew Jane. Later she remembered Calamity as a pleasant-
looking woman who lived in a shack and always wore the same faded
pink gown. Walker recalled that respectable people did not associate
with her because "swearing and drinking among women in those days
was absolutely unforgivable." Calamity continued to sell copies of her
autobiography to those interested in her life.

By mid-1903, however, it became clear that Calamity was nearing
the end of her colorful life. On August 1, 1903, Martha "Calamity Jane"
Canary died of inflammation of the bowels in the Calloway Hotel at
Terry, South Dakota. In an attempt to meld reality with fiction, her
death date was changed to August 2—to coincide with the killing of
her supposed true love Wild Bill Hickok. Montana newspapers
eulogized her as a woman who "lived and died in the West. The passion
for the free, untrammeled existence possessed her. The comely girl
scout long ago was blotted out by years and dissipation, but the
tremendous spirit of the woman burned brightly to the last."

So, just who was this Calamity Jane?

She could be whoever you wanted her to be. Although today she
might be categorized a "sleaze," Jane was definitely a product of her
upbringing and her times. If ever existed a true "striped person," as
described in the introduction to this volume, it was Calamity Jane.
The beautiful "Jane of the Plains" was entangled inexorably with the
"public nuisance." Although she had "a heart of gold," she was not
above maintaining her reputation as an obnoxious boor.

It was the Jane of the dime novels and the tender "angel of mercy"
that most Westerners preferred to remember—rather than the person
she truly was. While neither the romantic "Heroine of Whoop-Up,"
nor the bosom companion to Deadwood Dick and Wild Bill Hickok,
she eventually believed that she was both. And she was quick to relate
these fantastic adventures to anyone who would listen.

The historical Calamity Jane was and remains an enigma. She is
probably best remembered for the legend, rather than the reality.

~

Sources

No lack of information exists concerning Calamity Jane. Much of the material used in this chapter was gathered from two thick vertical/clippings files in the Montana Historical Society Library in Helena. Martha Canary Burk's pamphlet autobiography, *Life and Adventures of Calamity Jane, By Herself* (no publisher, no date), is, of course an excellent source of information on how Martha perceived herself during the last years of her life. Other sources include Roberta Beed Sollid's *Calamity Jane: A Study in Historical Criticism* (Missoula, Mont.: Montana State University, 1951); Estelline Bennett's *Old Deadwood Days* (Lincoln: University of Nebraska Press, 1982); Doris and Bill Whithorn's *Calamity's in Town* (Pray, Mont.: Livingston Enterprise, 1978); and a host of other secondary sources.

All of these references represent an accurate portrayal of Calamity as both a real person and a fictional character, combining the fabrication with the reality. It is sometimes difficult, however, to determine whether these authors are talking about the same person—or if there was a small army of Calamity Janes, both fantastic and obnoxious, wandering through the West in the late nineteenth century. Perhaps the best of the most recent pieces on Calamity is James D. McLaird's "Calamity Jane's Diary and Letters," which appears in the Autumn/Winter 1995, issue of *Montana, The Magazine of Western History*.

Montana's 1889 Constitutional Convention
The Founding Fathers—The Floundering Fathers
by Lyndel Meikle

Early in 1889, the United States Congress broke an extended partisan impasse and enacted the Omnibus Bill. This legislation provided a format for several Western territories—including Montana—to join the Union. The key step in this process was a "constitutional convention." Its elected delegates would draft a state constitution for the approval of the state's (male) voters.

When the Montana convention opened in Helena on July 4, 1889, optimistic journalists drew parallels to Philadelphia in 1787: George Washington, Benjamin Franklin, James Madison, George Mason. Unfortunately the comparison proved a stretch.

Fortunately, a verbatim transcript of Montana's 1889 floor debates is extant. It provides disappointing fare for the reader seeking dynamic leadership, vision, and high ideals. This document most certainly spawned some of Montana's subsequent political, economic, and social difficulties. Finally, in 1972, Montanans convened another "constitutional convention," and voters (male and female) replaced the 1889 document.

–Dave Walter

IT IS WITH MUCH PLEASURE THAT I CALL THIS CONVENTION to order, a convention that meets for the purpose of framing a constitution for one of the largest states in the Union, the great gold and silver State of Montana. . . .

L. A. WALKER, SECRETARY OF THE TERRITORY OF MONTANA, JULY 4, 1889, IN HELENA

The men who participated in the Montana Constitutional Convention of 1889 received high praise—in their own biographies. Those ponderous "subscription history" compilations produced around the end of the nineteenth century particularly honored these delegates. However, the biographical sketches contained in the works of Michael Leeson, of Joaquin Miller, and of their successors were really either *auto*biographies or eulogies written by family members. Naturally, they contain little criticism of their subjects.

On the other hand, the volume *Proceedings and Debates of the Constitutional Convention* is comprised of direct quotes from the seventy-five delegates, representing Montana's sixteen counties. Those words do not always reflect well on the speakers, on their fellow Montanans, or on the widespread attitudes of the era.

A reading of the *Proceedings and Debates* reveals several topics on which the delegates' opinions make us uneasy or embarrassed. By today's standards, their beliefs would not be acceptable in the public arena. By today's standards, the standards of 1889 are difficult to defend.

The issues of suffrage (not just woman suffrage, but suffrage in general), the expulsion of the Chinese, and the proposed termination of Montana's Indian reservations are cases in point. The Indian question proves particularly convoluted, yet revealing.

During the convention, Montana's soon-to-be Congressional representative Thomas H. Carter, of Helena, vented his anger to a newspaper reporter. Carter was outraged to find that, on Montana's

Meeting of the members of the 1889 Constitutional Convention at the Montana Club, taken in November 1911.

COURTESY MONTANA HISTORICAL SOCIETY, CULBERTSON PHOTOGRAPHER

Crow Reservation, "these women" were hanging around the agency school. When no one was looking, "these women" were attempting to snatch their children away. By today's understanding, it is ridiculous to condemn Crow mothers for trying to save their own children from the reservation's white educational system. Yet, in 1889, Carter's outrage received widespread understanding.

On the subject of suffrage, constitutional delegate Charles S. Hartman (Gallatin County) proposed a requirement that a voter must be able to read and write. He said,

> As citizens it is only right for us to take precautions against the scum of foreign nations. The United States has opened its door to anarchists and foreign laborers, and I say they should not have a voice in the government of the state.

Hiram Knowles, an attorney from Butte, disagreed. He argued that there were educated Germans, Scandinavians, and others who were lovers of liberty "and if he [the foreign-born immigrant] be so, . . . he is a patriot of this country, whether he can read or write."

Even in an era when illiteracy was much more widespread than it is today, this enlightened counterpoint was remarkable. Hartman's proposition reveals his own ignorance that his proposal would disenfranchise a large segment of the American-born population.

C. R. Middleton, a lawyer from Custer County, supported Knowles. He asked Hartman:

> Is it a fact that an ignorant man, who cannot read or write, should be unable to express his opinion in an honest way? In Chicago, the head men of the anarchists [inciters of the Haymarket Square riot of 1886] were intelligent men and, according to this article, they would be able to vote. And you would exclude the honest, hardworking man who cannot read or write?

Delegate Hartman's proposal also would have barred foreign-born men from voting if they could not read and write *in English*—even if they could read and write in their native language. Hiram Knowles again rose to point out that the country supported scores of German, French, and other foreign-language newspapers that discussed public matters. He added, "You wish to shut out all men who have not learned the English language, as though all there was about liberty was written in the English language!"

In this context, one of the convention's most offensive statements came from delegate Charles Warren, a mine operator from Butte. He pompously pronounced:

> If the questions could be divided in such a way as to permit certain foreigners to vote, I would be in favor of it. Take, for instance, the German or the Irish. When they come to this country, as a rule, they burn the bridges behind them and become as good citizens as we have. On the other hand, you take other foreigners, notably the Italians. They come here and declare their intentions to become citizens, and as quick as they accumulate $150 or $200 they go back to Italy, and that is the last you see of them. In the meantime, if they have an opportunity to sell their votes for a couple of dollars, they are on hand.

Vote-selling was a fairly common practice during the late nineteenth century in Montana, but it was never restricted to foreign-born men. An enterprising politician with access to a saloon could purchase just as many votes from English-speaking people! In fact, opponents of woman suffrage used this practice widely.

To the debate over allowing foreigners to vote, Charles Warren then read a published article into the record. He claimed that the article voiced his sentiments better than he could.

> It is somewhat uncomfortable to reflect that a citizen of intelligence, property, good moral character, and a keen sense of responsibilities and dignities of his duties as an American citizen may have his ballot offset by an Italian *lazaronne*, exuding garlic at every pore of his otherwise unpleasant body, whose intelligence does not equal that of the monkey for whom he grinds the organ, and upon whose sense, industry, and honesty he depends for his maintenance and macaroni.

The official transcription of the *Proceedings and Debates* parenthetically notes that members of the assembled convention greeted Warren's remarks with "laughter and applause." The impact of this scurrilous reference deepens when one understands that a *lazaronne* is "a homeless idler of Naples who lives by chance, working or begging."

So, who was this Charles Warren, who made such a bigoted charge condemning all Italians? Well, he was a man who, upon arriving in Montana, was absolutely homeless. He slept under a wagon!

Warren's "subscription history" biography states that, in August 1866, he camped, under his wagon, in a spot later occupied by the *Helena Herald* newspaper office.

> . . . Fate did not smile on his aspirations at this period. Yet, sustained by his lofty and resolute spirit, he packed his blankets all over the Territory in search of the opportunity he felt convinced was waiting for him—somewhere.

Warren apparently did not believe that Italians might come to "the land of opportunity" for the same reasons he did. Maybe he just thought that they had run out of street corners for their organ-grinding back in Naples. Granting Italians the vote would have made little difference anyway. At this time the German, Scandinavian, and Irish population of Montana was about twenty thousand—which was more than thirty times greater than the Italian population. The 1890 federal census did not mention how many monkeys lived in the state—or how many of them may have been delegates to Montana's 1889 constitutional convention.

Regarding Warren's view that all Italians were beggars, no evidence exists that the delegate panhandled as a young man. His biographical sketch, however, does mention that at one point he had to borrow $15 to take himself up to Butte, after an "unprofitable" stint as the sheriff of Deer Lodge County. It is possible that this removal to Butte is to Warren's credit, for what citizen would want a sheriff who could describe his stint as "profitable."

Delegate Warren's prejudice against Italians was not unusual during the late nineteenth century—and it was not the only form of prejudice popular at the time. On the East Coast, the Irish had suffered considerable discrimination. Yet, as they came west, encountered more opportunities, and became prosperous, some Irish passed the prejudice down the economic line, to the Chinese.

In the 1870s, Dennis Kearney founded the Workingman's Party in San Francisco. Montana's constitutional delegates seized on one cornerstone of that party: the expulsion of the Chinese from the U.S.

"Proposition #7" to Montana's 1889 constitution—submitted by Allen R. Joy, an attorney from Livingston—reads:

> No corporation now existing or hereafter formed under the laws of this state, shall, after the adoption of this constitution, employ directly or indirectly in any capacity, any Chinese or Mongolian. . . . No Chinese shall be employed on any state, county, municipal, or other public work within this state, except as punishment for crime. . . . The legislature shall discourage by all means within its power the immigration to this state of all foreigners ineligible to become citizens of the United States.

Since 1882, the federal Chinese Exclusion Act had made Chinese immigrants ineligible for U.S. citizenship.

"Proposition #7" continues:

> All contracts for Chinese or coolie labor to be performed in this state [are] to be void. All companies or corporations, whether formed in this country or any foreign country, for the importation of such labor, shall be punished by such fines and penalties as the legislature may prescribe. The legislature shall delegate all necessary power to the incorporated cities and towns in this state, for the removal of Chinese without the limits of such cities, and every other location within prescribed portions of those limits.

Delegate Joseph Hogan, a miner from Butte, agreed with Joy:

> I do not believe any person that is brought here under contract is worthy to be an American citizen. They are generally a class of people that are not identified with the American people or their institutions. They are an injury to everybody.

Interestingly Hogan's late May 1900 obituary in the *Butte Miner* noted, "As a member of the Constitutional Convention . . . Mr. Hogan enjoyed the full respect of his more highly educated colleagues, and he was never a party to anything that wasn't right."

"Proposition #7" did not pass the convention, but the impact of its proposal proved sufficient. Anti-Chinese sentiment increased in Montana after the convention. Some of the young state's uglier anti-Chinese incidents occurred in the Butte area (Joe Hogan's hometown) during the early 1890s.

Some delegates wanted to deny the Italians the vote; other members wanted to expel the Chinese. Women, however, faced a different problem: they were not people.

Timothy E. Collins, a Cascade County banker, made this point during the convention's very lengthy debate on woman suffrage. He sarcastically reminded the delegates favoring "Proposition #14" (a measure to establish woman suffrage) that they first needed to assert a basic declaration. Collins said: "I respectfully request that the gentlemen who are championing this particular question make a motion that a woman is *a human being or person.*"

By today's standards, this request appears ludicrous! To their credit, however, the delegates did devote a tremendous amount of time during the Constitutional Convention to the question of woman suffrage. Unfortunately—and *not* to their credit—they did not pass the woman suffrage proposition.

A lawyer from Virginia City, James E. Callaway, found considerable support among his colleagues for his contention that military service should be the basic requirement for the vote. He feared that "national security" would be endangered if women held the vote.

While he thought that his wife would "vote very nicely," Callaway also expressed delight that she did not hold any ambition to become a military hero (in fulfillment of his military-service requirement). However, Callaway's primary concern stemmed from his wife's extreme popularity. He remarked,

> It might be that the people of Montana would want to elect her Governor and, in that case, when I walked along the streets, my friends would say, "There goes the husband of the Governor." *That,* Mr. Chairman, would be unjust discrimination. I would not like it. . . . I think it would be better for her to stay at home and take care of her babies, where she does very well.

To this statement, Republican John Rickards (Silver Bow County) countered: "Unless there is better material for . . . governors on the other side of the house than on the side that has just spoken, he will never be the husband of a Governor."

Opinions from other delegates also stretch the imagination. Henry Whitehill of Deer Lodge opposed woman suffrage because it went against "natural law," against a relation that had been "divinely implanted."

Martin Maginnis (Lewis and Clarke County) opposed it because he did not want women to be "contaminated" by politics. This is a refreshingly candid comment, coming from a politician who had served as Montana's territorial delegate to Congress from 1873 to 1885. Maginnis also said that,

> . . . if the women of this country wanted the franchise, they would have it, no matter who stood in the way. Right or wrong, wise or unwise, we would give it to them. But they do not. We have no right to force upon them that which they do not want.

Then, in another burst of candor, Maginnis confessed that one reason he had always feared woman suffrage was that preachers might influence Montana women in the cause of statewide temperance. Of course he was correct. Once Montana women received the vote (1914), Montanans lost their liquor (1919)!

One other argument surfaced among delegates. James Callaway stated:

> I have studied this question for a good many years, and I am rather favorable to the proposition of woman suffrage, but I am a conservative man, and perhaps somewhat of a fogey. Perhaps I am not up with the times, but I do not want to see anything put in this constitution that is liable to endanger it. I sincerely believe that, if this provision goes in, you will endanger the adoption of the constitution.

Joseph K. Toole (Lewis and Clarke County), soon to be Montana's first state governor, agreed:

> We are just launching the ship of state. The primary and paramount consideration with us is admission to the Union. We have long cried and clamored for the supreme hour when

we might formulate our fundamental law and be received into the family of States. The hour has arrived, and, in my judgment, it is neither wise nor expedient for us to load down our constitution with this much-mooted question. Our work must first be ratified by the people before it has any binding force. We should be circumspect and discreet if we desire it to meet with popular approval.

Toole—in a much-admired speech referring to other states seeking admission to the Union—firmly urged:

... Do not dam up the river of progress. Let us remember that delays are dangerous, that now is the time, and here is that place.

Their delay in securing the vote proved *very* dangerous for Montana females. Wyoming had given women the vote in 1869, and Utah followed in 1870. However, it was another twenty-five years before women received the vote in Montana. It was fifty-four years before Congress allowed the Chinese citizenship. And it really was not until the civil-rights movement of the 1960s that "ethnic" jokes began to become socially suspect.

None of this discussion would matter today: *if* there were no longer any Polish jokes, or Irish jokes, or North Dakota jokes; *if* it were not still claimed that women do not want equal rights, or that the "national security" would be imperiled if women received equal rights; *if* some Montanans still did not fear that Asians are taking over the West Coast with their cheap labor and industriousness—and soon will own all the big ranches in Montana.

It just would not matter. We could close the books, and we could forget the whole issue of unbridled prejudice. But those things are being said—and feared—today.

By looking at the Montana past and comparing it with the Montana present, we can begin to change our attitudes about the Montana future. Then our descendants will not have to blush for us—as we must blush for the revealed prejudices of our founding fathers at the Constitutional Convention of 1889.

~

Sources

The primary document for this study is the Constitutional Convention's 1,015-page transcript: *Proceedings and Debates of the Constitutional Convention Held in the City of Helena, Montana, from July 4th, 1889 to August 17, 1889* (Helena: State Publishing Company, 1921), *passim*.

Contemporary comment on the convention—from myriad perspectives—can be found in the territory's daily and weekly newspapers, focusing on the period from July 1 to November 8, 1889. These papers are available on microfilm for interlibrary loan from the Montana Historical Society Library in Helena: the *Billings Gazette*; the (Bozeman) *Avant Courier*; the *Butte Inter Mountain*; the *Butte Miner*; the (Deer Lodge) *New Northwest*; the (Fort Benton) *River Press*; the *Great Falls Tribune*; the *Helena Herald*; the *Helena Independent*; the (Missoula) *Weekly Missoulian*; the (White Sulphur Springs) *Rocky Mountain Husbandman*.

Like other states, Montana produced a "subscription history" series, published between 1885 and 1957. Most often such a work appeared in multiple volumes—the first volumes relating the state's history and the last volume filled with biographical sketches of "prominent Montanans." Typically the author financed the publication of his historical text by selling space and portrait pages in the biographical volume. These biographical sketches are invariably laudatory. Hence the nickname for these volumes: "mug books."

The Montana series includes: *M. A. Leeson, ed., A History of Montana, 1739-1885,* (Chicago: Warner, Beers and Company, 1885); Joaquin Miller, *An Illustrated History of the State of Montana* (Chicago: Lewis Publishing Company, 1894); *Progressive Men of the State of Montana* (Chicago: A. W. Bowen and Company, ca. 1902); *An Illustrated History of the Yellowstone Valley* (Spokane, Wash.: Western Historical Publishing Company, ca. 1907); Helen Fitzgerald Sanders, *A History of Montana*, 3 vols. (New York and Chicago: Lewis Publishing Company, 1913); Tom Stout, *Montana: Its Story and Biography*, 3 vols. (New York and Chicago: American Historical Society, 1921); Robert George Raymer, *Montana: the Land and the People*, 3 vols. (New York and Chicago: Lewis Publishing Company, 1930); Merrill G. Burlingame and K. Ross Toole, *A History of Montana*, 3 vols. (New York: Lewis Historical Publishing Company, 1957).

Late-nineteenth-century Montana politics is addressed in: Clark C. Spence, *Territorial Politics and Government in Montana, 1864-1889* (Urbana: University of Illinois, 1975); Spence, *Montana: A History* (New York: W. W. Norton, 1978); Michael P. Malone, Richard B. Roeder, and William L. Lang, *Montana: A History of Two Centuries*, rev. ed. (Seattle: University of Washington, 1991).

Too Many Cooks
The Carlin Hunting Party Lost in the Lochsa
by Dave Walter

Make "man's inhumanity to man" a criterion for "jerk" status, and you produce a bevy of candidates. Whether it is the corporate executive shafting the public or the individual who victimizes his neighbor for perceived advantage, the West teems with overqualified nominees.

Among the hands-down winners is the Carlin hunting party. These three young, eastern "sportsmen" packed into Idaho's Lochsa drainage— right over the Bitterroot Mountains from Missoula—in the fall of 1893. After hiring a local outfitter and a cook, the trio anticipated a singular experience. They got it.

A combination of unseasonable weather (if such a thing exists in the Bitterroots) and bad judgment placed the expedition in jeopardy. Still, they could not conceive that tragedy would befall them. Then their inexperience and arrogance mixed with a perverse form of Western hunting etiquette to produce an ethical nightmare.

Five men went into the Lochsa, and only four came out. The story of the cook, George Colgate, remains a sobering one.

SEPTEMBER 16TH, 1805: BEGAN TO SNOW ABOUT 3 HOURS before Day and continued all day. the Snow in the morning 4 inches deep on the old Snow, and by night we found it from 6 to 8 inches deep. . . . I have been as wet and as cold in every part as I ever was in my life, and indeed I was at one time fearfull my feet would freeze in the thin Mockirsons which I wore. . . . Killed a Second Colt which we all Suped hartily on and thought it fine meat.

> William Clark on the Lolo Trail,
> above the Kooskooskee [Lochsa] River

The federal Superintendent of the Census declared, in 1890, that the Western frontier officially had disappeared. Nevertheless, one of the most remote and the wildest areas in the Northwest remained the

Lochsa/Clearwater drainage—just over the Bitterroot Mountains from Missoula.

Whites had learned early from area natives that the Lochsa was tough country. In September 1805 the members of the Lewis and Clark Expedition had wrestled desperately, painfully—but successfully—with the snowy, mountaintop Lolo Trail through the Clearwater country. That party's ultimate success hinged, at least in part, on its leaders' abilities to anticipate difficulties, to adapt to severe circumstances, and to assume themselves at the mercy of nature. In fact, on one level, that entire expedition is a triumph of man's ability to respect nature and to adjust to various environments.

Almost exactly eighty-eight years after Lewis and Clark struggled through the Clearwater, three Eastern nimrods entered the same country on a hunting expedition. Precisely *because of* its primitive nature, Will Carlin chose the Lochsa for a traditional "sportsmen's hunt" in September of 1893. It promised to be a memorable outing for the nimrods—one that still carries valuable lessons for hunters in the northern Rockies.

Imbued with a cockiness bred of inherited wealth, the Industrial Age, and Manifest Destiny, these youthful "sportsmen" believed that the American male could dominate nature. Their American could penetrate primitivism on his own terms and emerge unscathed, the victor—with scores of excellent hunting trophies and lots of macho stories to tell.

Thus the story of the Carlin hunting party is really a tragedy—a catastrophic scenario played out along the Lochsa River in deepest, most remote wilderness.

Carlin outfitted for the five-week expedition in Spokane, Washington. Since the party already was embarking too late in the season to hunt mountain sheep, the men would concentrate on mule deer, elk, moose, and bear at the headwaters of the Clearwater. On September 18, 1893, the expedition off-loaded on the depot platform at Kendrick, Idaho: hunters, crew, mounds of supplies, and various livestock.

William Edward "Will" Carlin led the party. He was the twenty-seven-year-old son of Brigadier General William P. Carlin—the U.S. Army commander at Fort Vancouver, Washington—and had spent much of his youth in the Northwest. Although he now lived in New York, Will had accompanied his father on numerous wilderness expeditions as a boy. A nationally recognized horseman, pistol shot, and an expert in fishing and photography, Carlin epitomized the American sportsman of the day.

Will's closest friend was Abraham Lincoln Artman Himmelwright, a twenty-eight-year-old civil-engineering graduate of Rensselaer Polytechnic Institute in Troy, New York. "Abe" had engaged in some surveying for the Northern Pacific Railroad in Idaho before returning to engineering jobs in New England. In the fall and winter of 1888-1889, Abe and Will had shared a six-month sportsmen's hunt in the Coeur d'Alene and St. Joe regions of Idaho.

The third Eastern huntsman was twenty-year-old John Harvey Pierce. John was associated with his father in a Buffalo, New York, business house and recently had married Will Carlin's sister. Pierce had done some bird shooting in the East, but this expedition constituted his first trip to the Rockies. The Rocky Mountain climate had been recommended to John by his physician, to help him recover from a recent bout with malaria. Pierce would prove to be a different type of fellow from either Carlin or Himmelwright. He was *not* the archetypical sportsman!

As a hunting guide, Carlin hired Martin P. Spencer, a twenty-seven-year-old native of Iowa who had guided in the Idaho wilds for eight years. In fact, Spencer had taken a hunting party into the Clearwater the preceding fall. He had brought those 1892 hunters out on October 20 to avoid heavy snows. Spencer planned to return Will's party to Kendrick by October 15 this year—just to be safe.

The final member of the Carlin party was George Colgate. He was a slight, fifty-two-year-old Englishman who had immigrated to the United States in 1877 and currently served as a justice of the peace in Post Falls, Idaho. In 1888-1889 Colgate had accompanied Will and Abe on their hunting trip in the Coeur d'Alene country, and his cheerful work as a cook and camp tender recommended him for the Clearwater expedition.

Off-loaded with the mounds of supplies at Kendrick were five saddle horses, five pack horses, two terriers (named "Montana" and "Idaho") for bear hunting, and Colgate's black spaniel to retrieve grouse. Will and Abe carried two specially made three-barreled "paradoxes," designed to shoot both cartridge ball and buckshot. In addition the party carried three repeating rifles, four revolvers, abundant fishing tackle, and two of the most modern cameras.

Organized by Spencer, the mounted hunters and their pack train trailed out of Kendrick on September 18, shortly after noon. In two days they intersected the Lolo Trail near Weippe and began pushing east along the six-thousand-foot ridgetops that parallel the Lochsa River to the north.

The horsemen encountered incredible mazes of downed timber on the steep, rocky trail, as well as six to eight inches of snow at their campsites. As members of the Lewis and Clark Expedition had learned eighty-eight years earlier, the Clearwater was frightfully rugged country—where snow came early in the season, piled to remarkable depths, and remained late in the spring.

Near the "Indian Post Office" monuments, Spencer led his sportsmen down precipitous, timber-littered slopes, out of the snow— almost three thousand feet to the narrow, shaded Lochsa River valley bottom. Spencer located their camp along the river and set Colgate to work preparing comforts for their employers.

Colgate complained that his legs were swelling up, but he managed to hobble around the campsite. It was September 26, and it had taken the party nine days to thread its way back into the wilderness camp. Abe described the scene:

> At the edge of a flat, in the midst of a young growth of pine and fir trees, we made our camp. At our feet rushed the clear, foaming, roaring waters of the river; while all around us towered the awful mountains, rising to altitudes of from two to four thousand feet above the river, many of them covered with snow and glistening in the bright sunlight. It was a beautiful spot, where we planned to spend about two weeks, if we had decent hunting luck. But time was precious.

The Carlin camp was situated between two riverside hot springs. The waters from these springs created natural mineral licks for game animals. So, in effect, the hunters would be shooting over salt licks!

Quite near the camp, the hunters were surprised to find two Montana woodsmen preparing to spend the winter. Jerry Johnson was a sixty-year-old prospector who planned to winter in the Lochsa to search for the "long-lost Indian Prospect." His companion was Ben Keeley, a Missoula trapper in his twenties. The younger woodsman already had established trap lines on the nearby tributaries of the Lochsa. The two partners had almost finished their cabin, and they obviously welcomed the company of the hunting party.

Then the rain and the cold overcast settled in. Day after day it alternated between a steady downpour and a drizzle, swelling the Lochsa and making hunting for big game most disagreeable. Trailing through the sopping underbrush left the sportsmen soaked to the skin, so they made fewer and fewer trips to the two licks.

John Pierce and Martin Spencer assumed the cooking and camp duties—as Colgate's body continued to bloat, and the man grew increasingly weak. The best that the older fellow could offer was that he would recover soon, when the good weather returned.

Finally, on October 1, Carlin shot a huge, six-point bull elk at the lower lick, and there was fresh meat in camp. This success prompted Abe to hunt the upper warm springs, where he bungled a clean shot at a grizzly—but together he and Will bagged a second bull elk there.

The next day, under repeated questioning, Colgate finally revealed that he had suffered from prostate and bladder problems for twenty years. For some unaccountable reason, he had failed to bring his catheters with him from Post Falls. Thus he could not relieve his bladder, and he continued to fill up with body fluids. As he wanted badly to accompany Will and Abe on this hunting expedition, he had not mentioned this problem either in Spokane or in Kendrick. Slowly Colgate's legs and hands had doubled in size. He now found it almost impossible to walk, and his condition was deteriorating rapidly.

Spencer, the outfitter, argued that the party should immediately abandon its hunt and pack Colgate out on horseback over the Lolo Trail to Kendrick. The guide cautioned that precipitation falling as rain in the valley bottom could be accumulating as snow on the Lolo Trail mountaintops above them. However, the three sportsmen, in council, decided (two-to-one, with John in opposition) to wait for the rain to subside. In the meantime they would continue to hunt the licks.

The rain, however, did not subside, and the temperature began to drop noticeably. At last, on October 10, the party struck camp, bade farewell to Jerry Johnson and Ben Keeley, lifted an immobile Colgate into his saddle, and began the steep ascent to the Lolo Trail. They left six inches of snow at the Lochsa campsite, which became sixteen inches atop the first ridge, and thirty-six inches well short of the crest of the range. And they were still sitting below the six-thousand-foot Lolo Trail. Spencer estimated that the snow would be at least forty-eight inches deep at the "Indian Post Office" monuments.

Thus was created a time for decision. The dilemma involved several factors. The party held provisions for only eight days of travel; finding game was uncertain on the ridgetops; the horses could last in this deep snow for only two or three days without feed; Colgate could not walk out on snowshoes.

Thus Will Carlin made the decision. He ordered the party to return to its campsite along the Lochsa and to investigate a valley-bottom escape route that followed the river. So the crew returned to its old campsite, repitched the tents, and tried to comfort the exhausted Colgate.

On October 11 the sun shone for the first time in more than two weeks. Despite what Spencer said, Carlin and Himmelwright were sure that "Indian summer" had finally begun. The sportsmen convinced themselves that they had plenty of time to pursue their canyon-bottom escape from the Lochsa. Young Carlin negotiated a deal with Keeley to purchase (for $250) his winter provisions and his assistance to accompany them down the river. Will assigned Spencer and Keeley to help finish the roof on Jerry Johnson's cabin—a four-day project—while he and Abe hunted elk, and John cared for Colgate.

Since Colgate no longer could travel overland, Carlin determined to build rafts and float out of the mountains—down the Lochsa, to the middle fork of the Selway at Lowell, and then into the Clearwater at Kooskia. Spencer argued against this water-level route. He knew that the only white explorers of the drainage had been two Army survey

Carlin hunting party returning to the Lochsa.

Originally printed in *In the Heart of the Bitter-Root Mountains: The Story of "the Carlin Hunting Party"* by A. L. Artman Himmelwright

(New York: G. P. Putnam's Sons, 1895)

crews, in 1881 and 1886. Both of these groups reported deep canyons, impassable rapids and waterfalls, and rampaging water. And these observations were logged in the best of summer conditions—not after two weeks of rain!

Nevertheless Will decided that the party would need two five-by-twenty-six-foot log rafts for the trip. October 15 was the day that guide Spencer had projected the party would return to Kendrick. On October 15 Spencer and Keeley established a raft camp in a cedar grove near the lower lick and began building the rafts.

The pair received little help from the sportsmen: Will developed a nasty boil on his ankle and stuck close to camp; Abe had pulled some muscles in his back while hunting and stayed near the fire; John's time was consumed alleviating Colgate's pain. By this time Colgate had swollen to two hundred pounds, and he could not lie flat because liquid would fill his lungs.

Spencer and Keeley finished the first raft (the "Clearwater") on October 23, and the party moved their tents down to the "raft camp." The second raft (the "Carlin") was not completed until October 30. In the meantime, Spencer had attempted two trips up the mountainside to check on snow levels. On October 18 he found six feet of snow on the Lolo Trail and tracks showing that their horses had tried to escape by that route, before turning back because of the drifts. On October 30 he discovered even more snow on the trail, and he completely abandoned the idea of any escape along the ridgetops.

For a couple of days the party assembled provisions for their projected seventy-mile float. Carlin arranged with Jerry Johnson to keep their horses and some supplies through the winter. The swelling in one of Colgate's legs burst on November 2, providing him some relief. Will forecast a one-week float down the river; Johnson predicted a four-day run. Nevertheless the party packed provisions for fifteen days. Both Carlin and Himmelwright wrote letters to their families and left them with Johnson—"just in case."

The party launched their two rafts on November 3. It had begun raining during the night, and that rain turned to sleet. The river ran high, with slush-ice floes. The lighter "Clearwater" carried Ben Keeley, Martin Spencer, and most of the supplies. The "Carlin" boarded Will Carlin, Abe Himmelwright, John Pierce, George Colgate, and the dogs. The rafts covered about three miles before the "Carlin" ran aground and dumped its men.

That night and the next two days were spent off-loading the

supplies, drying men and equipment, and arranging with Jerry Johnson to care for even more of their supplies, to lighten the loads. Among the items Johnson packed back to his cabin were Carlin's prized elk antlers and capes.

On November 7 the rafts again took to the current, running about seven miles through several bad sets of rapids and a gorge. In four days the party had floated about ten miles. For the next six days, the party endured a cold, wet, bone-crunching ride through high waves and frightful, bouldered rapids, often between sheer cliff walls. They lowered the rafts through rapids on ropes and chopped ice from the logs to prevent their poles from slipping.

Each scouting trip downstream produced even more dire descriptions of conditions. Will noted on November 12:

> It is still cold and clear. We walked down the river a long way this morning and were horrified to find that we were absolutely "stuck." Half a mile below camp is a ledge of rocks and a rapid through which we cannot take a raft. Below this are two more places still worse. Every one gave his opinion of his own accord, that we could not get our rafts farther down the river.

The six men had made, at most, twenty miles from the "raft camp" of November 3. And now it was November 12, with Colgate unable to walk and the party so low on provisions that the men decided that they could not carry him out. Will Carlin wrote in his diary:

> As nearly as we can estimate, we are 50 or 55 miles from civilization. The dreaded Black Canyon is yet before us. Colgate's condition grows worse hourly. His legs are in a frightful condition, and the odor that comes from them is almost unendurable. He is perceptibly weaker than he was yesterday, and his mind is so far gone that he has lately appreciated no efforts that have been made to make him comfortable. . . . We all feel that it is clearly a case of trying to save five lives or sacrificing them in order to perform the last sad rites for poor Colgate.

After laying over a day, the party divided their remaining provisions among the five pack sacks: Carlin, Himmelwright, Pierce,

Spencer, and Keeley. On November 13, Carlin wrote:

> We made Colgate as comfortable as we could, left him what
> necessaries we thought he might require in the brief period
> he had yet to live, and, shouldering our packs, we started
> sadly down the river. Although Colgate's head was turned
> toward us, he made no motion or outcry as he saw us
> disappear, one by one, around the bend.

For the next ten days, the Carlin party trudged down the Lochsa,
over steep shale slopes and piles of downed timber—sticking as close
to the north edge of the river as its banks and cliffs permitted. As the
men became weaker, they discarded all extraneous items from their
packs, to lighten the loads. And they learned to relish the grouse and
fish that comprised their diet.

The weather provided a constant mixture of rain, sleet, snow,
piercing winds, and slippery footing. The hunters seemed never to be
warm, and seldom dry. Working their way through Black Canyon taxed
their strength severely, as this area seemed devoid of game. On
November 17, they shot Colgate's black retriever and stewed him; on
November 20, they ate the last of their pan bread; on November 21,
six small fish provided their only meal.

On November 22, in two inches of new snow, about seven miles
above the confluence of the Lochsa and the Middle Fork of the Selway
(at Lowell), Spencer stumbled around a rocky bluff to encounter
Sergeant Guy Norton and Lieutenant Charles P. Elliott of the 4th U.S.
Cavalry stationed at Fort Vancouver. Within an hour, Keeley, Pierce,
Himmelwright, and Carlin straggled out of the trees. The Carlin
hunting party finally had been rescued!

At the behest of General Carlin—Will's father, the commander
at Fort Vancouver—Lieutenant Elliott had mounted a rescue squad
that had been in the field since November 9. Elliott's party consisted
of four military men, three civilian boatmen, and two boatloads of
provisions. Indeed, he had figured that the lost hunters would try to
exit the Clearwater wilderness by working down the Lochsa River.

Spencer's guiding partner—William H. Wright of Missoula—
had alerted General Carlin early in November that the sportsmen might
have encountered serious difficulty, if they had not yet returned from
the Clearwater. The general immediately promised to pay all search
expenses and offered a $2,500 reward for the safe return of his son

and the hunting party. Within days, private and military rescue teams were attempting to penetrate the Clearwater: from the east, via Lolo Pass; from Weippe, via the western end of the Lolo Trail; from the southwest, up the Clearwater, the Selway, and the Lochsa (Elliott's route). As the first two routes were clogged by unusually deep, drifted, early-season snows, Elliott's speculation alone bore fruit.

The Carlin party rested for several days in Elliott's camp on the Lochsa and then floated down the Lochsa, the Selway, and the Clearwater to the mouth of the North Fork of the Clearwater. From there they traveled overland by wagon and horseback to Kendrick, arriving on November 30, just in time for Thanksgiving Day dinner at the St. Elmo Hotel.

In Spokane, General Carlin and his son met with members of the Colgate family. Evidently the Carlins assured them that abandoning George Colgate on the Lochsa was a necessity, for the family never criticized either the nimrods or outfitter Spencer in the newspapers. Yet the whole saga of the Carlin party had played large in the national press, and scores of critics stepped forward to excoriate the sportsmen's decision to abandon Colgate.

In November, national headlines had keyed on the man-versus-nature drama: "LOST IN THE PEAKS"; "NEW YORKERS SNOWBOUND IN THE MOUNTAINS"; "RESCUERS DRIVEN FROM THE WILDERNESS BY RAGING STORM." Then, once Elliott had rescued the survivors, the print discussion continued—although it focused on the ethical question of abandoning Colgate: "THE MOUNTAINS SURRENDER; THE ROMANCE IS ENDED!"; "COLGATE'S BONES"; "COWARDLY DESERTION OF THE ENFEEBLED COOK"; "OH! MAN'S INHUMANITY!"

And, indeed, that is the crux of the Carlin story. Without the young men's unanimous decision to desert Colgate, the tale of the Carlin hunting party would be simply one of daring escapade and survival. But "the Colgate question" raises ethical issues that a hunter might face in the Rocky Mountains today.

During the winter of 1893-1894, seven distinct search parties attempted to enter the Clearwater wilderness to learn the fate of George Colgate. Although two men drowned while ascending the Lochsa, none of these attempts proved successful.

In late May 1894, Will Carlin and Abe Himmelwright hired Martin Spencer, his partner William H. Wright, and George R. Ogden of Missoula to enter the upper Lochsa via Lolo Pass. After crossing twenty-

The hunting party photographed in Spokane, Washington, after the rescue. From left: John Pierce, Ben Keeley, Will Carlin, Martin Spencer, and Abe Himmelwright.

ORIGINALLY PRINTED IN *IN THE HEART OF THE BITTER-ROOT MOUNTAINS: THE STORY OF "THE CARLIN HUNTING PARTY"* BY A. L. ARTMAN HIMMELWRIGHT (NEW YORK: G. P. PUTNAM'S SONS, 1895)

foot-deep snow fields in the Bitterroots, the party dropped down to Jerry Johnson's cabin on June 7. His provisions were almost exhausted, and he reported that the snow had reached depths of ten feet at the site of the Carlin hunting camp. All the horses had perished during the winter, but the sportsmen's trophies and camp equipment, left with Johnson, were found in excellent condition.

After pushing twenty-three miles farther downstream, the party reached the spot where Colgate had been abandoned. The men here found blankets, tent canvas, a shirt, and rope fragments along the shore; the site obviously had been washed by high spring runoff. Although they followed downstream an additional three miles, they found no evidence of Colgate's body. The entire party returned to Missoula on June 21, 1894.

During August, Lieutenant Charles P. Elliott—the same officer who had commanded the successful rescue party the preceding November—led a surveying cadre into the Lochsa Valley. Approximately eight miles below the place where Colgate had been abandoned, he found some of the cook's remains in a grisly bundle, obviously mangled by animals.

Elliott gathered the leg bones and some other body parts, as well as a match box, some fishing line, and a few personal items belonging to Colgate. He carried these effects upstream to the lower hot springs, where the Carlin party had built its two rafts. With some military solemnity, the officer buried Colgate's remains on a bench overlooking the Lochsa.

Today, at a Forest Service site called "Colgate Licks," immediately adjacent to U.S. Highway 12, George Colgate's unmarked grave stands in silent testament to the tragedy that occurred in that narrow, heavily-timbered valley more than one hundred years ago.

One cannot gaze long on this gravesite—knowing the circumstances of the Englishman's death—and avoid taking sides in the controversy. For issues larger than Western etiquette or hunting courtesy apply here. The Carlin hunting party of 1893 violated some of the basic tenets of humanity.

Without qualification, both Will Carlin and Abraham Himmelwright deserve heartfelt awards as full-fledged "jerks." John Pierce has earned at least "associate jerk" status. In the name of George Colgate, all three deserve it!

Sources

Although Will Carlin kept a diary on the 1893 expedition, he never formally published his account of the trip. Nevertheless, Carlin's version of events is evident in the several newspaper interviews that he granted immediately after the rescue. Abe Himmelwright, on the other hand, produced *In the Heart of the Bitter-Root Mountains: The Story of "The Carlin Hunting Party," September-December, 1893* (New York: G. P. Putnam's Sons, 1895) within two years of the event.

Writing under the pseudonym "Heclawa," Himmelwright's work includes portions of Carlin's diary as well as contemporary newspaper accounts of the trip, pertinent illustrations, and material concerning the rescue parties. An edited version of Himmelwright's original publication (marketed using "Heclawa's" original title) was released in 1993 by Mountain Meadow Press of Wrangell, Alaska.

For background information, see: Ralph Space, *The Clearwater Story: A History of the Clearwater National Forest* (Missoula, Mont.: USFS Region One, 1964); Borg Hendrickson and Linwood Laughy, *Clearwater Country!—The Traveler's Historical and Recreational Guide* (Kooskia, Idaho: Mountain Meadow Press, 1990).

Journalist Ladd Hamilton retells the Carlin story in *Snowbound* (Pullman: Washington State University Press, 1997), adding some supplemental materials. The author holds Colgate responsible for the expedition's tragedy, and that interpretation taints his presentation. Hamilton acknowledges, however, three worthwhile periodical sources: George R. Cerveny, "Human Spirit Broke Down; When 1893 Hunters Left Cook in Idaho Wilds to Die," *Pacific Northwesterner* (Summer 1975); Edmund Christopherson, "Tragic Trek," *Montana, The Magazine of Western History*, Vol.VI, #4 (Autumn 1956); Joe Baily, "The Tragic Story of the Carlin Hunting Party," (Spokane) *Spokesman-Review*, February 19, 1956. Add to this collection: Dave Walter, "The Carlin Party: Lost in the Lochsa," *Montana Magazine*, #116 (November-December 1992).

The very best contemporary sources remain local and national newspapers that covered the lost party, the rescue attempts, and the search for Colgate's body. Particularly worthwhile are the *New York World*, the *Spokane Review* (predecessor of the *Spokesman-Review)*, the *Lewiston* (Idaho) *Tribune*, the (Missoula, Montana) *Weekly Missoulian*, and the *Anaconda* (Montana) *Standard*. However, *all* of the newspapers in the Northwest carried the story of the Carlin Party to some degree—including editorial writings addressing the leaders' ethics.

Missoula's Murderous Madam
The Life of Mary Gleim
by Jodie Foley

Arguments about the nature of the Western prostitute have raged for generations. Was she an angel, or a savvy entrepreneur, or a soiled dove, or an unfortunate? The discussion continues among sociologists and historians to this day, without resolution. Mary Gleim, who reigned over Missoula's "red-light district" for twenty-five years, combined several of these traditional stereotypes in a powerful, rotund, lethal package. The terror that she brought to "the trade" set the bar quite high for her competitors—those who survived her anger. To say that Mary "cut a wide swath" down Front Street remains historically accurate.

Mary's story again raises the historian's challenge of documenting female "jerks" from Montana's past—particularly those involved in prostitution. Sources are sketchy, frequently euphemistic; few madams wrote their memoirs; fewer "working girls" kept diaries; business records are virtually unknown. Perhaps with "Mother" Gleim, we snuggle up as close to a Montana madam as we want to get.

–Dave Walter

PROSTITUTES HAVE BEEN THE SUBJECT OF DEBATE AS LONG AS "THE skin trade" has been plied. Questions about the character of the women, the reasons they come to "the life," and the forces that keep them there have been debated at length. Each new generation of Western historians has provided different answers to these questions.

Early histories of the American West portray madams, and their "girls," as queens holding court over a romanticized world of swinging saloon doors, player pianos, colorful faro dealers, and flying whisky bottles. In this view, the prostitute becomes the harlot with "a heart of gold." She makes the best of a sordid life, with a smile and a drink for any man who comes her way—for a price, of course . . . but what's a girl to do?

Late nineteenth- and early twentieth-century writings provide a more sinister perspective. Skulking through the shrouded underworld of the "white slave trade," these historians reveal lives defined by addiction, depravity, and violence. Here the madam is the villain. Once a victim herself, she joins unscrupulous men in luring innocent women to their doom. She is both evil and tragic, a willing dupe to the greed and lusts of men. The story of her life is a cautionary tale used to control a generation of women disillusioned with the confines of traditional female roles.

Among the social historians of the 1960s, the prostitute in the West becomes a sexual maverick or a savvy entrepreneur. She serves as a vital cog in the fledgling financial machine that drives Western boom towns.

By this explanation, women—especially poor, uneducated, and abandoned women—come to the trade looking for a way to make a great deal of money, fast. In all but a few cases, their dreams are thwarted either by addiction to alcohol and drugs or by the brutality of the relationships they form with patrons and with each other. Despite their considerable financial acumen, they are consumed by the predatory underworld they are forced to inhabit.

None of these interpretations fully explains the forces that brought women to the flesh trade. What is more certain, however, is that the lives of the prostitutes were often "nasty, brutish, and short." In some cases this phrase could be used to describe the temperament and physical characteristics of the women themselves. Mary Gleeson Gleim, the heavyweight "Queen of Missoula's Bad Lands" (the popular name for the town's red light district), was the epitome of such women.

At 5 feet 4 inches and nearly 200 pounds, Ms. Gleim cut a wide swath through civic and court affairs, from her arrival in Missoula in 1888 until her death in 1914. With an iron fist, Mary reigned over the brothels and saloons of the "Garden City's" legal underworld, located on West Front Street. Her impressive arsenal included weapons of economic and pugilistic force.

As is the case with most sporting women, little is known of Mary's early life. Mary Gleeson was born in Ireland in 1845, at the height of the Potato Famine. Her father Thomas, was rumored to be an "Irish Squire," or a non-royal landowner. How and when she migrated to the United States is unknown, but she reportedly lived in San Francisco, then in New York, and finally in St. Louis. Working in St. Louis, she amassed a sizable fortune, presumably through the skin trade, but also as a result of a profitable marriage.

John Edgar Gleim was a man of some wealth and little brain—a perfect mate for the ambitious Ms. Gleeson. He came from a respectable, upper-middle-class family, but was addicted to the fast, seamy life. Gambling and alcohol threatened to cut short both his wealth and his unremarkable days on earth. Ms. Gleeson stepped in and, once the couple married, she took charge of the family fortune.

In 1888 Mrs. Gleim insisted that the pair leave St. Louis and follow the opportunists to the gold fields of Alaska. The couple tried to cross the Canadian border twice, but they were refused entry each time. Perhaps Mary's reputation as a notorious smuggler was the cause of these rebuffs. The full extent of Ms. Gleim's exploits prior to coming to Montana will never be known. It was rumored, however, that her picture once graced the "Rogue's Gallery," a lineup of New York City's most notorious fugitive felons.

Mary's reasons for choosing Missoula as a home base likewise are unknown. It is probable, though, that the community's central location, the newly arrived Northern Pacific Railroad, and the large numbers of "unattached" young men were deciding factors.

Missoula, in the 1880s, was awash in bachelors looking for quick riches and enjoying their first taste of freedom. Businesses grew to meet the needs of these young men—including saloons, bordellos, dance halls, and gaming establishments. Missoula's "city fathers" officially tolerated these enterprises, as long as they could be restricted to the West Front Street district.

Missoula also was an important hub for western Montana and Canadian trade, used by legitimate and not-so-legitimate business people. A nefarious northern trade route was rumored to have crisscrossed the Rocky Mountain West in the late nineteenth century, extending from Denver to British Columbia. The Montana segment ran from Billings in the southeast, through Butte and Missoula, to Thompson Falls in the northwest. The "merchandise" included diamonds, lace, opium, and humans—particularly Chinese laborers and women of the flesh trade. With these facts in mind, the Gleims made Missoula their new home in 1888.

Ms. Gleim quickly set to building a clientele. Under the thin veneer of selling excess furnishings, Mary made a plug for her first women's boarding house in the *Missoula Gazette* (May 19, 1889).

Mrs. M. Gleim begs to inform the public that she has returned from Chicago with two car loads of the newest and latest styles in furniture. Having more than she requires for her new lodging house she will sell bed-room sets . . . at cost price. Don't forget to call at the big new red house on Main Street . . . no reasonable offer will be refused.

Obviously Mary was referring to more than just the furniture.

In less than a year, Ms. Gleim expanded her holdings on West Front Street to include eight commercial buildings. These constituted nearly one-half of the existing structures on the nefarious thoroughfare.

Almost as quickly as she accumulated property, Mary accumulated enemies, both real and imagined. She earned a reputation as a "relentless hater," appearing frequently before the county judge on charges stemming from her drunken rages. Court records show convictions ranging from uttering "loud and unusual noises" in the early morning hours, to various verbal and physical assault cases. It should be remembered that many of Mary's victims were not the sort of people who would rush to the police. As a result, her convictions represented only the most severe cases.

In addition to criminal cases, Ms. Gleim was also a frequent participant in civil cases. These disputes primarily involved her refusal

Front Street in Missoula, 1894.

COURTESY MONTANA HISTORICAL SOCIETY, F. J. HAYNES PHOTOGRAPHER

to pay contractors for work done on her houses, and her foreclosures on the unhappy tenants who could not make their rents or mortgage payments. In 1893 alone, Mary Gleim was sued ten times for back wages—including one suit brought by her own lawyers. In most of these cases, Mary lost and was forced to pay the wages, plus court costs. The costs often tripled as a result of her intransigence.

Mary's lack of common sense and seemingly boundless rage extended beyond her financial interests in the red-light district. In January 1892, "Mother Gleim"—as she was facitiously called—was

One of Mary Gleim's eight buildings, 265 West Front Street, Missoula. Built in 1893, shown here restored in 1989.
COURTESY MONTANA HISTORIC PRESERVATION OFFICE, MONTANA HISTORICAL SOCIETY

convicted of physically assaulting a group of Catholic priests in their rectory. On a drunken whim Ms. Gleim took it upon herself to advise the priests concerning their clerical duties.

During the course of her instruction, Mary attempted to punctuate her point a tad too forcefully. She tore the frocks of Father J. Neale and Brother Pascal Megazzini, and she destroyed several pieces of furniture. When the priests refused to defend themselves, Ms. Gleim stormed out of the rectory and into a waiting carriage. She then vented her frustration by pummeling the driver. This escapade resulted in three assault charges: two involving the priests; one concerning the hack driver.

In her defense, Mary stated that she had "called on the *imitation* priests (I don't believe there are any genuine priests in this country) . . . [and] asked for candles for the McCormicks' child." (This followed the custom of placing "ecclesiastical lights" in a house of mourning to protect the soul of the dead person and to encourage community prayer.) Mother Gleim claimed that she had voiced her opinions in Latin, but that the priests had not responded. So she told them that they ought to learn the language where "Romulus and Remus were suckled by the wolf on the banks of the yellow Tiber."

Disgusted with the clerics' ignorance, Mary attempted to leave and tripped, grabbing the fathers' robes to save herself a fall. The prosecution argued that the opinionated Ms. Gleim, had attempted, in fact, to tear the robes from the clergymen because she believed that they were not fit to wear such holy raiments.

The court found Mary Gleim guilty and fined her $50. Once again her disrespect for the court cost her a great deal more than the basic fine. For each of the charges Ms. Gleim forfeited her bond because she refused to appear for appointed court dates, contradicted her lawyers by calling for a trial when she previously had pled guilty, and neglected to show up for sentencing. In total, fines and bonds cost Mary $736.30.

This cost and notoriety, however, did not dissuade the lady from further tirades. Just two weeks after she had attacked the priests, Mary appeared before the court on another assault case, this time for breaking a beer bottle over the head of one A. Hollenbach.

On this occasion, Mary used her court appearance as a forum to vent her opinions of the legal profession and all those people who were out to destroy her (*Gazette*, February 17, 1892):

The woman hardly opened her mouth yesterday without

applying vile epithets to the court, the prosecuting attorney
and some of the witnesses. . . .When this was resented by
the prosecuting attorney, . . . Mrs. Gleim squared herself off
at him and dared him to do anything. The affair looked more
like an incipient prize fight than a proceedings before a court.

Mother Gleim's performance earned her two counts of contempt.
One count was cleared by her attorney on his promise that it would
not occur again. When it *did* occur again, Mary was fined $50 in
addition to the court costs already pending.

In her numerous court appearances, Ms. Gleim and her lawyers
proved adept at using continuances, demurs, and requests for changes-
of-venue to keep her out of jail. Mary was also a talented dissembler.
When asked about an encounter with a doctor in a Front Street saloon,
Mary blatantly refused to cooperate (*State of Montana v. Mary Gleim*,
September, 1895):

Q. Walking along Higgins Avenue not long ago didn't you
    meet a young gentleman in a saloon?
A. I never saw a gentleman in a saloon.
Q. A man then?
A. A man is not a gentleman who will insult a lady.

And on she went until the lawyer lost his train of thought or
"Mother" became enraged. While she was skillful at redirecting the
conversation, she also could be an easy mark for a lawyer who knew
how to draw out her infamous ego:

Q. Don't you get drunk and get into fights?
A. No. I never go outside of my door to hunt a fight.
Q. Didn't you have a fight with "Big Bertha" out on the street
    and she whipped you?
A. No! She didn't whip me!

As one might conclude, Mary had developed an arrogant
disregard for the law. After a hard-fought perjury conviction was
overturned (*State of Montana v. Gleim*, #116, 1892), Mother went on a
celebratory romp through the district. She purchased a bottle of wine
for a man who had been a member of the jury and then hollered to a
crowded bar room, "That man and my money set me free!"

This was not a particularly prudent statement. In fact it proved one that would come back to haunt her during a later trial. Despite Mary's outrageous behavior, her money did buy her a pack of talented lawyers who were able, for a time, to keep her out of jail.

Eventually, however, Ms. Gleim's contempt for the law and for her fellow humans caught her in a snare from which she could not so easily bully or buy her way out. In the fall of 1894, Mary was convicted of the attempted murder of a long-time nemesis, Mr. C. P. "Bobby" Burns. Burns was one of Mother's business rivals and was well known among members of Missoula's rougher element. He earlier had been a primary witness against Ms. Gleim in a fight over some Front Street property. That case went all the way to the Montana Supreme Court, where Mary lost.

Mary had several more run-ins with the hapless Burns. During one particularly vicious encounter, Burns was whipped and dragged half a block by a team of horses. Mother Gleim's hatred for Burns finally led her to concoct a plot that landed her and an accomplice on trial for attempted murder. Ms. Gleim's conduct before, during, and after this trial (*State of Montana v. Mary Gleim*, 1895) reveals the extent to which Mary believed herself invincible, and the lengths to which she would go to protect her assets.

In the early-morning hours of February 12, 1894, Missoula's red-light district was rocked by an explosion that leveled the home of "Bobby" Burns. Burns miraculously survived the blast and immediately offered a $500 reward for information leading to the capture of the culprits. Local newspapers indicate that he had a pretty good idea who was behind the attack and that he was helping the authorities to collect evidence.

Two arrests were made within a few weeks. Authorities took into custody Patrick Mason, a longtime resident of "the Bad Lands," and William Reed, a Black private in the 25th U.S. Infantry stationed at Fort Missoula. The Missoula County sheriff held Mason without bond, but later released Reed on his own recognizance. Reed proved to have played a smaller role in the attack than officers first thought. He subsequently became a key witness for the prosecution.

It was not until August 1894 that the case moved to trial, and the full details of the conspiracy were revealed. Mary Gleim then was accused of orchestrating the plot to kill C. P. Burns—despite the fact that, at the time of the explosion, she was in San Francisco looking after some of her financial holdings.

Officers took Mother into custody and held her until a bond could be secured. She requested that a wealthy Missoula attorney sign as bondsman. He would have signed for her, but the judge in the case objected. He ruled that the attorney, who was currently practicing before the district court, could be held in contempt and severely fined if he provided Mary's bond. As a result Mother could not find a bondsman, and she remained in custody until the trial.

Despite this setback, the ever-resourceful Ms. Gleim kept herself occupied. Local reporters noted that Mary entered the jail with enough booze to keep her quite happy for several days. Upon consuming her libations, she spent the first evening verbally abusing the only other female inmate, a woman who would be transferred to the state penitentiary the next day. After spending that charming evening with Mother Gleim, the woman was probably more than happy to be on her way to quieter accommodations in Deer Lodge.

Ms. Gleim used her wealth to secure expert counsel for her co-defendant. Patrick Mason was "throughout his trial surrounded and defended by some of the brightest legal talent in the state" (*Daily Missoulian*, September 1, 1894). Despite his legal dream-team, however, Pat Mason was convicted and received the maximum sentence of fourteen years. He was swiftly escorted to the state prison in Deer Lodge, notwithstanding legal attempts to postpone the move until after Gleim's trial. The judge stated that the Missoula County jail was not a safe place for a man like Mason.

So, Gleim's lawyers prepared for her trial with the conviction of her accomplice already on the books. Her impressive legal representation included Judge Newton W. McConnell of Helena and Joseph K. Wood of Missoula. The team set about to build the same kind of legal web that Mary had used in the past.

They first requested that Mother Gleim be released on her own recognizance, as her "considerable girth" made it impossible for her to hide. They then attempted to gain both a continuance and a change of venue. All three requests were denied, and the trial was set for Friday, September 8, 1894. With "a small army of witnesses," the prosecution solidly established the connection between Patrick Mason and Mary Gleim.

Unfortunately, Mary had never been very careful about how loudly she expressed her opinions of Mr. Burns or what might be done to remove him. Several prostitutes and a former employee were brought in to testify about threats and plotting that they had overheard—

including discussions of poisoning Burns' sugar. The prosecution also provided several eyewitness accounts of the destruction wrought on the Burns residence by the explosion.

By this time, William Reed, the Black soldier arrested with Mason, had been cleared of all charges. In return, he delivered the most damning testimony of the trial. Under oath, Reed stated that Patrick Mason had confessed the plot to him while they shared a cell in the Missoula County jail. The private provided all the particulars of the plan concocted by Mason and Gleim to kill "Bobby" Burns.

Mary Gleim's attorneys put her on the stand as the final witness for the defense. But, rather than making a show of good character or pleading her innocence, she used the platform to expound upon her peculiar theories. Mother Gleim described a conspiracy that kept her on the wrong side of the law, for no reason other than that she dared to defend herself from the constant attacks of those wishing to destroy her.

On September 14, 1894, Mary Gleim was found guilty. The following day the judge sentenced her to serve fourteen years at hard labor in the state penitentiary. Given her infamous bad humor, many observers believed that Mary would lose her composure and explode during the sentencing. Instead she could not be moved to make even a statement on her own behalf. When all the people around her gasped at the severity of the sentence, Mary remained calm.

Although it is impossible to know what was transpiring in her mind, it seems unlikely that Mother was looking forward to her stay in Deer Lodge. Perhaps her pride would not allow her to give the court the satisfaction of an emotional outburst. Perhaps she had another card to play. Nevertheless, on September 16, 1894, Mary Gleim entered the women's portion of the state prison. Her attorneys immediately filed an appeal of the guilty verdict.

In November of the same year, this petition was heard in the Fourth District Court in Missoula. The bases of the appeal were that one of the jurors was not a citizen of the United States and that two of the principal witnesses for the prosecution were convicted felons. The suit was dismissed. Mary's lawyers quickly appealed *that* decision to the Montana Supreme Court. The Supreme Court overturned the lower court's decision and granted Ms. Gleim a new trial. Because most of the witnesses—habitues of the demimonde—had long since left the area, observers considered the retrial a mere formality and Mary's freedom assured.

On October 30, 1895, Mother Gleim made a triumphant return

to Missoula for her new trial. In an interview with a *Missoulian* reporter, Gleim confided,

> ... There is not a woman in the world who has been more persecuted more than I. I have lots of data laid aside [that] I will show to the people when the time comes. They have had their day, but mine is coming.

When asked about her upcoming trial, Mary coldly remarked (*Missoulian*, October 31, 1895),

> I have no fear of the results of a new trial. Two of the witnesses who were hired to swear against me have committed suicide, and God only knows where the rest are.

Mary's new council, Edwin W. Toole of Helena, was successful in reducing the bond from the original $15,000 to $7,000. Mary promptly paid this amount, and she was released, awaiting her retrial. Her first act as a free woman was to regain control of her holdings in "the Bad Lands." She had transferred ownership of these properties to her husband while she was in prison. With deeds in hand, Mary was back in business.

While waiting for her new trial, however, Mary could not keep herself out of trouble. Within months, she brutally attacked one of her tenants, "French Emma," nearly killing the woman. When "French Emma" made her court appearance nearly two weeks later, she resembled (*Missoulian*, February 28, 1896):

> ... A piece of high decorative art. Her eyes black and swollen... [with] a deep brown-colored oil painting covering the side of her nose. One of her hands were [sic] lacerated, said to have been done by Mrs. Gleim's teeth.

During this trial Mary testified that, in the encounter, a knife had fallen out of "French Emma's" dress—a knife which Mary believed Emma meant to use to kill her. Mary said that she further believed that the visit was part of a plot cooked up by "Bobby" Burns to get rid of her once and for all. According to Mary, the reason that she viciously beat the petite Ms. Emma was self-defense.

On March 1, 1896, Ms. Gleim was found guilty of assault and

fined $250. She also paid $300 in attorney's fees. A few days later, an anonymous, ominous note appeared in the *Missoulian*:

> French Billy, James Hayes, and a score of others who testified against Mrs. Gleim will please change their Front Street addresses.

A request that was promptly heeded, no doubt!

Two weeks later Mother Gleim received a real stroke of luck. "Bobby" Burns, the only remaining material witness in the attempted murder case, died of a heart attack. On May 23, 1896, the state dropped its case against Mary Gleim, and she became truly a free woman.

For eight months Mary managed to behave. Then, in February 1897, she embroiled herself in a new rash of assault cases: one verbal; one second-degree; one third-degree. After this flurry, however, she failed to appear on the Missoula County jail registry until 1905, when she was indicted as a co-defendant in an assault-with-intent-to-kill case.

In this instance, Mother and two men were accused of assaulting C. A. Clayton by entering

> ... the plaintiff's house and with bludgeon, loaded weapons, or instrument did cruelly and maliciously, wantonly, and unlawfully assault [him] by violent hitting, hammering, and striking him over the shoulders, in the face, [and] on the head and neck. . . .

Mary once again claimed self-defense. Mary once again attributed her woes to a conspiracy. After some deliberation, the jury found Ms. Gleim and her co-defendants not guilty. This time, our heroine—at the age of sixty!—had narrowly escaped the possibility of a second prison term.

In 1895 Mother Gleim had reported to the press, while awaiting the "Bobby" Burns retrial, that she gladly would leave Missoula if she were set free. However, she never did leave. On February 22, 1914, Mary Gleeson Gleim died of influenza "in a hovel on West Front Street," at the age of sixty-nine. Despite the fact that Mary had recently lost a $135,000 investment in a failed brick-making business, attorneys estimated her assets at more than $148,000. Those 1914 dollars are comparable to several million dollars today. She died without a will, leaving a niece and a nephew to dig their way through her diverse assets. Her holdings included property in Missoula, St. Ignatius, Ronan, Sanders County, and Canada.

Mary Gleim's obituary pays tribute to her considerable physical strength, her education, her financial acumen, and her spontaneous acts of kindness. These "acts of kindness" are not specified, however, so it is difficult to bestow praise where it might be due.

Even in death, Mother Gleim stirred up life in Missoula. She long has been credited with making the sentimental request that her tombstone face the railroad (when all the nearby headstones faced the opposite direction), "so her boys could wave goodbye to her." Since she left no will, however, this request cannot be substantiated. These community memories may just stem from the need to remember the dead kindly, or to fit local personalities into the larger myth of the West.

Perhaps the true nature of Western prostitutes lies somewhere outside the boundaries of the historians' theories. Perhaps they are "all of the above": sometimes harlots with "hearts of gold"; sometimes successful businesswomen in a man's world; sometimes vicious predators; sometimes just nasty women with nasty habits. Mother Gleim's life indicates just such a complex mixture, with the nasty habits taking center stage most of the time.

What seems certain, however, is that those unlucky souls caught in the whirlwind of her temper did not recall—at the time of her death—any of her "acts of kindness." Rather, they remembered Mary Gleim's arrogance, her paranoia, and her cruelty. For it is these dominant traits that made the "Queen of the Bad Lands" a queen among Montana's "jerks!"

~

Sources

Mary Gleim surfaced almost a decade ago in my research for a seminar paper on prostitution in Missoula, 1870-1916. At the time I was a student in the History Department at the University of Montana in Missoula. Since then I have sporadically gathered additional information on her. In this pursuit I am particularly indebted to Ms. Carol Israel of the Western Montana Genealogical Society in Missoula. Carol encountered Ms. Gleim while working on a project at the Missoula City–County Library to index back issues of the *Daily Missoulian*, and she shared her findings with me.

Similarly I received invaluable assistance from Ms. Marcia Porter, the Missoula County Records Manager in the county courthouse. She directed me to several sets of records on which I have relied: Missoula County Clerk and Recorder, County Deed Books, 1887-1948; Missoula County Clerk of Court, Jail Registers, 1890-1914; Clerk of Court, Civil and Criminal Case Files, 1890-1914; Clerk of Court, Probate Files, 1914-1916.

The extant county-court records contain only trial summaries of Mary's cases. In contrast, the files of the Montana Supreme Court present actual transcripts of cases involving Mary Gleim. Material concerning Mother's encounter with the Missoula Jesuits, some of her early Missoula assault charges, and auxiliary incidents involving "Bobby" Burns is contained in: *State of Montana v. Mary Gleim* (Montana Supreme Court, #S736; 1895). Specifics about the "Bobby" Burns case can be found in: *Kate McCormick v. Mary Gleim* (Montana Supreme Court, #S425; 1894). Both of these cases are on file in the Montana Historical Society Archives in Helena.

Given the nature of the period's sensational journalism, perhaps the most vivid sources for information on Mary Gleim are Missoula's daily and weekly newspapers. In gathering information on Ms. Gleim, I have surveyed: the *Weekly Missoulian* (1888-1907); the *Daily Missoulian* (1889-1914); the (weekly and daily) *Missoula Gazette* (1888-1895). Two other items have provided explanatory, supportive material for the newspaper accounts: R. L. Polk and Company, *Missoula and Hamilton City Directory* (1901; 1903; 1905; 1907; 1909; 1911; 1913; 1915); Sanborn Fire Insurance Company, *Structure Maps of Missoula, Montana* (1884; 1888; 1890; 1891; 1902; 1912; 1921; 1953; 1963).

One can find detailed discussions of prostitution in the American West—exhibiting its several interpretations—within the following works: John C. Burnham and Robert E. Riegel, "Changing American Attitudes Toward Prostitution, 1800-1920," *Journal of the History of Ideas*, Vol. 29 (July 1968), 437-452; Anne M. Butler, *Daughters of Joy, Sisters of Misery: Prostitutes in the American West* (Urbana: University of Illinois, 1985); Mark Thomas Connelly, *The Response to Prostitution in the Progressive Era* (Chapel Hill: University of North Carolina, 1980); Marion S. Goldman, *Gold Diggers and Silver Miners: Prostitution and Social Life on the Comstock Lode* (Ann Arbor: University of Michigan, 1981); Barbara Meil Hobson, *Uneasy Virtue* (New York: Basic Books, 1987).

See also: Mary Murphy, "The Private Lives of Public Women: Prostitution in Butte, Montana, 1878-1917," in: Susan Armitage and Elizabeth Jameson, eds., *The Women's West* (Norman: University of Oklahoma, 1987), 193-206; Paula Petrick, *No Step Backward: Women and Family on the Rocky Mountain Frontier, 1865-1900* (Helena: Montana Historical Society, 1987); Ruth Rosen, *The Lost Sisterhood: Prostitution in America, 1900-1918* (Baltimore: Johns Hopkins University, 1982); Elliott West, "The Scarlet West, The Oldest Profession in the Trans-Mississippi West," *Montana, The Magazine of Western History*, Vol. 31, #1 (Spring 1981), 16-27.

Ike Gravelle
Montana's First Unabomber
by Salina Davis

Even "jerks" validate the frequently misquoted George Santayana maxim—to the effect that "Those who cannot remember the past are condemned to repeat it." Ted Kaczynski may have grabbed national headlines with his capture in 1996—and held them to the present—but Ted lives in the shadow of an earlier explosives man: Ike Gravelle— "Montana's first Unabomber." For months in the summer of 1903, Gravelle paralyzed passenger travel on the Northern Pacific Railroad. His bombings of N. P. tracks, bridges, and tunnels, and his attempted extortion of $50,000 from the railroad frightened and fascinated readers across the nation.

However, Ike was not the brightest of criminals. A cellmate in the Deer Lodge State Prison, Harvey Whitten, proved the mastermind of their initial extortion scheme. Then, when Ike had to improvise tactics without Harvey's advice, he could not. Given the requirements for "jerk" nomination (Rule #1: To be eligible, a "jerk" must be deceased), Ted Kaczynski's application remains in limbo. Montanans stamped "approved" on Ike Gravelle's file long ago.

–Dave Walter

THE MOST VICIOUS CRIMINAL IN THE HISTORY OF MONTANA Issac Gravelle was the most desperate criminal that has ever been before the courts in Lewis and Clarke County. He was a horse thief, a dynamiter, and a burglar, and—if Tony Korizek dies—he will also be a murderer. He was the first man in the annals of the state who deliberately planned to wreck a train carrying 200 innocent passengers, and to throw that train into the river—his sole object in that attempt being to force the Northern Pacific Railroad Company to pay him money.

The Helena Daily Independent, August 12, 1904

On April 3, 1996, federal authorities surrounded and captured "Unabomber" Ted Kaczynski in his cabin outside Lincoln, Montana. Most Montanans were amazed that such a notorious criminal could be residing peacefully in their midst. The surprise arrest created a barrage of national media coverage that poked fun at Montana's sparse population, its "live and let live" good-neighbor policy, and its general naivete.

What the national media did not acknowledge is that Montana holds a long and legitimate legacy of extortion, retribution, and bombing. That legacy includes the "father" of Ted Kaczynski: one Isaac Gravelle who, for months in 1903, held the entire state in abject fear of his bombing escapades. At the time, both reporters and lawmen called Gravelle "the most vicious criminal in the history of Montana." Throughout the autumn of 1903, newspapers across the country featured dramatic stories of Ike's criminal exploits.

By all accounts, Ike Gravelle possessed a gentle nature and a belief that he had been victimized by society. What career criminal has not believed the same? Born in Montreal and raised in Canada, he had emigrated to Montana in 1885, at the age of sixteen. He was employed by the Morrow Brothers in Fort Benton for two years, and then he settled near the brand-new frontier community of Lewistown.

For several years Ike worked as a cowhand, breaking horses on Judith Basin ranches. He gained a reputation as an amiable, hard-working, reliable employee, and he became known for his marathon horseback rides, sometimes exceeding sixty miles in a single day. Then, in 1891, he stole a harness from a Lewistown livery stable and was caught. A local jury convicted him of felony burglary, and a Fergus County judge sentenced him to two years and nine months in the state prison at Deer Lodge.

Released in September 1893—five months short of his full sentence—Ike secured a job breaking horses for an outfit in the Sun River valley. In late 1894, he moved to a relinquished ranch near Priest Pass, west of Helena. Here he raised hogs and operated a series of butcher shops in the state capital and in nearby Clancy and Rimini. At one time he was feeding as many as 150 hogs at the ranch.

Ike could undersell any other pork supplier in the Helena area because he had reduced his overhead to a minimum. He routinely rustled local cattle, butchered them at his Priest Pass farm, and rendered the animals—hides and all—in large cooking vats. With this nutritious, low-cost brew he slopped the hogs, and they thrived on it.

In 1897, however, a state stock inspector caught Ike red-handed, butchering two cows near Clancy. Unfortunately neither cow belonged to Ike. This time a Jefferson County judge sent the twenty-eight-year-old felon back to Deer Lodge on a grand-larceny conviction for a nine-year term, of which he would serve almost six years.

During his second stretch, Gravelle learned to read and write with the help of the Scranton School of Correspondence. He also gained a reputation as a skilled craftsman (*Helena Daily Independent*, August 17, 1904):

> The articles Gravelle turned out while he was an inmate of the penitentiary showed he was an ingenious fellow. He made bridles, hackamores, and other articles used by horsemen, and beside he turned some curious things. Among these is a souvenir that Bert Coty has. Gravelle took an ordinary beer bottle and, in the bottom of it, he built out of chips a house, over which he put the legend "Ike's Place." In front of the house he built a corral, and in it is a horse, lying down, and two hogs standing over it. This was indicative of the business Gravelle once carried on at the Priest Pass house.

While in prison this time, Ike shared a cell with one Harvey Whitten. Harvey was a bright, calculating, inventive young man, who was serving an eighty-nine-year sentence for killing a sheriff's deputy in Madison County. From Whitten's fertile mind unfolded a plan to extort $25,000 from the Northern Pacific Railroad Company. The Northern Pacific offered a choice target, since many Montanans already hated the corporation—seeing it as a faceless, heartless monopoly that victimized small farmers and businessmen with its arbitrarily high freight rates.

The scheme assumed Ike's release in the summer of 1903. The plan itself involved the threat to dynamite Northern Pacific mainline tracks, bridges, tunnels, and even moving trains. Unlike "Unabomber" Ted Kaczynski, however, neither Whitten nor Gravelle harbored a political agenda. This was extortion strictly for profit! Ike planned to use one-half of the ransom money to make a fresh start in Ohio. He would give the other half to Whitten's girlfriend, Stella Brothers, who lived in Bozeman. She would use it to hire an attorney to press for Whitten's release or pardon.

In their cramped cell, sometime during the spring of 1903, Whitten dictated to Ike four extortion letters, addressed to the board of directors of the Northern Pacific. The pair wrapped the letters (at Whitten's direction, written in Ike's hand) around the handle of a walking cane, over which Ike braided horsehair to conceal the paper. When the authorities released Ike from the State Prison on July 16, 1903, they permitted him to carry out the cane and several other horsehair-plaited pieces, for sale as pocket money.

Ike boarded the 2 P.M. train that sped him from Deer Lodge to Butte. Here he purchased several envelopes from a stationery store and stripped the horsehair braiding from the cane to extract the letters. Ike flattened the extortion messages as best he could and placed three of them in separate envelopes. He addressed one to Charles Fee, the Northern Pacific's publicity director, another to J. M. Hannaford, the corporation's second vice-president, and the third to the Northern Pacific's board of directors in St. Paul, Minnesota.

Not too brightly, Ike mailed the letters that evening—so the postmarks matched precisely the date of his release from Deer Lodge: July 16! He then rode the train to Helena, where he bought a saddle, a bridle, and a pair of distinctive Mexican-style spurs from noted saddle-maker F. J. Nye. He also ordered a pack saddle, which Nye delivered a week later.

The July 16 extortion letters gave N. P. officials fifteen days to signal their willingness to pay the $25,000 ransom. These executives, however, received hate mail on a daily basis. Not surprisingly, they ignored Ike's demands.

So, right on schedule, Gravelle acted. On the night of July 31, he broke into the McKay Hardware Company's powder house in Bozeman and stole 120 pounds of #2 "giant powder." Then, in the early-morning hours of August 2, an explosion seriously damaged an N. P. bridge that spanned the Yellowstone River three miles east of Livingston. Before track crews discovered the damage, a fully loaded freight train and an express carrying 225 passengers rumbled across the bridge, high above the river. Both narrowly averted disaster.

Two days later, on August 4, a Northern Pacific freight train hit a sack of dynamite on a feeder line one mile west of Bozeman. The tremendous explosion, heard everywhere in the townsite, derailed the entire train into the borrow pit.

Quickly Northern Pacific executives reappraised the July 16 extortion letters mailed from Butte. The company offered a $2,500 reward for the capture of the bombers. Montana Governor Joseph K. Toole immediately added $1,000 of state money to the reward.

Almost overnight, "citizen posses" began combing the trackside hills from Big Timber to Missoula, looking for what Montana newspapers stated was "obviously an entire gang of crazed bandits." Scores upon scores of local men, idled by the national depression of 1903, joined the search for Ike. Thus the N. P. gained hundreds of volunteer employees for the mere promise of the $3,500 reward. In addition, the railroad hired pairs of track-walkers to patrol three-mile segments of its Montana Division mainline—day and night, seven days a week—looking for buried dynamite charges.

To organize the company's response to the extortionists, N.P. officials detailed their Special Agent William J. McFetridge to Montana. Detective McFetridge was a bright, experienced, tenacious operative. He held "highball rights" on all Northern Pacific lines—that is, he could order *any* train, even a prestigious passenger express, to a side track so he could chase his prey. McFetridge also had designed a special car that provided bunks and a heated sitting room for several men and stalls for their horses. With his own locomotive and coal car, this high-speed "special" could dart up and down the mainline in pursuit of criminals.

The savvy McFetridge did not import his squad of specialists from St. Paul. Rather, from the Bozeman-Livingston area he hired Major James F. Keown, Captain Frank Latta, and Bert Reynolds—all experienced trackers, crack shots, bloodhound handlers, and fearless lawmen. Most important, these men knew the country in which the gang of extortionists was operating. McFetridge positioned his squad in Bozeman and awaited developments. He did not have to wait long.

On August 10, Northern Pacific officials in St. Paul received the second extortion letter. This demand also had been dictated by Harvey Whitten to Ike in their prison cell and smuggled out wrapped around the cane handle. It outlined the payoff procedure for the $25,000 ransom and designated August 23 as the time of payment. No experts were needed to reveal that the "August 23" date had been added to a blank in the previously-written letter.

For the next two weeks, the public fear and anxiety that had gripped Montanans since the initial August 2 bombing seemed to subside. A few passengers who had postponed trips on the Northern Pacific chanced buying tickets and traveling on the threatened carrier. Montana newspapers, meanwhile, offered daily speculation about the authorities' attempts to apprehend "this outrageous gang of extortionists."

At 7 P.M. on August 23, as directed, a light Northern Pacific train pulled out of the Livingston yards, heading for Missoula at thirty miles per hour. Following at a discreet interval was Detective McFetridge's special train of manhunters. Ike—red lantern in hand, poised to strike the match—remained concealed beside the track sixty-five miles away, near Townsend.

However, the lead locomotive soon developed mechanical trouble, lost power, and fell behind schedule. A frustrated Gravelle finally broke his cover and paced the right-of-way, listening in the dark for his payoff train. Had the mighty Northern Pacific been foolish enough to ignore his demand?

One full hour after the train's expected arrival, an irate Ike stopped stomping along the tracks, packed his lantern in his saddle bags, and mounted up for the return ride to Helena. Just then the engine steamed around the bend.

Ike frantically dismounted and fumbled for the lantern. He raced for his spot on the right-of-way. But, in the darkness, the panicked Gravelle pitched headlong into a hole beside the tracks. With a stiff wind blowing, he huddled over the red lantern and attempted to light it. But match stick after match stick blew out in the gale. As the train reached his hiding place, a pesky gust extinguished Ike's last match. He later told a cellmate that he had cried like a child as the train pulled out of sight, carrying all of his money into the darkness.

From his temporary residence at the home of Myron and Bessie May Shanks in Helena, Ike then wrote his own letter to the Northern Pacific's board of directors. In it he apologized for bungling the ransom delivery, and he rescheduled the payoff for September 2. Again the locomotive—shadowed by McFetridge's special train—left Livingston on time. Again it fell behind schedule, and again a truly furious Ike Gravelle finally abandoned his rendezvous.

This time he had burned the lantern continuously upon his arrival—but for naught. From a hilltop on the trail back to Helena, he saw the train finally appear in the distant valley, a full two hours behind schedule. Again Ike's disappointment turned to rage; again Detective McFetridge missed an opportunity to capture "the gang."

Ike's subsequent letter to the Northern Pacific demanded a third payoff for September 15. By this time, however, company officials had decided to ignore further threats. When the September 15 rendezvous failed to materialize, Ike retaliated. He wrote another letter to the Northern Pacific doubling the ransom demand to $50,000.

More important, he returned to guerrilla bombing. Gravelle first planted a dynamite charge that blew an N. P. switch engine off Walker's Spur, near Blossburg, west of Helena and Mullan Pass. He enforced this retaliation with another bombing in the Butte Flats on September 17. These two seemingly random explosions rekindled flames of fear in the Montana populace (*Helena Daily Independent*, August 12, 1904):

> Those days were filled with many anxious moments for all connected with the Northern Pacific Railway Company, from Charles S. Mellen, who was president at the time, to the brakemen running on the Montana Division, and to the section men. Mr. Mellen knew not what hour he would receive a telegram bringing the news that a train loaded with passengers had been wrecked by the dynamiter. And the brakeman knew not what hour, when running on his train, he would be hurled into eternity. And the section man was in constant dread he would come across the dynamiter in the dark hours of the night, when the blackmailer was engaged in putting dynamite on the track, and he would get a bullet for his discovery.

Gravelle continued to raise the emotional stakes on Montanans. On the night of September 20, he broke into the A. M. Holter Hardware Company's powder house on Helena's east side. From this cache, he carried away five twenty-five-pound boxes of Hercules "Giant Powder," which was 60 percent nitroglycerin. The implications of this heist were immediately clear to lawmen and newsmen: "the desperate gang" of blackmailers had armed itself for an extended reign of terror.

Indeed, Northern Pacific locomotives then detonated charges of dynamite buried in the Helena switch yards (September 22), at Sampson's Spur, three miles east of Elliston (September 24), and near the eastern portal of the 3,875-foot Mullan Tunnel (September 27). Particularly the September 22 explosion—right in the N. P. yards at Helena—terrorized Montanans, for it prompted some locomotive engineers to refuse any more trip assignments.

In response, Chief Detective McFetridge moved his base of operations to Helena. By this time the Northern Pacific, Governor Toole, and the City of Livingston had raised the reward to $10,500 for the capture of the criminals. What the authorities really needed, however, was a bald-faced break.

Practically on cue, they received that break! Early in the morning of September 29, Mike Sheridan, a ranch hand who rode for Nick Rorvig's Antelope Springs outfit, surprised a fellow sleeping in a fresh haystack. The Rorvig place was located between Winston and Townsend, and it fronted on the Missouri River. Interestingly, the haystack was within sight of a dramatic Northern Pacific bridge—quite ripe for destruction—that spanned the Missouri River.

On that morning, a flustered Ike grabbed his saddlebags and his rifle, jumped to his saddle, and lit out. But he left in the haystack some damning items: a thirty-five-pound burlap sack of dynamite on which was stenciled "A. M. Holter Hardware Company" and one distinctive silver spur.

Rorvig delivered these items to the authorities in Helena. Within hours, Agent McFetridge found two local livery-stable hands who could identify the peculiar spur as belonging to an ex-convict by the name of Isaac Gravelle. So, for the very first time, authorities could label one of their adversaries—although they still believed that he represented a larger gang of cutthroat extortionists.

Soon each Helena lawman carried a copy of Ike's prison photograph, and they stepped up their patrols of the N. P. mainline in the vicinity of the capital. In the meantime, in early October, Ike pursued his bombing spree. One charge (October 5) blew a lead engine off the tracks near Birdseye, just west of Helena, and another (October 14) derailed a fully loaded freight train west of Elliston. On October 17, track-walkers discovered a sack of dynamite wired to the N. P. rails near Clasoil, ten miles east of Helena. They removed it only minutes before the regular eastbound passenger express roared through.

Then, on October 18, another pair of track-walkers surprised Ike as he buried a dynamite charge between the mainline rails at Mile Post 23, west of Helena. They shot at him, and he escaped on horseback into the gathering darkness. The guards then wired McFetridge in Helena, and the special detective and his squad of crack trackers steamed to Mile Post 23.

At first light, Major James Keown, Frank Latta, and Bert Reynolds picked up Ike Gravelle's tracks beside the rails. For the next ten hours, the squad trailed a pack of yelping bloodhounds supplied by the state prison in Deer Lodge. Patiently they tracked Ike's meandering route through the mountainous McDonald Pass–Mullan Tunnel–Austin–Priest Pass–Blossburg district—country that Ike knew intimately. Finally, they ran him to ground at his old hog ranch near Priest Pass and, without firing a shot, captured their prey.

In most dramatic fashion, the Northern Pacific lawmen trailed Ike down into Helena, with his hands bound behind his back. The triumphant captors had telephoned ahead, and hundreds of

Ike Gravelle.

townspeople lined Helena Avenue to gawk at this blackmailer who had terrorized the entire state of Montana for three long months. A reporter for the (Helena) *Montana Daily Record* commented that, oddly, the suspect wore only one spur.

Ike's trial began in Helena district court in mid-December 1903. The state charged him with "sending threatening letters for the purpose of extorting money from the Northern Pacific Railroad"—a felony. The prosecution had meticulously assembled the many pieces of circumstantial evidence needed to build the case. Special Agent McFetridge doggedly supervised this activity.

The Northern Pacific also supplied its Montana attorney-on-retainer, Helenan William Wallace, Jr., to "assist" Lewis and Clarke County Attorney Lincoln Working. Because Gravelle was indigent, the court had assigned the young Leon A. LaCroix to defend him. The *Helena Daily Independent* reported (December 15, 1903):

> He [Gravelle] wore a neat striped suit, his linen was spotless, and he was clean-shaven. Gravelle has a strong face, his hair is jet black, and he has piercing black eyes. He is short, but well-built, and has the appearance of a man of great strength. During the selection of the jury, he paid close attention and frequently consulted his attorney. He paid little attention to the crowd in the courtroom, and during the recesses he quietly puffed a cigarette.

The prosecution's tone became evident in William Wallace's opening statement (*Helena Daily Independent*, December 31, 1903):

> Isaac Gravelle has engaged in the most dastardly plot for the purpose of extorting money that is known in the history of the country. He endangered not only the lives of the trainmen and others in the employ of the railroad, but in his efforts to get the money he cared not if he sacrificed the lives of hundreds of innocent travelers. Although in the form of a man and endowed with the intellect of one, his act is so perverted as to place him on a level with the beasts.

In the course of the two-week trial, the state paraded eighty-two people before the jury—setting a new Montana record for prosecution witnesses. The defense countered with a mere twelve witnesses. Rather, it relied heavily on Gravelle's own testimony, in which he accounted for his travels and activities—always far removed from the sites of the bombings.

Some of the most damning testimony in the whole trial was delivered by Bessie May Shanks, the young wife of Gravelle's friend Myron. Obviously well rehearsed by Agent McFetridge, Bessie testified that Ike had stayed with the couple in Helena on the night of September 2—when the second payoff attempt had fizzled. The next morning Ike had borrowed a writing tablet from Bessie May and had written two letters while seated at the dining-room table.

During the agonizing composition of the letters, Ike had asked Bessie May how to spell three words—"monkey" and "double" and "Garrison." Prosecutor Wallace then produced the extortion letter of September 3, containing the phrases "monkey work," "double the ransom," and "by way of Garrison." Bessie May sealed the deal when she revealed that she had found a red lantern in their barn and that Ike had told her it was his. On cross-examination, Shanks denied that Gravelle had asked her how to spell "dyn-o-mite."

For two additional days, attorney Wallace compelled Ike to write phrase after phrase used in the series of extortion letters. The experience was visibly painful for the defendant. On occasion Ike asked Judge Henry C. Smith for spelling tips, but the court declined. A handwriting expert then compared the samples with the letters and concluded that Ike was the writer of all of the exhibits. The *Montana Daily Record* observed (December 22, 1903):

> Gravelle for the last two days seems to have lost his sense of humor. There was nothing in the proceedings of the day that made him smile, and he kept his head bowed in his hands. . . . During the first week of the trial, Gravelle frequently had talked with his counsel. But for two days now he has had scarcely a word with his lawyer. The strain is beginning to tell on him. He looks as if he believes the penitentiary is awaiting him.

After long, heartfelt summaries, the jury received the case on December 31. It argued the case for only four hours before returning a verdict of guilty. The *Montana Daily Record* commented (December 31, 1903):

> Gravelle appeared less agitated than he had yesterday. Then

he was pale and showed evidence of the strain under which he has been resting since the trial was begun. He sat facing the jury with his face in one hand, his left elbow resting on the arm of the bench. He did not move a muscle when the verdict was read by the foreman.

On January 4, 1904, Judge Smith sentenced Isaac Gravelle to the maximum: ten years of hard labor in the state prison; a fine of $5,000, "worked out" at $2 per day. State newspapers called the proceedings "the most notable criminal trial in the history of Montana courts." Preparation and execution of the two-week trial cost Lewis and Clarke County $2,500. The Northern Pacific Railway Company expended an estimated $50,000 to guard its tracks and to apprehend Gravelle.

No one was surprised by Ike's ten-year prison term and fine, but Detective McFetridge was outraged that even the maximum sentence was so light. He immediately lobbied county officials to prosecute the three-time felon on the September 20 dynamite heist from the A. M. Holter Hardware Company's powder house. If convicted of this fourth felony, the courts could designate Ike a "habitual criminal" and remand him to the state prison for the rest of his life.

Finally the Lewis and Clarke County attorney relented. He filed charges against Ike for the theft of five twenty-five-pound boxes of 60-percent Hercules "giant powder" from the Holter powder house on September 20, 1903. This trial opened on June 6, 1904, in the same Helena courtroom, featuring the same witnesses and the same principals: Gravelle, his attorney LaCroix, Judge Smith, County Attorney Working, and Northern Pacific counsel Wallace. The *Helena Independent* remarked (June 7, 1904):

Gravelle looks to be in good health, despite his confinement in the penitentiary. He is not so stout as he was last winter, when he was on trial on the charge of dynamiting the Northern Pacific tracks, but he has every appearance of being strong and rugged. He wears the same suit he did during his last trial. But, owing to the fact that his hair is cut close, he looks a little different than he did on his first trial.

The seven-day June trial featured testimony already heard during the December proceedings. In a new wrinkle, however, the prosecution referred repeatedly to Ike Gravelle's "93 Days of Peril." Once again,

Ike's defense comprised a litany of his horseback travels, none of which placed him at the scene of either a dynamite theft or a dynamite explosion. Defense attorney LaCroix's summary argument focused on "the paltry resources of the little man pitted against the Northern Pacific Railroad's massive wealth and power."

Then the best-laid plans of the prosecutors failed: a single juror—Michael Corbett—hung the panel. Jury members argued for sixty hours, setting a new Lewis and Clarke County record for deliberation. They logged more than fifty ballots, but Corbett remained intractable. A disappointed Judge Smith finally discharged the jurors on June 17.

McFetridge and the Northern Pacific quickly renewed their demands for officials to try Ike on the powder-house theft. County Attorney Lincoln Working secured a retrial on the court's August calendar. As a result, authorities did not return Gravelle to Deer Lodge, but confined him in the Lewis and Clarke County Jail for the interim.

During the summer, Ike raised money for his defense by braiding horsehair (*Helena Daily Independent*, August 12, 1904):

> He made bridles and other paraphernalia for horsemen, and he sold a number of them at prices ranging from $4 to $7. He made quite a bit of money as a result. He was the recipient also of a contribution made by convicts in the penitentiary to be used for his defense at this trial. With this money he engaged the services of lawyer Leon A. LaCroix, who has defended him in all of his recent trials.

At Judge Smith's request, District Judge E. K. Cheadle of Lewistown presided at Ike's retrial. These proceedings opened in the same Lewis and Clarke County Courthouse chamber on August 6, 1904, before a packed house. The audience thinned, however, during the first three days of the prosecution, because the evidence presented lacked any new information. Such was also the case during the morning session on Thursday, August 11.

When not in the courtroom, Ike remained locked in his county jail cell, directly across Ewing Street to the east. Special Deputy Tony Korizek escorted the unshackled Gravelle between his cell and the courtroom. Ike informed both Korizek and attorney LaCroix that he would poison himself rather than return to spend his life in Deer Lodge, but both dismissed these comments as "jailhouse braggadocio."

After Thursday's morning session, Korizek was leading Gravelle through the courthouse, when Ike suddenly declared an emergency and asked to use the first-floor men's room. The deputy remained at the lavatory door while Ike used a stall within. In that stall, Ike picked up a loaded pistol—planted there by "a party or parties unknown." He concealed the revolver in his trousers, and the pair resumed their trek to the jailhouse. Here jailer James G. Jones locked Ike in his cell and delivered his dinner tray.

Precisely at 1:45 P.M., Deputy Korizek returned to the jail to escort Ike back across the street for the court's afternoon session. Once the cell door had been unlocked, Ike produced his loaded weapon and backed Jones and Korizek into the jailer's office. When he attempted to disarm Korizek, the two wrestled for the deputy's gun. Ike discharged three shots into the deputy, and Korizek dropped to the marble floor, bleeding heavily.

Concealing both handguns under his coat, Ike calmly walked out the front door of the jail and down the stone steps to Ewing Street. Hank Monroe—a witness against Gravelle, who had heard the shots— ran from the courthouse, brandished a gun, and ordered Ike to stop. The fugitive broke, fired a shot over his shoulder, and ran around the corner. The *Helena Independent* recounted (August 12, 1904):

> Gravelle ran up Breckenridge Street past the Murray Stable. Near the corner of Rodney Street, a horse was tied. He started to untie the animal when he noticed that Monroe was not to exceed 15 feet behind him. Gravelle quickly turned, leveled his gun at Monroe and fired. Monroe dropped to the ground, and Gravelle gave up the horse and ran down Rodney Street.

By this time, four armed men from the courthouse were chasing Ike. He sprinted into an alley, heading west. In the heat of the action, John Raab, attired in a bloody white apron, charged out of his butcher shop on the corner of Fifth and Rodney and joined the chase. At first Raab foolishly was wielding only a meat cleaver, but he then stopped at a corner saloon to pick up a revolver.

Meanwhile, Gravelle circled back to Courthouse Square and dropped behind a hedge on the corner of Ewing and Fifth Avenues— the location of Governor Joseph K. Toole's brand new mansion. After lunch the governor had returned to his office in the Capitol, but Lily Toole and their two young sons were home, playing in a second-floor sitting room.

Arriving near Governor Toole's residence, Raab joined with those firing at the prisoner. The *Montana Daily Record* described the scene (August 11, 1904) :

Raab had redoubled his efforts to overtake Gravelle. Arriving near Governor Toole's residence, he joined with those firing at the prisoner.

Raab said, "I lay behind the curbstone and fired five shots at Gravelle. He was among the flower beds. He then went down into the cellar way, and I tried to flank him by going around to the back door of the governor's house, but I could not get in."

Ike Gravelle had attempted to enter Governor Toole's mansion through the coal-room door, but it too was locked. With his escape lanes blocked and shots whizzing over his head, Ike put Korizek's stolen revolver to his temple and pulled the trigger. Lawmen later recalled the thirty-five-year-old dynamiter's threat that he would kill himself rather than return to the state prison for the rest of his life. The entire escape and chase lasted less than ten minutes.

The *Record* concluded (August 11, 1904):

Fifteen minutes after Gravelle had killed himself, the body was carried out into the alley, up Ewing Street, and to the basement of the Courthouse. Blood dripped from a gaping wound in Gravelle's head. His left hand was bloody and blood covered his shoulder. The body was followed to the Courthouse by a great crowd. The coroner arrived soon afterward.

Anton Korizek died the next day of the wounds inflicted by Gravelle. His funeral drew hundreds upon hundreds of mourners, and the *Helena Independent* immediately started a subscription fund for the relief of his wife and three children. In contrast, Ike was buried in the county's "Potter's Field" section of the Benton Avenue Cemetery, with "no pall bearers, no service, no flowers, and no mourners." Thus ended the career of "the most vicious criminal in the history of Montana," by his own hand. For months in the summer of 1903, Ike Gravelle—at the direction of his wily cellmate Harvey Whitten—had held Montanans hostage to his extortion demands. Only good fortune had prevented the loss of life due from his bombings. Ultimately six citizens shared in the $10,500 reward posted for the capture and conviction of "the bomber."

Ironically, Ike never received a penny of ransom money from the Northern Pacific Railroad Company. Yet he did severely disrupt the railway's Montana operations, and he did cost the corporation more than $75,000 to protect its property and to track him, capture him, and prosecute him. Somehow, even Ike's desperate chase through Helena's courthouse district seems a fitting conclusion to the convoluted career of this desperado.

Although it remains premature to nominate Ted Kaczynski as a certifiable "Montana jerk," more than ample evidence exists to grant that dubious honor to Ike Gravelle—"Montana's first Unabomber."

~

Sources

Montana State Prison records (Manuscript Collection 197, Montana Historical Society Archives, Helena, Montana) provide basic biographical information on both Ike Gravelle and Harvey Whitten.

Portions of the Ike Gravelle story have been told as newspaper features. See, for example: the Montana Newspaper Association's Insert editions for November 28, 1938, and March 21, 1941; the Christmas special edition of the *Anaconda* (Montana) *Standard* for December 22, 1921; the (Helena) *Montana Record-Herald* special edition for July 12, 1939; Salina Davis, "More from the Quarries of Last Chance Gulch," (Helena) *Independent-Record*, May 2, 1996. A sensationalized version is told by Daniel Boyle and Jack Keenan, "Montana's Train Wrecker," *True Detective Mysteries* (May 1933), 20-25, 79-81.

The most fertile sources remain Montana—and particularly Helena—newspapers. See both the *Helena Daily Independent* and the (Helena) *Montana Daily Record* for the series of newspaper stories covering: the three-month bombing spree (August 2–October 18, 1903); activities related to Ike's trial on the charges of extortion (October 18, 1903-January 4, 1904); Gravelle's mistrial on the charge of dynamite burglary (June 6-June 18, 1904); Ike's retrial on the burglary charges, his escape, and his death (August 6-August 17, 1904).

"WHATEVER HAPPENED TO HARVEY WHITTEN?"

Harvey Whitten was the "brains" behind the scheme to extort $50,000 from the Northern Pacific Railroad Company. His fertile mind produced the plan that Ike Gravelle executed during the summer of 1903. The (Helena) *Montana Daily Record* called Whitten (July 15, 1913) "the brainiest and wiliest prisoner in Deer Lodge."

Harvey had been born in Cedar Rapids, Iowa, in 1876, and in his teens he had come to Montana to work as a cowboy. He had been convicted of murder in the second degree in Madison County. His crime involved the killing of Deputy Sheriff Jack Allen, who had attempted to arrest him for rustling. Whitten had been sentenced to the state prison in Deer Lodge for eighty years; he began his term on March 31, 1898.

Ike Gravelle and Harvey Whitten shared a cell in Deer Lodge for two years prior to Ike's release in 1903. While in prison, Harvey also masterminded two other capital crimes on the outside. The first involved a released prisoner named James McArthur (Fleming), who killed the father of incarcerated prisoner Clinton Dodson, after forcing the elder Oliver Dodson to sign a false confession to the murder committed by his son. The second crime propelled two ex-convicts into a deadly shootout, following their successful $30,000 robbery of a Livingston bank.

Through the efforts of his family and his Bozeman lover (Stella Brothers), Whitten received a parole in September 1911—after serving only thirteen years of his eighty-year sentence. He lived a straight life in Butte until August 1912, when he helped two Montana convicts escape to Nevada. In Nevada he took the name "Jim Ross" and engaged in horse stealing. Caught, convicted, and remanded to the Nevada State Prison in Carson City, Whitten escaped to Idaho after three months—only to be returned to Carson City with an increased sentence.

Paroled in 1922 from Nevada, Whitten moved to California and assumed the name "James B. O'Neal." In 1924 he was tried and convicted of robbery in the second degree in Los Angeles and sent to the California State Prison at Folsom. Paroled again in March 1933, he violated that parole (suffering a conviction for first-degree robbery) and was returned to Folsom in 1934.

Based on his four felony convictions, Whitten then was adjudged a "habitual criminal" and given a life sentence. He died in Folsom during World War II, at the age of sixty-seven.

To the Last Gasp: Deer Lodge Valley Ranchers v. the Anaconda Copper Mining Company

BY LYNDEL MEIKLE

By now you have noticed that the "jerks" in this volume often suffer from the sin of arrogance. On a personal level, this flaw can make life chaotic. On a corporate level, it devastates entire communities. The Anaconda Copper Mining Company (ACM) illustrates the point. For the first sixty years of the twentieth century, this international corporation dominated Montana's economy, politics, and journalism—even the state legislature. Historians who talk of Eastern depletion of Western natural resources, or of Western states' "colonial economies," land quickly on how the Anaconda Company ruled Montana for decades.

Nothing reveals "the Company's" collective arrogance better than the protracted litigation brought by the ranchers of the Deer Lodge Valley in 1905. As the recipients of deadly pollution from the ACM's smelters in Anaconda, these downwind farmers assumed the mantel of David. In this instance, however, the Anaconda Company demonstrated how Goliath had earned his reputation. In the end, the entire state became the victim of this corporate arrogance.

–Dave Walter

ALTHOUGH THIS INVESTIGATION PITS THE RANCHERS OF MONTANA'S Deer Lodge Valley against the mighty Anaconda Copper Mining Company (ACM), the story really begins with Butte's copper mines.

From the mid-1870s into the 1890s, companies both mined and smelted copper ore in Butte. In addition to the more familiar, conventional smelter operation, Butte processors used open-heap roasting. This procedure took two or three weeks and involved the laying of alternate layers of timber and ore, one upon the other, until a heap one-city-block wide and several feet high was built. When the heap was fired, many of the undesirable elements of the ore were burned away—chiefly arsenic and sulphur dioxide.

As a result, thick, acrid smoke blanketed the city of Butte. During the winter—locally called the "smoke season"—atmospheric inversions pressed the smoke down on the city. At times the smoke grew so thick, particularly in the daytime, that workingmen became lost trying to find their way to the mines. Some days, street lights burned from dawn to dusk. Trolley cars crept through the streets, ringing their bells continuously for safety. At night the conductor walked ahead of the trolley, holding a lantern, to prevent collisions. Out-of-state newspapers soon labeled Butte "that smoky city of sin."

In the days before the copper mines, Butte was not much different from other western Montana valleys. Its timbered hills and grassy lowlands might have provided solid farming and ranching opportunities, had not the area's mineral resources made the valley much more profitable for mining.

Timber men cut much of Butte's surrounding timber to fire the ore heaps and to feed underground mine construction. However, local timber also died from the conversion of all that sulphur dioxide (SO_2)—mixed with moisture—into "acid rain." The pine, fir, and spruce succumbed, leaving little but stunted juniper, which is resistant to SO_2.

Yet not only the trees, grasses, and wildlife suffered. In the town of Butte, the death rate exceeded any comparable location where smelting did not occur.

Nevertheless, "Copper King" William Andrews Clark claimed that the smoke was actually beneficial—that it was a disinfectant that destroyed germs. As for the arsenic, Clark noted that some women of that day used arsenic externally and internally to achieve a fashionably pale complexion. During Montana's 1889 Constitutional Convention, Clark testified that

> . . . the ladies are very fond of this smoky city [Butte] . . . because there is just enough arsenic . . . to give them a beautiful complexion.

This remark provoked laughter from his fellow delegates. Undeterred, Clark continued:

> . . . I believe this fact will be offered—because the interests of the ladies are paramount—as one reason why the [state] capital should be [located] in Butte.

The physician then in charge of Butte's health department, Dr.

Heber Robarts, did not agree. He kept meticulous records that enabled him to lay the blame for Butte's high death rate and its higher number of respiratory complaints directly on the smelting processes. Between July and October 1890, he attributed almost two hundred deaths in the city to smoke poisoning.

The technology of the day permitted the conversion of much of the sulphuric smoke into sulphuric acid. However, no ready market existed for sulphuric acid at the time, so smelter executives dismissed that solution as impractical—i.e., "unprofitable." The welfare of people, animals, and plants was rarely sufficient inducement for industry to change its procedures, unless its profits benefited too.

As pressure grew to reduce the smoke, the mining companies introduced a new and highly effective weapon from their arsenal: rumor. Whenever public criticism gathered momentum, a rumor would circulate that one of the city's major employers was about to shut down because of the complaints. The rumor asserted that jobs by the hundreds, even the thousands, would be lost if the company were forced to change its reduction methods.

Meanwhile, various solutions to the smoke problem were discussed. At one point, experimenters tried to burn up the smoke. A demonstration was arranged, and witnesses watched as the smoke entered a furnace, where it appeared to vanish. Outside, no smoke appeared for several inches above the top of the stack, but farther up, a dense cloud formed. Those advocates who wanted a quick solution to the smoke problem—one that would cost neither jobs nor profits—focused on the few inches of clear air. The realists saw the smoke above.

In 1891 the Butte City Council finally passed an ordinance prohibiting open-heap roasting. However, the Boston and Montana Consolidated Mining Company kept building heaps. Its executives contended that the ordinance was against *roasting the ore*, not against *building the heaps*. Then, in December 1891, company Superintendent Thomas Couch instructed his employees to set fire to the heaps, and he left town.

The time of year and the weather guaranteed that the smoke would blanket the town for days. After struggling for a week with the choice between economic loss and human loss, city officials moved to extinguish the heaps.

When Superintendent Couch returned to town, he explained that he had fired the heaps to prove his sincere belief that the smoke from the heaps never descended on the town. "I was mistaken," he admitted.

In the end, what saved Butte from this severe air pollution was the fact that its abundant copper-ore deposits were not complemented by an equally abundant water supply. "Copper King" Marcus Daly decided, as early as 1883, to build a smelter and a community where more water was available. So the town of Anaconda—almost thirty miles west of Butte—was born, a child of Daly and his Anaconda Copper Mining Company.

For almost two decades, the Deer Lodge Valley ranchers and the smelters coexisted, because the Company located its first set of smelters in the nearby Warm Springs Valley. Prevailing valley winds carried the smoke from these "Old Works" stacks to the south and the southwest, away from the town of Anaconda and the Deer Lodge Valley.

Then, in 1902, the Company constructed a brand-new smelting complex near Anaconda. The Washoe Smelter was the largest ore-reduction plant in the world; it represented an investment of nearly 10 million dollars.

Unlike the Company's "Old Works," the Washoe complex perched on a hill high above Anaconda, with four 225-foot stacks tall enough to pierce a different set of valley wind patterns. At stack level, the prevailing winds pushed north, down the Deer Lodge Valley, toward Garrison. From the first day that the Washoe Smelter's stacks belched smoke, Deer Lodge Valley residents were in real trouble.

The valley had been settled in the 1850s, before Montana's placer-gold rush; its first white residents were traders and ranchers. Mountain men such as Jim Bridger passed through the area as early as 1831. By all

---

"The Smoke of the Smelters"
Anonymous

O say, can you see, by the dawn's early light
What so proudly we hailed at the twilight's last gleaming?
Whose blue clouds and white mists, through the long legal fight
Over mountain and vale were so gallantly streaming?
And the furnaces' glare, the whistles' keen blare
Gave proof through the night that our smoke was still there!
The smoke of the smelters! Long may it flow
In the heavens above, o'er the earth here below!

Source: [A.C.M.-owned] Anaconda Standard, June 11, 1906

accounts it was a haven— a lush valley bottom well-watered by the Clark Fork River. Early visitors noted its abundant grass, game, and fish.

The animals in the valley were the first to complain about the new Washoe Smelter. Since they could not speak, they showed their displeasure by dying. A recitation of the symptoms of arsenic poisoning is grim fare. Yet the symptoms were clear: ulcerated noses; nostrils swollen shut; rough, scruffy hair; the inability to shed; inflamed and weeping eyes; the loss of appetite; exhaustion; loss of flesh; the incapacity to breathe (especially cattle); partial paralysis of hind legs (especially horses); labored heart action; dilation of the pupils; partial paralysis of the diaphragm.

When chemists performed autopsies on the Deer Lodge Valley animals, they found high concentrations of arsenic in their tissues. Within nine months of the smelter's first firing, corpses of hundreds of horses and cattle littered the valley. The dead livestock not only had been exposed directly to the Washoe effluent, it had also consumed vegetation that absorbed the poisoned air.

Particularly hard hit was Peter Levengood, whose land sat just northwest of the smelter. In an affidavit filed with the U.S. Department of Justice, he testified that his hay had decreased 75 percent in quantity and more than 75 percent in quality.

Another rancher, Nick Bielenberg, testified that, during the last months of 1902 and the first months of 1903, he had lost one thousand head of cattle, twenty head of horses, and eight hundred sheep. In desperation, he had moved his surviving stock to the Big Hole Valley, more than fifty miles to the south.

The ranchers hired two professors—W. D. Harkins from the University of Montana in Missoula, and Robert E. Swain, from Stanford University in California—to investigate the causes of the die-off. The academicians took soil and plant samples, collected falling particulate matter, and analyzed animal tissue from a one-hundred-square-mile area around the smelter. Of the animals that were dying at an ever-increasing rate, dissection revealed that nearly all showed evidence of acute arsenic poisoning. Four miles from the smelter, one animal exhibited 88 parts per million (ppm) of arsenic trioxide and 708 ppm of copper in its tissues. These amounts grossly exceeded arsenic and copper levels found in nontoxic areas elsewhere in Montana.

Two local veterinarians agreed with the professors' findings, as did Dr. M. E. Knowles, the Montana state veterinarian. Knowles added that the only other area where he had seen this condition before was around Great Falls, Montana—another smelter city.

The farmers threatened to sue, and the Anaconda Company offered to settle. The ACM's terms, however, did not satisfy the farmers: $330,000 in total damages, no payments for losses beyond a five-mile radius from the smelter, and a relinquishment of all rights to future damages. So the ranchers determined to fight the Company in defense of their families, their lives, and their livelihood.

In 1903 the Company constructed a new stack system at the Washoe complex. Its nucleus was a single 300-foot stack, 31 feet in diameter at its base and 30 feet at the top. Because the stack sat on a hilltop, its top rose 1,100 feet above the floor of the Deer Lodge Valley.

This mitigation was designed to throw the smoke higher into the air. The height was important because Professors Harkins and Swain estimated that the capacity of the Washoe Smelter in 1903 was 8.5 million pounds of copper ore per day (it would reach 20 million pounds by 1907). So, theoretically, the additional height would spread the ever-increasing smoke plume so far that, by the time it reached the ground, its poisons would be diluted and would cause no harm.

At least that was the public explanation. In fact, the new flue and stack system permitted the Company to collect a good deal of additional flue dust. And the resmelting of flue dust into copper had profited the Company by more than 6 million dollars in 1902. Once again, the adage holds: public good rarely provides an inducement for change, unless that change also increases profits.

Then the benevolent Company gave a banquet for the ranchers of the Deer Lodge Valley. At the gathering, Company officials assured the locals that the new stack would solve all existing problems. If it did not, the executives promised, the ranchers would be compensated fully for their losses.

The new stack did, indeed, spread the smoke over a wider area. By 1905 the average amount of arsenic emitted was 59,270 pounds per day. In addition the stack spewed sulphur trioxide and an astonishing 4.5 million pounds of sulphur dioxide—daily! With the new stack, the smoke traveled thirty miles north, beyond Deer Lodge, all the way to Garrison.

The two professors hired by the ranchers found that no measurable improvement could be documented, except in the immediate vicinity of the stack. They concluded that this benefit was the direct result of the pollutants being carried farther away before falling to earth. They also noted that the velocity of the smoke inside the stack was too great to allow the arsenic to settle out immediately. Interestingly, it would take more than ten years for a U.S. Bureau of Mines engineer to confirm the findings of Harkins and Swain.

Through 1904, the farmers in the valley were unable to sell their hay, despite an active market. In fact, brokers *were shipping in hay* at an average cost of four dollars more per ton than the Deer Lodge farmers' asking price. Ranchers statewide obviously knew that Deer Lodge Valley hay was tainted with arsenic.

Local farmers again complained to the Anaconda Company. The ACM investigated the charges and concluded that there was no basis for these complaints. The Company refused to pay any claims; it vowed to invest no more money in research to reduce stack emissions; it promised to fight the farmers on every front.

Locals created the Deer Lodge Valley Farmers' Association (DLVFA) early in 1905. The organization presented Company attorneys with verified claims for $1,120,731 and sought relief. When the Company did not respond, the DLVFA next offered to sell title to the claimants' property for $918,147. The ACM again provided no response to the organization's offer.

Anaconda smelter in 1903.

So, in May 1905, the association filed suit in the name of Fred Bliss. Bliss owned 320 acres just five miles southwest of the Washoe Smelter. He claimed that the farm's rental value had dropped from $1,000 per year to $300 and that the value of the land itself had been slashed by one-half. In addition, he declared that the formerly fertile farmland had been rendered barren and desertlike, and that nearly all of his trees in the downwind "smoke zone" had been killed.

Anaconda Company Secretary Cornelius F. Kelley countered that the Deer Lodge Valley had never been either rich or fertile and that the soil was, for the most part, "thin and poor and in many places charged with alkali." By contrast, pioneer cattleman Conrad Kohrs noted that, when he first arrived in the area in 1862, "The Deer Lodge Valley was one of the most beautiful stretches of bunchgrass country imaginable. The grass waved like a huge field of grain."

Kelley also claimed that the smoke from the smelter caused no harm (*Butte Inter Mountain*, May 19, 1905):

We have a perfect right to carry on a legitimate business and, if incidentally we should pollute the atmosphere, nobody has the right to complain until specific damage gives him a cause of action.

Then Secretary Kelley raised the specter of unemployment—always a highly successful technique, and understandably so. For much of the economic activity in both Butte and Anaconda depended on the Washoe Smelter's operation. Fresh in the minds of Montanans was the Anaconda Company's "Shutdown of 1903," during which it ceased all operations. That blatant manipulation paralyzed the entire state's economy for weeks, until finally the Company triumphed. In the end, a reluctant Governor Joseph K. Toole called a special session of the Montana legislature, which passed the legislation sought by the ACM.

The ranchers' hopes rose briefly when a federal district judge in Salt Lake City issued an injunction preventing any Utah smelters from treating ore containing more than 10 percent sulphur or from permitting the escape of *any* arsenic from their stacks. In his decision, the judge noted that arsenic emissions had resulted in the death of Utah horses and cows and that sulphur emissions, on contact with moisture, became sulphuric acid, which killed vegetation.

The farmers initially raised $40,000 to launch the Bliss suit. Agents of the ACM warned the litigants—through the Company-owned

Anaconda Standard—that they would "not have enough money left to buy breakfast" if they chose to fight.

And the litigation *was* expensive for the ranchers. Locating and hiring expert witnesses proved especially costly. Some potential experts frankly declined to "enter the field against the defendants." Of the toxicologists, pathologists, and microbiologists (histologists) contacted by the farmers, all but a single witness refused to participate in the case.

One of the veterinarians—Dr. Charles Greswell from Swansea, Wales—who would have testified for the farmers, died on an operating table in Denver before he could give a deposition. The farmers' other veterinarian, Dr. Olaf Schwartzkoph of Fort Assinniboine, suddenly was transferred by the U.S. military to a remote part of the Philippine Islands before the trial.

Some of the witnesses provided by the ACM were able—based on figures supplied to them by the Company—to give expert testimony without all the tiresome time and bother of actually visiting the Deer Lodge Valley site. For example, one Company-hired meteorologist, a Dr. Strange, testified that between 11:30 P.M. and 1:05 A.M. the wind velocity over the stack ranged from 81 to 134 miles per hour!

The plaintiffs' attorney disposed of this testimony by pointing out that, as of 1905, the highest wind velocity ever recorded in the United States was 87 miles per hour, and that the highest wind speed ever recorded *anywhere* was 92 miles per hour, in a typhoon in the Indian Ocean.

Professor Joseph Blankinship of Montana State College at Bozeman testified on behalf of the Company. He said that the damage to vegetation was caused by a disease that he himself had discovered. He called it "the drying-up disease." Blankinship was confident that other scientists would confirm his findings.

The professor assured the court that only because he had not yet made his discovery generally known was he unable to name any experts who would agree with him. However, under cross-examination, Blankinship did acknowledge that he had discovered this disease in only one other locale. Oddly enough, that place was Great Falls, the home of the ACM's other smelter.

At one point in the trial, behind the scenes, the Company tried to buy out Bliss at whatever price he demanded and, thus, end the litigation. However, the rancher was unable to sell, even if he wanted to, because his attorney held the title to the ranch property, as surety against his bill.

Oddly, the agent sent to Bliss by the Company in this attempt to silence his charges was Dr. Otey Yancy Warren of Warm Springs—the son-in-law of one of the major landholders in the valley, Conrad Kohrs. The Company also made lucrative offers to Kohrs and to his half-brother Nick Bielenberg, as well as to other leaders of the farmers' association.

One expert witness for the plaintiffs, Dr. Daniel Salmon, testified that he had been offered a $10,000 bribe to abandon the case. The Anaconda Company summarily fired any of its employees with relatives who kept their membership in the Deer Lodge Valley Farmers' Association.

Throughout the litigation, the ranchers received little support in the state's "captive press." The copper barons each had owned at least one newspaper during the several phases of the "War of the Copper Kings:" W. A. Clark published the *Butte Miner*; Marcus Daly produced the *Anaconda Standard*; F. Augustus Heinze ran the *Butte Reveille*.

The Anaconda Company's 1959 sale of its newspaper network to Lee Enterprises revealed that the ACM had accumulated the *Billings Gazette*, the *Anaconda Standard*, the (Butte) *Montana Standard*, the *Butte Daily Post*, the *Livingston Enterprise*, the *Daily Missoulian*, the *Missoula Sentinel*, the (Helena) *Independent-Record*, the (Libby) *Western News*, and the (Superior) *Mineral Independent*.

Early in the century, the Company had learned that it could control the news by what it printed *and* by what it declined to print. "Company journalism" made effective use of both techniques— inclusion and exclusion. What chance did the Deer Lodge Valley farmers have against this "captive press?"

The ranchers next appealed to the federal government, and particularly to President Theodore Roosevelt, a personal friend of cattleman Conrad Kohrs. They believed that Roosevelt, as a conservationist, would support them. The government did investigate the effects of sulphur dioxide on national-forest lands, and it contemplated action against smelters in both California and Montana.

Unfortunately the price of copper was low at that time because of an oversupply, compounded by foreign competition. Government investigator Ligon Johnson concluded:

A suit at the present time would more than likely be seized upon as a pretext [for the copper companies] to close [the copper mines and smelters] and let the cry go out that, under

the persecution of the administration, thousands of miners
had been thrown out of work.

Leaving office in 1908, Roosevelt delegated the matter to the
William Taft administration to pursue. The Taft men finally filed suit
against the Anaconda Company in 1910. But that was too late for the
Deer Lodge Valley and its ranchers.

In 1909 Judge William H. Hunt had rendered his decision in the
Deer Lodge farmers' suit. He ruled that they had failed to prove their
claim and that no substantial injury had been done to the valley since
the building of the big stack. Furthermore he concluded that the
Company's smelter operation was of such economic importance to
the area that to shut it down would work contrary to the real justice of
the case.

In his conclusion, Judge Hunt applied the principle of "the greatest
good for the greatest number." Unfortunately he had not benefited
from the wisdom of renowned American jurist Oliver Wendell Holmes,
Jr. Holmes once said: "The greatest good of a minority . . . may be the
greatest good for the greatest number in the long run."

Throughout the protracted case, the Company claimed that it
was using the most effective methods available to reduce emissions.
With Judge Hunt's decision, no incentive existed for the ACM to change
those methods. Anaconda spokesmen acknowledged, in 1913, that
arsenic loss through the stack had increased to more than seventy tons
per day.

The emitted arsenic could have been collected by means of a "bag
house" system. However, Edgar Dunn, who supervised the testing at
the Washoe, noted that the arsenic's

> . . . recovery and its entry into an already dull and sagging
> market means breaking present prices to the vanishing point.
> . . . There can be no question that the installation of any
> device for catching the fume . . . on the enormous scale
> required by the daily volume of stack emanation is not a
> commercial proposition.

In keeping with the operating tenets of the Anaconda Company,
if the proposition was not commercially profitable, the proposition
was not implemented.

Even today, on some of the ranches in the Deer Lodge Valley, sizeable areas called "slickens" exist. Nothing grows on this ground. Some of these "slickens" have been caused by airborne pollutants. The majority of them, however, are the result of an overflow, several decades ago, from the Company's settling ponds, combined with some soils redeposited during floods. On a graph plotting copper, arsenic, zinc, lead, and other contaminants located between Butte and Missoula, ranches featuring Deer Lodge Valley "slickens" sit near the high point.

After 1910 engineers developed more effective processes and equipment to reduce emissions from the Anaconda stack. Finally the ACM was able to claim that arsenic emissions had been reduced from the average of 75 tons per day, reported between 1914 and 1918, to a mere 190 tons for the entire month of October. However, that was *October 1976!*

The Atlantic Richfield Company (ARCO) purchased most of the Anaconda Company holdings in Montana in 1976. ARCO operated the Anaconda smelter for several years, but found it cheaper to mine and smelt copper ore in less developed countries than in the United States. In 1980 ARCO shut down the smelter. Most of the complex's buildings no longer exist, although a local citizens' committee saved the massive stack from demolition.

The various techniques employed by the Anaconda Company between 1883 and 1976 enabled it to create what is now the U.S. Environmental Protection Agency's largest Superfund cleanup site in the nation. The Company's control of the press, its dire threats of unemployment, its delaying tactics, its spurious experts, its political shenanigans, and its legal maneuvers served to defeat the Deer Lodge Valley farmers. Some of these ranchers eventually crafted individual settlements with the Company. Some simply gave up. A few adapted and survived.

The farmers' association's loss in the Bliss case proved the key event in this whole David-and-Goliath scenario. The matter had seemed cut-and-dried. The ranchers' livestock was dying, and the smelter clearly was responsible. They appealed to the judicial system and found no justice.

Nevertheless, incidents of court action involving the Washoe Smelter and the Deer Lodge Valley ranchers dragged on for years after 1910. Environmental horror stories continued for decades. Even today, when a section of the valley's Clark Fork riverbank caves in, fish kills can result for miles downstream—the result of toxic-waste deposits falling into the stream flow.

One would like to believe that Montanans had learned from the case of the Washoe Smelter complex and the Deer Lodge Valley ranchers. One would like to believe that the problem of soil, water, and smoke pollution in the Deer Lodge Valley had been solved. Yet an eyewitness account testifies that such is not the case.

Lucille Davis taught school in the Deer Lodge Valley. She told of looking out her classroom window one day to see smoke whirling to earth:

> . . . in a vast black pall. Within seconds, the sun was obliterated, the valley enshrouded, and the sinister fog was creeping uphill toward the schoolhouse. I drew the blinds and turned on the lights. "The spelling lesson will continue," I told the children quietly. But soon it was hopeless. Seeping through the window sills, the floorboards, the ventilators— even the keyhole—the sulphur- and fluoride-laden smoke began to fill the schoolhouse. The children hid their heads in their arms. They tied handkerchiefs over their faces. They tried to take refuge under their desks. Nothing availed. As the morning wore on, I tried vainly to comfort the children. But the acrid smoke grew denser. It seared the children's eyes and throats, made their tongues crack and bleed, and left them choking and gasping. Some staggered around the room. Others sat dazed and motionless. It was not until late afternoon that a breeze sprang up, lifting the black pall enough so that the children could grope their way home. Peering through the gloom, the tow-headed grandson of a local rancher pointed at the roaring smokestack in the distance. "Do you think it'll do that until it makes us all die?" he asked.

This story did not come from the Anaconda end of the Deer Lodge Valley, but from the north end, at Garrison. This incident did not occur in 1903, but in 1963. Not until the mid-1970s did the Rocky Mountain Phosphate Company permanently close its smelter in Garrison.

Defenders of the Garrison plant used the same political, economic, media, and pseudo-scientific ploys that the Anaconda Company had employed sixty years earlier. Now the sprawling mess left after the demolition of the Garrison smelter is dotted only with junipers—the sole survivors of acid rain.

The controversy continues in Montana today, as opportunistic companies apply to burn hazardous wastes and international mining corporations fight to protect the cyanide-leach process for gold. The arguments remain the same: "It's perfectly safe"; "It will provide jobs"; "If any problems are discovered, the plants will be shut down immediately."

Hmmmmmmmmmmm. One wonders. The Clark Fork River, as it meanders through the Deer Lodge Valley, still flows past miles and miles of deeply toxic soils—a permanent, silent monument to corporate greed.

~

Sources

The research done for this chapter would have been redundant if Donald MacMillan's *Smoke Wars: Anaconda Copper, Montana Air Pollution, and the Courts, 1890-1924* (Helena: Montana Historical Society, 2000) had been consulted. It is the best work on the environmental pollution record of the Anaconda Company. This work is based directly on the author's doctoral dissertation, "A History of the Struggle to Abate Pollution from Copper Smelters of the Far West, 1885-1933," (University of Montana, 1973). Another sound piece by MacMillan is his chapter, "Butte's Struggle to Abate Air Pollution, 1885-1891," in: Robert Bigart, ed., *Environmental Pollution in Montana* (Missoula, Mont.: Mountain Press, 1972), 1-14.

A summary of the court opposition between the Deer Lodge Valley farmers and the Anaconda Company is provided by Gordon M. Bakken, "Was There Arsenic in the Air?," *Montana, The Magazine of Western History*, Vol. 41, #3 (Summer 1991). See also Mary C. Horstman, "Historical Events Associated with the Upper Clark Fork Drainage," Project #8241, Montana Department of Fish, Wildlife and Parks, August 15, 1984 (Helena: Department, 1984).

Court documents at the heart of this case include the multivolume "Abstract of Testimony," *Bliss v. Anaconda Copper Mining Company* transcript, a copy of which is held by the Montana Historical Society Archives in Helena. See especially the findings of the Special Master for the case in *167 Federal Reporter* (1909).

Complementary, contemporary pieces that exhibit the findings of both sets of experts include: E. M. Dunn, "Determination of Gases in Smelter Flues, and Notes on the Determination of Dust Losses at the Washoe Reduction Works, Anaconda, Montana," *Transactions of the American Institute of Mining Engineers*, Vol. 46 (1913); R. J. Formad, "The Effects of Smelter Fumes upon the Livestock Industry in the Northwest," U.S. Department of Agriculture, Bureau of Animal Industry *Twenty-fifth Annual Report* (Washington, D.C.: Department, 1908).

See also: W. D. Harkins and R. E. Swain, "The Chronic Arsenical Poisoning of Herbivorous Animals," *Journal of the American Chemical Society,* Vol. 30 (1908); Harkins and Swain, "The Determination of Arsenic and Other Solid Constituents of Smelter Smoke, with a Study of the Effects of High Stacks and Large Condensing Flues," *Journal of the American Chemical Society,* Vol. 30 (1908); J. K. Haywood, "Injury to Vegetation and Animal Life by Smelter Fumes," U.S. Department of Agriculture, Bureau of Chemistry *Bulletin #113* (Washington, D.C.: Department, 1908).

Newspaper sources frequently provide the most vivid accounts of this battle. See particularly: the *Anaconda Standard* (1889-1970); the *Butte Inter Mountain* (1881-1912); the *Butte Daily Miner* (1885-1928); the (Butte) *Montana Standard* (1928--); the *Butte Reveille* (1900-1909); the (Deer Lodge) *New Northwest* (1883-1897); the (Deer Lodge) *Silver State* (1893-1925); the (Deer Lodge) *Silver State Post* (1925--).

For background on the Anaconda Company's newspaper chain—Montana's "captive press"—see: Richard T. Ruetten, "Togetherness: A Look into Montana Journalism," *The Call Number,* Vol. 21 (Fall 1959); Ruetten, "Anaconda Journalism: The End of an Era," *Journalism Quarterly,* Vol. 37 (Winter 1960); John M. Schiltz, "Montana's Captive Press," *Montana Opinion,* Vol. 1 (June 1956).

The story of Lucille Davis, the Garrison school teacher, can be found in: Ben Merson, "The Town That Refused to Die," *Good Housekeeping* (January 1969).

"You'd Better Be Careful, or I'll Send You to See Ed Morrissey!" A Case Study of Hooliganism in the Butte Police Department, 1910–1922

by Jon Axline

A historian searching for "jerk" candidates rarely unearths a truly despicable human being—someone rotten to the core. Ed Morrissey, however, is not a striped "jerk"—that mixture of good and bad. Nothing mitigates his black character. This disgusting fellow swaggered through the seamier side of Butte society for two decades, most of the time protected by the Butte City Police Department and the Anaconda Company.

Chief of Detectives Morrissey represented all that was corrupt and disgraceful in America's early-twentieth-century urban police forces. And Ed then extended that demeanor to his wife, his family, and his dogs. If the lawman's career served any purpose, it was that he became the prime focus of Butte's police reform campaign. That is a thin epitaph for an ignoble scoundrel, in a town full of ignoble scoundrels.

—Dave Walter

THE EXCESSES OF POLICE OFFICERS HAVE GENERATED DISCUSSION AND controversy almost as long as law enforcement has existed. Much of that debate has examined the role of the police in urban society. Even more often the questions raised have been "what constitutes 'excessive'?" and "what kind of person should be a policeman?" In the nineteenth and early twentieth centuries, governmental authorities most frequently hired police officers from the working class or from the lower-middle class. They gave them minimal training, if any, and put the men on the street.

Police wages were low, and in the case of Butte, Montana, the officer had to provide his own uniform, weapons, and badge. The taking of bribes to augment their meager paychecks was an act common to many policemen. Although not publicly sanctioned, business owners—both legitimate and shady—accepted the practice of bribery as a way to curry favor and to provide the extra protection of the law for their enterprises. In Butte, the bribe sometimes took the form of free booze at the local saloons. One cop even had his own keg of beer in the basement of a prominent establishment.

Butte "city fathers" created the community's police department in the 1880s, when the boom in copper caused a tremendous expansion of the formerly small gold and silver camp. Like its big-city counterparts, Butte's police force represented a variety of nationalities, but was predominantly Irish, Finnish, and German. Also like its big-city complements, Butte became saddled with a police force that was not always scrupulous in its handling of crime.

The Butte newspapers are full of accounts of policemen brought before the Police Commission to answer for improprieties while on duty. These transgressions included drunkenness, sleeping on duty (sometimes with prostitutes), offensive language in mixed company, and the excessive use of force while subduing persons for rather minor violations of the law. Unlike the situation in other cities, however, Butte sported a political and economic arbiter of all activities of the day: the Anaconda Copper Mining Company (ACM).

"The Company" overshadowed life in Butte so completely that most citizens of "the Mining City" rightfully believed that the ACM controlled the police. Evidence of this control—although indirect— can be found in how the police enforced the peace, in police behavior during times of labor unrest, and surprisingly, in the appearance of officers before the Police Commission.

If a policeman were "politically correct," he could and would be granted a certain amount of latitude in how he enforced the law. If he were not of the preferred political persuasion (i.e., if he were a Socialist), the Police Commission often showed bias against him. One favored officer appeared before the commission nine times before the commissioners finally fired him.

Of all the policemen active in Butte during the early part of the century, Ed Morrissey best exemplifies what was wrong with the system. Although frequently drunk, prone to the use of violence, and generally obnoxious, Ed Morrissey proved typical of policemen in many urban areas. He also became the first victim of the city's attempt to clean up its image during the 1920s. He serves as an interesting case study not only for the early-twentieth-century Butte police force, but also for just how rotten a human being can become when he puts his mind to it!

Born on Christmas Day 1874, in Waterford, Ireland, Ed Morrissey arrived in Butte two decades later. When war with Spain broke out in 1898, Morrissey served with a Montana volunteer regiment. Discharged in 1899, he had spent most of the war either in an American hospital in the Philippines or in the stockade, allegedly for a self-inflicted shoulder wound. Returning to Butte in 1900, he found employment at the Anaconda Company-owned Modoc Mine. In 1906 the Butte Police Department hired him. Within four years, Morrissey had become chief of detectives.

In 1910 he conducted a lone raid on a Colorado Street boarding house owned by a reputed Socialist. He carried no search warrant, but brandished a large revolver. (One pundit later observed that "without a large revolver, Ed Morrissey is not much of a man.") He lined the roomers up in the building's hallway "pouring unprintable abuse upon the shirking ears of women and the furious ears of men. . . ." The detective never did clarify the purpose of the raid. The episode ended when Chief of Police Jere Murphy and another officer arrived and escorted Ed from the building. Although a female boarder and her husband filed charges with the Police Commission against Morrissey, the case was never heard.

In 1911 newly elected Socialist mayor Lewis Duncan dismissed Morrissey because of his alleged Anaconda Company affiliations. Duncan replaced Morrissey with a Socialist, George Ambrose. Ed then became a watchman at Hennessey's Department Store, the headquarters for the Anaconda Company. Democratic mayor Charles H. Lane reinstated him as chief of detectives in 1916, after Ambrose discredited himself by consorting with known prostitutes and pimps while on duty.

A series of incidents in June and early July 1917 led to Morrissey's suspension from the force. The events typified many policemen of the time but, because Morrissey was chief of detectives, his actions were much more publicly visible.

In mid-June, Morrissey became involved in a one-sided fist fight with E. A. Milligan, a prisoner in the city jail. The chief of detectives had mistaken Milligan for a forger who was wanted in Anaconda and had jailed him. A co-worker's verification of Milligan's real identity forced the prisoner's release—but then the lawman attempted to assault Milligan outside the jail.

Morrissey struck Milligan in the stomach and the jaw with brass knuckles. Mayor W. H. Maloney, who was present at the jail, advised Milligan to sue the chief of detectives. During the trial, however,

Maloney testified in behalf of the detective and condemned Milligan as a troublemaker. Morrissey also labeled Milligan a malcontent and claimed that he had attacked Milligan only in self-defense.

Witnesses for the plaintiff stated that the attack appeared unprovoked. Milligan testified that Morrissey had approached him menacingly and snarled, "Now I'll get you!" The plaintiff further stated that the detective hit him with his left hand while holding a gun in the other hand. At the conclusion of the trial, Justice of the Peace John Doran ruled that Morrissey had used no more force than was necessary and that he had chosen the correct methods to subdue Milligan. The bench dismissed the suit.

While making an arrest a few days later, Morrissey attacked and severely beat a man whose only crime was public intoxication. The victim filed charges of police brutality with the Police Commission. On July 14, the police commissioners suspended Morrissey for his attack on the drunk.

In the 3 A.M. darkness of August 1, 1917, a black convertible drew up outside the Steele Block at 316 North Wyoming Street—the boardinghouse where Industrial Workers of the World (IWW) organizer Frank Little was staying. While one man remained with the car, his five masked compatriots entered the building.

The men erroneously broke down the door to an empty room, waking Mrs. Nora Byrne. By the time she had reached her door, the thugs had begun to beat on it. As she barred the door, Byrne asked the men what they wanted. The leader replied, "We are officers, and we want Frank Little!" Mrs. Byrne told them that Little's room was the one across the hall.

The "vigilantes" then turned to Little's room, broke down the locked door, and forced him outside. Believing that these men were law officers, Byrne waited awhile before she became suspicious and called the police. Later Byrne reported that, although she had not seen any of the men's faces, she believed that they were all young because of their vigorous movements. The *Butte Miner* (August 1, 1917) reported, "One [man] was 5 feet, eleven inches tall and not more than 20 years old; another was described as 'short, chubby, and five foot four inches tall.'"

A brief distance from the boarding house, Little's abductors stopped. One assailant pulled the IWW organizer from the car and tied him to the rear bumper. They then dragged Little, screaming, behind the car for about four blocks. Then the car stopped again, and

Little was untied and pulled inside. The vehicle proceeded to the Milwaukee Road railroad trestle on Centennial Avenue. Here the kidnappers hanged the unconscious man from the trestle, hoisted by a rope tied to the bumper of the car.

Ed Morrissey's long affiliations with the Anaconda Company and its hired gunmen make him a likely candidate for the murder of Frank Little. His career certainly suggests that he was not particularly scrupulous. His dismissal from the Police Department in 1911 and his subsequent employment as a watchman for the Company verify his close connections with ACM. Moreover, at different times between 1916 and 1919, the Company employed Morrissey as a guard at its Swan Lake retreat, while he continued to draw a salary from the City of Butte as its chief of detectives. Finally, Morrissey's suspension from the department in July 1917 made him conveniently available at the time of Little's death.

In 1919 the Socialist *Butte Daily Bulletin* claimed that a drunken Morrissey was escorted from a local saloon shortly after the killing and was "watched tenderly until he was normal and safe." Mrs. Byrne's description of one of the "vigilantes" as "short and chubby" closely resembles Morrissey's physical appearance.

The similarity to Morrissey also might help to explain why the Police Department did not make a serious investigation into the crime. The arrest of the chief of detectives for murder would look bad for the department and would raise embarrassing questions about the Company's participation in the lynching. The Little murder remains unsolved.

Ed Morrissey remained a colorful figure on the Butte police force after the controversy surrounding Little's death subsided. After March 1919, however, the detective's fortunes waned. Following a rash of misdeeds involving the detective, *Daily Bulletin* editors launched a campaign against him in the paper. This effort eventually galvanized a reform-minded mayor into seriously investigating the internal affairs of the Police Department.

On March 25, 1919—during the mayoral Democratic primary election—Ed Morrissey, accompanied by ACM and East Butte Mining Company guards, harassed and intimidated a number of voters and polling judges in two city wards. That party primary pitted Socialist activist and *Butte Daily Bulletin* publisher Bill Dunne against real-estate developer and World War I veteran William Cutts.

In the first incident, an intoxicated Morrissey physically assaulted a young man, Joe Torpey, who was visiting a friend at the polling place. When Torpey questioned Morrissey's actions, Ed called him a "slacker"—although Torpey had just been discharged from the U.S. Navy. Morrissey advanced threateningly toward the young man. Then Torpey's older brother William jumped "Eat-'em Up Ed" from behind and threw him to the ground. After regaining his feet, Morrissey arrested both of the Torpey brothers and escorted them to the city jail.

In the second case, at Precinct B in Ward 8, Morrissey verbally assaulted three middle-aged women acting as ballot judges. After confronting Charles Weiss, Frank McGee, and Dennis Harrington, Ed physically ejected the three World War I veterans and two of the women—one a mother of six children.

Two days later, Morrissey raided a bootlegging operation and confiscated twenty-eight cases and numerous loose bottles of whiskey. He delivered only twenty-four cases to the Police Department, however. Judging from the following week's events, it is readily apparent what happened to the other four-plus cases.

On March 28, 1919, the Silver Bow County coroner was summoned to the Morrissey home at 211 North Idaho Street. Ed's wife of four months, Katherine Ronan Morrissey, had died during a heated argument with the policeman. Kate, who was alcoholic and who suffered from obesity and heart trouble, apparently died of natural causes.

Allegations of spouse abuse, however, forced the coroner to convene an inquest on the following day. The Socialist *Daily Bulletin*—seeing an opportunity to repay the detective for the previous week's misadventures at the polling stations—accused Ed of murder. The inquest lasted almost one week and included the testimony of ninety-six witnesses, including the principals' friends, neighbors, and relatives.

For nearly a week prior to her death, Kate and Ed Morrissey had fought steadily. Most of the tumult occurred in the backyard of the apartment building that they owned. Several witnesses reported seeing Ed drag his wife up the back stairs by either her hair or her leg—no mean feat, since the woman weighed nearly three hundred pounds. On one occasion, the irate man sicced his dogs on the woman, who had passed out in the backyard.

In fact, many of Kate's actions can be attributed to the fact that she was repeatedly drunk. A neighbor, Ethel Bailey, testified:

Well, a week ago last Sunday, . . . I saw her lying on her back on the back porch. Mr. Morrissey pulled her into the house by her feet. We heard her again the same day. I looked out the window, and she was lying again on her back. She was dragged in again by her feet. Bailey said that she was later. . . startled by the apparition of Mrs. Morrissey bursting from the back door of her residence screaming for help. She was pale with fear, her wild terror-stricken eyes were staring from her head, her form only wrapped in a loose kimono.

In addition to dragging her around by her feet and hair, Ed also punched her in the mouth, locked her in the porch, and beat her head against a door knob. The Morrisseys were apparently suffering from the effects of bad bootleg whiskey.

Another neighbor, Anna Nellis, testified that she was a dinner guest of the Morrisseys on the night before Kate's death. She could initially remember nothing other than that "the eats were good." The coroner summoned her the following day, and she then remembered hearing a scream followed by a thud later that tragic night.

Kate's uncle, Dan Comba, who was present when Kate died, stated that when the woman collapsed and died on the living-room floor, neither he nor Ed thought anything was wrong with her. So they did not call the police until the next day. Before the coroner's inquest

Butte Police Detectives, 1917. Ed Morrissey is third from the right.
COURTESY BUTTE-SILVER BOW COUNTY ARCHIVES

concluded, however, Ed was admitted to St. James Hospital, diagnosed with the delirium tremens. (This affliction would be proven at Ed's own coroner's inquest, held three years later.) He thus was unable to testify at his wife's hearing.

At the conclusion of the inquest on April 5, the coroner's original verdict stood: Kate Morrissey died of natural causes aggravated by alcohol abuse and obesity. The jury's verdict caused the *Daily Bulletin* to step up its campaign against the detective. Upon Ed's discharge from the hospital, the newspaper speculated: "Perhaps, at intervals, weary lids dropped over those cold hostile eyes and blessed slumber allowed his cruel brutish nature to soften momentarily and to assume the semblance of human instincts for a little brief minute."

The *Bulletin*'s crusade against "this notorious tool of the corruptionists" increased. Almost daily, articles slandering Morrissey appeared on the front page of the newspaper. In one case, a piece equating him with "the bogey man" appeared the day after Easter Sunday.

> A lady was hurrying along the street, all rigged out in Easter togs. She dragged an infant by the wing. . . . An older child, perhaps of 5 or 6 years, attended her progress, but persisted in navigating on his own hook, unattached to his mother's person. Like a curious puppy, he trotted up to every object of interest along the way and felt it. He also lifted it if it was loose, and appropriated it for his own enjoyment until another prize dimmed its attraction. The young man's suit was plainly suffering by his activities, and so also was his mother's patience. "Woodrow," panted the exasperated lady with that slow severity which hints at an ultimatum, "Woodrow, if you don't keep out of the gutter and walk along like a decent child, I will send you to see Ed Morrissey!"

On May 10, 1919, Kate Morrissey's sister, Mayme Juckem, filed a probate to prevent Ed from disposing of his deceased wife's substantial estate. In the probate, Juckem alleged that Ed had married her sister to gain access to her property. She also charged that

> He . . . did . . . feloniously, wilfully, and unlawfully make several assaults on said Katherine Ronan Morrissey and did seize her with his hands by the head and did forcibly strike and bump

her head against iron pipes firmly established in the wall.

Further, Juckem claimed:

> . . . Morrissey is in the habit of getting drunk and had frequently, during the last two months, been in a drunken and semi-drunken condition, to such an extent that he has at divers[e] times suffered from delirium tremens and thereby rendered himself wholly unfit and unable to attend to business or to properly discharge the duties of [estate] administrator . . . ; that the said Morrissey has procured for himself by dishonest and unlawful means (the exact method . . . being unknown) large quantities of intoxicating liquors, which the said Morrissey is preserving for his own use and with the intent to consume same. . . .

The case went to court on June 2, 1919. Juckem successfully prevented Morrissey from discharging Kate's estate or sharing in any of its advantages.

On June 14, attorney David Wittenberg, on behalf of four individuals who were present at Ward 8 on March 25, filed charges of misconduct and conduct-unbecoming-an-officer against Ed Morrissey with the Butte Police Commission. (Wittenberg previously had represented the Socialist *Butte Daily Bulletin* in several legal entanglements.) The charges accused Morrissey of harassment, false arrest, and the murder of his wife. The accusations further stated that Morrissey was "brutal by nature and addicted to drunkenness" and that "on several occasions, in fits of brutality, he had assaulted peaceable citizens without any cause or reason."

The charges were specified in four counts:

(1) That Morrissey had entered a polling place while drunk;
(2) That he had used vile and indecent language "in the presence of a number of people, some of whom were ladies";
(3) That he had assaulted Dennis Harrington, Charles Weiss, and Frank McGee;
(4) That at Ward 8 he had forcibly ejected two women.

Wittenberg filed a second charge for John Boyle, a Pipestone-area rancher who claimed to have been assaulted by Morrissey the preceding year. Boyle declared that, on the night of October 29, 1918, he had entered police headquarters at City Hall to inquire about a policeman. He said that Ed Morrissey accosted him in the building, accused him of being intoxicated, and then arrested him for disorderly conduct. When Boyle protested, Morrissey punched him in the face and pushed him down the jail's stairs. Although later exonerated of the charge of disorderly conduct, Boyle apparently had nursed his resentment of Morrissey until the opportunity for revenge presented itself.

Police Commission chairman D. S. Jackman set a trial date for June 30. Because of public pressure—some of it applied by the Butte Good Government Club—Chief of Police Murphy suspended Morrissey from duty until after the trial. The *Daily Bulletin* also increased its campaign against Morrissey, comparing him to the German Kaiser and accusing him of fraternizing with ACM thugs.

The trial began on June 30, 1919, on the third floor of the Silver Bow County Courthouse. ACM attorney Peter Breen defended Morrissey. In the face of frequent objections from Breen, the charges against Morrissey were restated on the first day of the trial. Both the *Daily Bulletin* and the ACM-owned *Butte Daily Miner* covered the trial in detail.

From the transcripts published in the *Miner*, Breen's primary objections involved the testimony to be presented by the *Bulletin*. He attempted to discredit Wittenberg's witnesses and to disqualify the prosecutor's evidence. The Police Commission overruled most of Breen's objections.

Of the five charges brought against Morrissey, the commission discarded only one: Ed's alleged murder of his wife Kate. It was, the commissioners believed, beyond the scope of their jurisdiction and irrelevant to the main charges brought against him. Wittenberg also complained of threatening phone calls that he had received from people identifying themselves as Butte policemen.

Breen described his client as a "gallant officer" and charged that the *Daily Bulletin* was "a Bolsheviki organ on Galena Street . . . waging a battle to injure and discredit a gentleman, a martyr, and a patriot." Breen further impugned the reputation of Wittenberg and questioned his motives for representing the *Bulletin* in its vendetta against the police detective.

On July 1 and July 2, the people whom Morrissey had wronged gave their testimony. Their descriptions of the incidents closely paralleled the accounts reported in all of the Butte daily newspapers at the times of their occurrence.

On July 3, Morrissey testified in his own behalf. He portrayed himself as a sober, industrious, and gentlemanly police officer who never drank on duty. Breen bolstered his client's presentation by stating that the "Wobblies" (IWW members) wanted Morrissey out of the way so that they could "raise hell and escape." The attorney, however, never denied that the events leading to Wittenberg's charges had occurred.

In only one case—that of Joe and William Torpey—did Morrissey's account differ substantially from that of the witnesses. Indeed, he claimed that he was attacked by the Torpeys without provocation because they were "Wobblies." Two fellow police officers, Ed Hannigan and Mike Dwyer, vouched for Ed's "sobriety and virtue." (Mike Dwyer subsequently fell victim to Butte Mayor W. T. Stodden's crusade against undesirable elements in the city's police force.) Although Morrissey's testimony was detailed, it failed to raise sufficient reasonable doubt to absolve him from all the outrages attributed to him by the *Daily Bulletin*.

On July 8, the commission found detective Morrissey guilty, and Mayor Stodden dismissed him from the police force on the following day. According to the *Daily Bulletin*, the Police Department heaved a collective sigh of relief when Morrissey left its headquarters for the last time. An anonymous letter in the *Bulletin* asserted: "My wife and daughter may now walk downtown without fear of being insulted by a brute of the type of Morrissey, who, because of the star he wore on his breast felt authorized to insult women of respectability."

The evidence submitted before the Police Commission by the prosecutor, however, was far from conclusive. And, it is conceivable that Mayor Stodden wished to distance himself from his chief of detectives—since Morrissey had received so much bad publicity in the months prior to his dismissal. In fact, Morrissey might have become a severe liability both to the mayor and to the Police Department.

Morrissey's trial was the first held under Stodden's administration, and it became the test trial for his plan to rid the department of policemen of dubious character. As such, it set the precedent for trials during the following months. Morrissey was the first and the most visible "victim" of the new mayor's campaign for effective police reform in Butte.

After Morrissey's dismissal, he dropped out of sight for about one month. On August 20, 1919, he was arrested for impersonating a federal Prohibition officer. When arrested, Morrissey claimed he was working undercover in Butte for the Gallatin County district attorney. No evidence existed to support this contention, and the former detective was found guilty and fined $250 for the crime. In December 1919, Morrissey was hired as a federal Prohibition officer for Silver Bow County.

Morrissey's career as a federal-government agent proved almost as colorful as had his tenure on the Butte police force. Continually under fire from his dead wife's family (who still believed he had killed her), Morrissey was forced to resign his position under allegations of misconduct and of retaining confiscated alcohol for his own use. At the time of his death in 1922, rumors circulated through the city that Morrissey had been taking bribes from some bootlegging gangs, at the expense of other hoodlums.

From 1920 until his death, Morrissey drifted in and out of numerous jobs. In January 1922, he was involved in a fight at the Crown Bar, a local speakeasy. A "big, tall, slim fellow" struck Morrissey in the head during the altercation. A few weeks later, Ed's frozen, partially mouse-gnawed body was found by his brother in the same apartment in which his wife Kate had died. Although published reports stated that Morrissey had died as a result of poison moonshine, the coroner's inquest determined that he had succumbed to a blood clot that developed from the blow he had received in the Crown Bar fight. The murderer was never apprehended. Upon his death, Morrissey's only possessions were his clothes, his guns, and a "couple of worthless dogs."

Edward Morrissey represented all that was corrupt and disgraceful with many urban police forces at the turn of the century. He was not averse to enforcing the law with violence in a city renowned for such behavior. Although police work, even today, draws criticism, disrespect, and hostility from the citizenry, Morrissey's scurrilous activities drew more than a little attention from the news media.

The *Butte Daily Bulletin* characterized Ed Morrissey as little more than an alcoholic Neanderthal with a police badge—"Dragnet's" Joe Friday he was not! By current standards, the newspaper could be sued for libel, at the very least. No evidence exists that either Morrissey or his attorney Peter Breen attempted to do so.

Even the *Butte Miner* depicted Morrissey's actions as somewhat extreme. No real dispute exists concerning whether the events involving Morrissey actually happened. At issue is whether Morrissey could have received a fair trial, based on the coverage he had received from the

Daily Bulletin. This much is clear, however: Edward Morrissey had never been one of Montana's better citizens. Even his death represented an ignoble end to a less-than-admirable career.

~

Sources

The primary sources of information for the colorful life of Ed Morrissey include: the *Butte Daily Bulletin*; the coroner's inquest for Kate Morrissey; the coroner's inquest for Ed. The *Daily Bulletin* was definitely the "Current Affair" or the "Entertainment Tonight" of its time. Although biased and often slanderous, its accounts of Ed's more outrageous activities seem essentially true. Whether the quotations attributed to concerned citizens (e.g., the Easter bogeyman story) are true must remain a matter of conjecture, since the original records—if they ever existed—are long gone. However, these quotations do paint an interesting portrait of how the *Daily Bulletin* sought to discredit further a man who was accomplishing that task quite well without the newspaper's help.

Even in the more staid *Butte Miner*, Ed Morrissey usually appeared only if he had done something wrong. To its credit, however, the *Miner* provided a rather complete obituary for the former police officer, with no mention of his less-heroic efforts at keeping the peace in "the Mining City."

Edward Morrissey's name also appears in passing in Oscar Rohn's World War I records in the Montana Historical Society Archives in Helena. (This collection—Record Series 19: Montana Council of Defense—also contains some unflattering remarks about Frank Little, provided by one of his fellow labor organizers.) The National Archives in Washington, D.C., also holds some information about Ed's military service during the Spanish-American War.

Finally, the probate filed by Morrissey's brother Mike provides the most poignant testimonial to Ed's life in Butte. It lists as assets nothing but his clothes, guns, fishing pole, and two dogs of no value. Still, it remains impossible to conclude that this "jerk" did not earn his designation.

These Are the Days of Our Lives
The Reverend Leonard Christler and His Nine Commandments

by Jon Axline

When scandal taints one of a town's leading citizens, officials frequently bend legal procedures and community rules to protect the elite. Such was the case in 1922 with the wife of Havre's popular Episcopalian minister Leonard Christler. Since 1907 the clergyman had built a solid reputation across the Hi-Line. He had constructed a new Episcopal church in Havre, and then he filled it with parishioners who came to bask in his vibrant rhetoric.

On the other hand, surely something was going on between the Reverend and Margaret Carleton, the attractive wife of a local judge. And the Reverend's long-suffering wife Anna had to fit into this equation somehow. Was she clueless? What did Anna think Leonard and Margaret were doing as they worked the Chautauqua circuit in the Midwest together?

Well, now that the minister and Mrs. Carleton have been shot dead in the rectory, we will certainly straighten out this whole soap-opera mess. There is strong "jerk" potential here.

–Dave Walter

EARLY IN THE MORNING OF OCTOBER 28, 1922, A TELEPHONE CALL summoned Doctors Carl Foss and D. Stuart MacKenzie to the home of Leonard and Anna Christler at 813 Third Avenue in Havre, Montana. Approximately fifteen minutes later, Anna made another call, to the police, with the announcement that her husband and Margaret Carleton were dead.

When the physicians (and their respective wives) arrived, they found Leonard's body in his bedroom and Margaret lying several feet away, in the hallway. Chief of Police Jim Moran and County Coroner James Holland reached the house twenty minutes later. They pronounced Leonard and Margaret dead at the scene, the victims of an apparent murder-suicide.

This tragic occurrence ignited a series of events that caused sensational newspaper headlines throughout the United States. It further raised embarrassing questions about the relationship between the two dead people and about the Reverend's adherence to the Seventh Commandment: "Thou Shalt Not Commit Adultery."

Anna Christler's role in the drama also proved enigmatic. She provided conflicting descriptions of the events leading to the shooting. More important, she lied to the coroner's jury about what happened on that October morning. Some evidence also indicates that Havre officials may have covered up the truth about one of Havre's—and Montana's—most prominent citizens.

Born in 1876 in Auburn, New York, Leonard Jacob Christler arrived in Montana in 1907. Since then he had ministered to the Episcopal Church's Havre-based Milk River Mission. Christler was responsible for the construction of Episcopal churches on the Hi-Line in Malta, Glasgow, and Gildford.

Elected to the Montana State Assembly in 1909, he introduced legislation for "the reformation of erring women and girls." He further attempted to make it illegal for a husband to live off the earnings of his wife while she was employed in a house of prostitution. Not surprisingly, only the former bill passed the legislature. The *Helena Daily Independent* praised Christler's ability as a speaker "fit to cope with the orators of the nation...." In 1914 he married Anna Wadsworth, a member of a prominent upstate New York family.

Sponsored by the Great Northern Railway Company, Christler lectured throughout the East, boosting north-central Montana and the agricultural opportunities of dryland farming. He also spent summers lecturing on social and spiritual issues for a variety of Chautauqua companies. The clergyman acquired a national reputation as a result of the works of Stewart Edward White—a writer of popular, melodramatic, and grisly westerns—who christened him "the Bishop of All Outdoors."

In 1918 Christler supervised the construction of St. Mark's Episcopal Church on Third Avenue in Havre. At the time he owned a substantial home called "Hill Crest," south of town, near Beaver Creek. In 1922 he and his wife also rented a house at 813 Third Avenue in Havre proper. Reverend Christler's reputation as a charismatic orator packed the church every Sunday. Not all of the congregation were Episcopalians, and most were women.

Margaret Davenport Lotz Carleton was born in Helena in 1889. The daughter of pioneer Montana mining entrepreneur Donald

Davenport and the granddaughter of Anaconda physician J. M. Sligh, she was among the social elite of "the Capital City." Margaret married Charles Lotz (or Loutz) in 1909, at the age of twenty. A clerk at the A. M. Holter hardware store in Helena, Lotz frequented the local saloons and occasionally beat his young wife. Margaret bore a daughter, Catherine, in 1910. Claiming spouse abuse, Margaret then divorced Lotz in 1912 and obtained custody of their daughter.

Still described as "pretty, vivacious, and of particularly jolly disposition," Margaret five years later married up-and-coming Helena attorney Frank Carleton. When Frank was appointed the judge for Montana's Eleventh Judicial District in 1920, the family relocated in Havre. Upon her arrival in the community, Margaret, a devout Christian, became involved with the Episcopal Church—and, presumably, with its Reverend Christler.

In 1921, rumored financial and marital difficulties between Frank and Margaret resulted in the separation of the couple—with Frank retaining custody of Margaret's eleven-year-old daughter, Catherine. Shortly thereafter Frank and the young girl left Havre for Los Angeles. The judge later would blame the breakup of his marriage on the machinations of Leonard Christler.

In the meantime, Christler encouraged Margaret to seek

Havre St. Mark's Episcopal Church, partially built in 1916.
COURTESY MONTANA HISTORICAL SOCIETY

employment with the Midwest Lyceum Bureau, a Chautauqua company based in Chicago. Coincidentally, Christler already had been offered a job with that company as a lecturer. For the next two summers, Leonard and Margaret toured the Midwest on the Chautauqua circuit. One long-time Havre resident remembered Anna Christler, during the summer months, diligently tending the flowers planted by her husband at St. Mark's Church, while her husband was away.

By late 1921, local gossip connecting Leonard Christler and Margaret Carleton led to an investigation by the Bishop of the Montana Diocese of the Episcopal Church. Although Bishop William Faber

The Reverend Leonard Christler.

ORIGINALLY PRINTED IN *GRIT, GUTS AND GUSTO: A HISTORY OF HILL COUNTY* BY THE HILL COUNTY BICENTENNIAL COMMISSION (HAVRE, MONT.: BEAR PAW PRINTERS, 1976)

received many letters that linked Christler with Carleton, no one came forward with specific information during the cleric's fact-finding visit to Havre.

Although Bishop Faber later admitted that he had never seriously investigated the charges, at the time he publicly concluded that the accusations against Christler merely constituted a plot created by his enemies to discredit him. Officially the bishop reported that the situation revealed no romantic involvement between the priest and Mrs. Carleton. Despite the bishop's conclusions, the Christler-Carleton rumors persisted—and in June 1922, took an even more bizarre twist.

While Frank Carleton practiced law in Los Angeles, he provided financial assistance to his estranged wife in Havre. Simultaneously Margaret's affair with Christler became more conspicuous. Long-time Havre resident Walter Mack remembered that, as an eleven-year-old boy, he had seen Leonard and Margaret walking briskly down Third Avenue together—with Anna bringing up the rear.

In June the Mutual-Elwell Chautauqua Bureau hired Margaret as superintendent for one of its stock companies. Leonard Christler had secured the position for her with a lengthy letter of recommendation. Company manager Charles Booth later stated that he had received the recommendation in the same envelope with Christler's own application-for-employment letter.

Before Margaret left for the Chautauqua tour, her physician, Dr. Carl Foss, "operated on Mrs. Carleton and removed certain conditions that she was troubled with. . . ." The "certain conditions" (possibly an abortion) had placed her in a highly emotional state, subject to deep depression and frequent anxiety attacks. To remedy the side effects of the operation, Dr. Foss prescribed sleeping powders to help her relax. Margaret departed for Chicago and the Chautauqua tour in early July.

While in Chicago, Margaret received numerous letters from both her estranged husband and Reverend Christler. Although Frank Carleton had attempted to reconcile with his wife on several occasions, he believed that her infatuation with Christler proved an insurmountable barrier to rekindling their marriage. Eventually, in August 1922, Frank suggested that Margaret file for an uncontested divorce. He told her:

> I know that you have no love for me, and why make the pretense? We have been apart a year, and there is absolutely no chance for happiness for you as my wife. . . .

Margaret forwarded the letter to Christler, who then was visiting his family in New York.

Christler replied with words of encouragement—in a letter found in Margaret's Havre hotel room after her death.

> . . . I want to see you clean the slate in Havre. Am coming to help. Your stock there is going up. Keep it going. Your own standard for pluck, common sense, and honesty in Montana . . . is going to be recognized and respected, if time, health, and God's blessing only permits [sic].

The clergyman also suggested that Frank's financial problems should be resolved before the divorce and thus abrogate any responsibility she might hold for these debts. Surprisingly, Frank's letters to Margaret had given no hint of financial difficulties.

True to his word, Christler shortly arrived in Chicago from New York. The couple spent the next two weeks together in "the Windy City." Chautauqua manager Charlie Booth later remembered that Christler and Carleton spent considerable time together and that there never rose any hint of trouble between the happy couple. Christler returned to Havre in September, and Margaret followed about one month later.

Upon her arrival in Havre, Margaret's depression again deepened, her anxiety attacks returned, and her behavior sometimes bordered on hysteria. To compensate, Dr. Foss increased the dosage of her sleeping powders. On October 26, Margaret's mother, Elizabeth Pyle, convinced her daughter to come to Butte—where Elizabeth lived with her second husband, Anaconda Company executive Joseph Pyle. A few hours after making this decision, however, Margaret attempted suicide with an overdose of sleeping powders.

Thirty hours later, on October 27, Margaret awoke to find Leonard Christler by her side. At 5:40 P.M., Elizabeth Martin—the head librarian at Havre's Carnegie Library and a neighbor of Margaret—was summoned by her husband to Margaret's room in the Havre Hotel. The librarian found her friend in near hysterics, with Christler attempting to soothe her. Leaving the room, Mrs. Martin remarked to her husband that she thought Margaret had tried to kill herself.

Reverend Christler left the room shortly thereafter to meet Father Charles Chapman, the rector of St. John's Episcopal Church in Butte who was visiting Havre. Margaret then destroyed most of the letters

Margaret Carleton, ca. 1917.

that she had received both from her husband Frank Carleton and from Christler. When the police entered the room on the following day, they found the remains of the correspondence and her partially packed suitcases.

After meeting with Father Chapman, Reverend Christler conducted the evening mass, with his wife Anna in attendance. Upon conclusion of the service—shortly after 11 P.M.—Anna suggested that the couple and their several guests go to a restaurant for supper, before Father Chapman boarded the train for Butte. From this point, the events of the evening become somewhat confused because of Anna's contradictory statements and because of the actions of the Havre chief of police and the Hill County coroner.

Inexplicably, Anna left her husband and friends to return to their rented home about a block-and-a-half north of the church on Third Avenue. At the coroner's inquest held two days later, Anna would not tell the jury why she went home. She would report only that the trip was of "a private nature" and "concerned nobody but [herself]." She did, however, tell *reporters* that her errand involved retrieving some forgotten keys.

When she arrived home, she noticed that the lights had been turned on in the living room. Despite the hour, she asked her neighbor, Oscar Hauge, to watch from his porch until she made sure that everything was all right.

When Anna entered the house, she found Margaret Carleton in the front room destroying photographs of Leonard. When later asked about Margaret's state of mind at that point, Anna replied that "the kindest thing to say about Mrs. Carleton was that she was not in her right mind." Margaret's speech was rambling and incoherent to Mrs. Christler. She obviously was still suffering from the effects of the suicide attempt.

The women spoke for a while before they left the house and walked together toward the railroad depot. Along the way, Margaret and Anna met Reverend Christler and his friends. The group then proceeded toward downtown Havre. Margaret remained behind the group when it reached the Havre Drug Store on the corner of Third Avenue and Third Street. She said that she would wait for them to return.

Chief of Police Moran found Margaret about a block east of that corner a few minutes later. He told the coroner's jury that, when approached, Margaret moved away as if she did not want to be recognized. He warned her that it was not safe to loiter around the streets that late at night. After Chief Moran recommended that she go home, Margaret replied that she was "waiting for a party."

The police chief believed that Margaret's behavior was odd, and he watched her for some time afterward. The newspapers reported that Moran also had seen her across the street from the Christler home earlier in the evening. Yet he made no mention of that sighting at the coroner's inquest.

After seeing Father Chapman off, Leonard and Anna returned home at approximately 12:40 A.M., on October 28. Margaret Carleton reached the house about twenty minutes later. Upon her arrival, the trio sat in the living room for about fifteen minutes. Anna claimed that only "ordinary conversation" passed among them, although she also reported that, at one point, Margaret turned to her and said, "There is no place in his life for you."

At that juncture, Leonard rose to prepare for bed. Anna stood to escort Margaret to the door. As she turned toward the door, Anna said that she heard two shots like "snapping fingers" and the sound of two falling bodies. She found her husband lying across the entrance of his bedroom. The body had wedged the door to the room almost shut. Margaret lay three feet away, face down in the hallway.

According to her testimony, Anna then called the telephone exchange to summon Doctors Foss and MacKenzie to the house. Although she did not specify why, the two physicians soon arrived with their wives in tow. During this short interlude, Anna called Bishop Faber in Helena to relate the terrible news. She also called the local Western Union office to send telegrams to the families of Margaret and Leonard. *Then* she called the police.

After determining that Reverend Christler and Margaret Carleton indeed were dead, Dr. MacKenzie removed a .38-caliber, double-action, Smith and Wesson revolver from the dead woman's hand and set it on a nearby table. He noted that three of the five-shot revolver's shells had been fired and that two rounds remained in the weapon.

Police Chief Moran and Coroner Holland arrived a few minutes later. According to both men, they had become lost and could not find the Christler house in the dark. The two officials promptly pronounced the shootings a case of murder-suicide and determined that no inquest would be necessary. Neither authority questioned Anna about the tragedy, although Dr. MacKenzie had tampered with evidence by removing the revolver from Margaret's hand. At that point, responsibility for the crime still remained an open question.

Shortly after breakfast on the morning of October 28, Anna addressed a solemn assembly of parishioners who had gathered to hear the details of their beloved minister's death. The story that the widow told them proved quite different from the ones that she subsequently told either to the media or to the coroner's jury.

To the parishioners, Anna claimed that she had seen the entire event: After shooting the clergyman, Margaret pointed the still-smoking gun at her [Anna] and wavered before she pulled the trigger; when the revolver misfired, Margaret turned the gun on herself, successfully firing it, and her body fell across that of the Reverend. Both the *Great Falls Leader* and the *New York Times* observed that this story also differed from what Anna had earlier told the police.

Margaret's mother, Elizabeth Pyle, became increasingly dissatisfied with the stories told by Anna Christler and with the report given by Havre police authorities. She believed that sufficient evidence existed to prove the innocence of her daughter. So Mrs. Pyle demanded that a coroner's inquest be held to determine the facts of the case. When the police and the Hill County coroner hesitated, she pressured Havre city executives through the Anaconda Company and her attorney, U.S. Senator Thomas J. Walsh. The officials quickly convened a coroner's jury on October 29.

The coroner's inquest lasted one day and produced mixed evidence. The jury ruled that Margaret Carleton had killed Leonard Christler while temporarily insane. Nevertheless jury foreman R. G. Linebarger raised such important questions that Mrs. Pyle's suspicions were not assuaged.

Hill County Attorney Max Kuhr and Coroner James Holland presided over the inquest. The jury comprised a "Who's Who" of Havre's professional elite. Witnesses included Anna Christler, Doctors Foss and MacKenzie, Police Chief Moran, and Margaret's neighbor/ friend Elizabeth Martin. Anna became the primary witness, since she alone was present at the scene. Again, her testimony differed from what she had volunteered to the police, what she had revealed to the media, and what she had reported to the Episcopal gathering.

When foreman Linebarger asked Anna to describe her actions immediately after the shootings, she reported that she had telephoned the physicians, sent telegrams to the victims' families, and then called the police. When asked to explain the logic of this sequence, the widow replied that she "wanted everybody there." Anna also proved reluctant to discuss the nature of the conversation just prior to the shootings.

She did reveal, however, that Margaret had done all of the talking.

Dr. MacKenzie's testimony included details of the bodies' locations, which of Margaret's hands had held the revolver, and the location of the entry wounds. The bullet that killed Leonard Christler entered his right breast at an upward angle, exiting just below the left shoulder blade. Death was attributed to a severed aorta. In her own case, Margaret's aim had been more accurate: she symbolically shot herself through the heart.

Dr. Foss's testimony became much more detailed when pressed by the jury's foreman. In this case, Linebarger's questions primarily concerned Margaret's mental and physical conditions at the time of the tragedy. He pointedly asked Dr. Foss if

> a person of high nervous temperament, who has been ill and greatly worried and confined to her bed off and on, taking lavishly of sleeping powders, would be out of her right mind?

Dr. Foss replied that such was quite likely, and he added that Margaret had needed the sleeping powders to calm her nerves before she went to work for the Chautauqua. When foreman Linebarger asked the doctor if Margaret were a sick woman, he replied that "anybody laboring under the condition of nervous tension she was, would be absolutely irresponsible."

Linebarger then questioned if it were possible for someone to hold a revolver so that the bullet could directly enter the body when fired. Dr. Foss stated—and Chief of Police Jim Moran later confirmed—that one could point the weapon directly at one's heart, but that the recoil would produce a bullet wound with an upward track.

The foreman then inquired if it were possible to shoot oneself with the degree of accuracy shown in this instance. Chief Moran replied that a slender person might be able to do so. He qualified his answer further by stating that it was easier for a woman to do so because her wrists were more flexible.

Moran also admitted during his testimony that he and Coroner Holland were unable to find the Christler residence and, therefore, arrived late at the murder scene. At the very least, however, Linebarger's line of questioning revealed that he was not convinced that Margaret had first killed the Reverend and then had committed suicide.

Once Chief Moran was dismissed, Linebarger recalled Dr. Foss to the stand. The jury foreman first requested the witness to discuss Margaret's bungled suicide attempt. Then he asked if, after sleeping for thirty hours, Margaret would have been in "a normal state." The physician replied,

> She would not be in a normal state after sleeping thirty hours, like . . . a state of post-anaesthesia [in which] one would not realize they [sic] were walking, not realize what they were doing or where they were.

Shortly after Dr. Foss was dismissed, the coroner's jury ruled that Margaret Carleton, while temporarily insane, shot and killed Leonard J. Christler and then killed herself. Anna announced that she would pay the funeral expenses for both her husband and Margaret.

The murder of Leonard Christler and the subsequent suicide of Margaret Carleton produced perfect fodder for the sensational journalism of the 1920s. Eager for a story, newspapers and news agencies from all over the country wired over fifty telegrams to Havre within a few hours of the tragedy. Coroner Holland remarked that "All they want is to try and make a sensation out of it." When asked by the *Great Falls Tribune's* reporter why he considered it sensational, Holland refused to answer. Stories about the alleged murder-suicide splattered over the front pages of newspapers not only in Montana but also as far away as New York City and San Francisco.

Finding no support among Havre's authorities, Margaret's mother sought the backing of the newspapers in her attempts to clear her daughter's name. She publicly labeled the coroner's inquest "a farce" and, on October 31, initiated her own investigation into the tragedy. "My daughter's memory was blackened by a clique of heartless men in Havre to shield others and to save the county further expense," she claimed.

Mrs. Pyle hired two Havre physicians, W. F. Hamilton and A. E. Williams, to conduct a second postmortem examination of her daughter. The examination revealed that the course of the bullet that struck Margaret had traveled in a downward path through the woman's body rather than at an upward angle, as reported to the coroner's jury by Dr. Foss. This would indicate that someone taller than Margaret had fired the shot. This discovery lent credence to Mrs. Pyle's claim that her daughter had not killed herself. She believed this evidence inconsistent with that for a self-inflicted wound and stepped up her campaign to prove Margaret's innocence.

That same day, the *Great Falls Tribune* made public a letter written by Margaret Carleton to Mutual-Elwell Chautauqua Company manager Charlie Booth. In a preface to the letter, Booth expressed his amazement that Margaret had committed the crime and stated that her correspondence "gave no evidence of mental derangement." Margaret's letter said,

> I am en route to Butte . . . where I will get my daughter and [I] anticipate returning east in ten days and accepting the Clinton position. However, my mother is protesting against me taking my little girl and, if I find it best not to, it is comforting to know that I can come back to the Midwest Lyceum Bureau. I shall keep you posted concerning my whereabouts and will surely call. . . .

Booth also commented on the two occasions when Reverend Christler and Mrs. Carleton were in Chicago and spent considerable time together.

Fueled by Booth's statements, Elizabeth Pyle's campaign to clear her daughter's name escalated. The mother became frustrated in her attempts to find the owner of the weapon used in the shootings, so she obtained a warrant to search the Christler home. Accompanied by Police Chief Moran, George Bourne (the owner of the rental house and Havre's mayor), and a host of newspaper reporters, Mrs. Pyle ransacked the Christler home to find evidence suggesting that Anna had fired the fatal shots.

When this ploy failed, she claimed that diamond rings known to have been worn by Margaret the night of the shooting had disappeared. This revelation added fuel to the newspaper accounts that suggested a "whitewash" by Havre city officials. Mrs. Pyle firmly believed that the rings had been removed so that the gun could be placed in her daughter's hand *after* the shooting occurred.

Mrs. Pyle's investigations later revealed that the gun used in the shootings had been used in a murder that occurred in Havre in 1919. Margaret's husband (Frank Carleton) had represented the accused murderer, and he kept the weapon when the trial concluded. Disappointed, Elizabeth Pyle took her daughter's body back to Helena for burial on November 1.

Before the funeral, however, she publicly blasted the handling of the entire affair in Havre. In a scathing interview published in the *Billings Gazette*, Mrs. Pyle declared:

> I could not even employ an attorney in Havre who would agree to go through with the case.... Margaret's husband ... had friends there, as did Margaret. I saw one attorney after the other, and they all shook their heads. . . . Those prominent attorneys on whom I called for help told me they did not care to help me as it was no use. "You'll get no satisfaction out of that inquest or as a result of your investigations, so why go to the expense," they told me.

Claiming that she was not even treated courteously by the Hill County authorities, Mrs. Pyle maintained that James Holland had promised that he would hold the coroner's inquest on October 30, but then rescheduled it for October 29 for the convenience of Anna Christler. When Pyle reminded him of his original promise, Holland set the inquest for 7:30 *that evening* (October 29)!

Margaret's estranged husband, Frank Carleton, telegraphed Elizabeth Pyle on October 31 and characterized the investigation as "an outrage." He also stated that the authorities were attempting "to whitewash" Leonard Christler's character, at Margaret's expense, to protect his reputation. Doubtless, Carleton's feelings were the result of the disintegration of his marriage.

Both Carleton and Margaret's mother admitted that the dead woman was infatuated with "the Bishop of All Outdoors" prior to her death. Frank blamed the minister for the impending divorce and cast aspersions on Christler's reputation through the newspapers. Carleton was aided in his crusade by an unwitting Bishop William Faber, Leonard's superior in the Episcopal Church.

Rumors of Reverend Christler's involvement with Margaret Carleton had circulated in Havre for months prior to the shootings. According to local sources, Christler's congregation included many non-Episcopalian women who were enamored with the minister. To many of them, perhaps, the death of this "very remarkable man" at the hands of a jilted lover came as no surprise.

The subject was obviously dodged by Havre's officials and the town's primary newspaper, the *Daily Promoter*. No mention ever was made of a romantic involvement between the dead people. Fortunately for posterity's sake, other Montana newspapers had no such compunctions about printing the innuendoes. Some of the headlines read:

MOTHER CONVINCED TRUTH OF KILLING
HAS BEEN SUPPRESSED

HAVRE'S CODE OF COURTESY KEEPS DOUBT UP IN TRAGEDY

TRAGEDY WHITEWASHED SAYS CARLETON;
REVOLVER PUT IN HAND, MOTHER ADDS

CARLETON AND CHRISTLER'S NAMES HAD BEEN CONNECTED
FOR THREE YEARS PREVIOUS TO TRAGEDY

The *Billings Gazette* and the *Great Falls Tribune* were Eastern newspapers.

Finally, the most damning evidence of an amorous relationship between Margaret Carleton and the Reverend Leonard Christler appeared in two letters printed in the *Great Falls Leader* and reprinted by other papers. The first was written by Christler's superior, Bishop William Faber of Helena. In it, he wrote:

> I believe, as a result of the investigation I have made of the tragedy . . . and after questioning those who knew about it, that if this woman had been able to work her will on Mr. Christler he would be alive today—unfaithful to his wife, but still living.

He concluded that "[Christler] was an eloquent speaker and a most magnetic man. He was unconventional and most human."

Infuriated, Frank Carleton replied to the Bishop's statements through the newspapers. Carleton charged that Bishop Faber had unjustly attempted to make Margaret the villain of the tragedy, and he denounced the cleric's investigation as a mockery that included only Christler's friends and protectors.

Carleton further damned Christler's influence over his wife and questioned the secrecy of their relationship. He wondered why the Reverend Christler had not practiced what he preached and, instead, chose to maintain his "hypnotic hold" over Margaret. Finally he declared that,

I too have known of Margaret's love for this man for several years, and it is only fair to her to say that she confessed it to me. I will not further violate her confidence, but I do want to state unqualifiedly and unreservedly that it is a fact that this preacher had led her to believe that he returned that love. I want to further say that I had plenty of opportunity and occasion to observe "this big man mentally and physically" time and again. I warned my wife and told her the results of my observations and pleaded with her to save herself before it was too late. On several occasions I believe I convinced her of the true situation. In conclusion, I want to say to the world that Margaret is not to be blamed for this affair, but that the real blame should justly be placed upon the man who paid the price that must be paid by all who prove unfaithful to their trust.

In a simple funeral service, Elizabeth Pyle buried her daughter in the family plot at Forestvale Cemetery in the Helena Valley. Amid much national publicity, an emotional Anna Christler buried her husband in Waterloo, New York, on November 3, 1922.

With these interments, the sensational furor that had followed the drama played itself out. There is little mention of the affair in any Montana newspaper just a few weeks after it occurred. Speculation and rumor in Havre, however, have continued even to the present.

The story also goes to prove three adages:

—You will be punished for breaking one of the Ten Commandments.
—Adultery can be dangerous.
—If you play with fire, you will get burned.

Shortly after Leonard Christler was buried, his substantial home south of Havre mysteriously burned to the ground, leaving just a stone chimney to mark its location. Some residents of Havre said it was arson perpetrated by one of the Reverend's rejected *paramours*.

Just who was the jerk or jerks in this sordid affair? If the rumors about Leonard Christler's relationship with Margaret Carleton were true, as indeed they appear to be, then the good Reverend was certainly a jerk. An uncommonly handsome man with a charismatic personality, he was not, apparently, above "fraternizing" with female members of his congregation. According to the existing documentation, he may have manipulated Margaret into seeking a divorce from her husband and, seemingly did little to hide his affair from his devoted wife.

Coroner James Holland and Chief of Police Jim Moran, moreover, attempted to hide the Reverend's indiscretion by whitewashing the events and tampering with evidence in an attempt to protect both Leonard and Anna's reputation. Both Margaret and Anna were the victims in the matter—victims of Christler's moral shortcomings and their own emotions.

Anna Christler returned to Havre for many years afterward, to tend the St. Mark's flower beds planted by her deceased husband. As for Margaret, someone placed a bouquet on her grave in the Helena Valley as recently as 1990.

~

Sources

All of the major Montana newspapers extensively covered the tragic Christler events in Havre. Most notable, however, were the *Great Falls Tribune*, the *Helena Independent*, the *Butte Miner*, and the *Billings Gazette*. In addition, the story was carried by newspapers in New York, Cincinnati, and San Francisco. For more detailed information, the transcript from the coroner's inquest—on file at the Hill County Courthouse in Havre—provides the best source for the event itself.

The house in which the shootings occurred still stands in Havre at 813 Third Street. While the interior has been renovated, the exterior of the dwelling looks exactly as it did in 1922. St. Mark's Episcopal Church, 533 Third Avenue, also still stands. Both the church and the dwelling are located within the Havre Residential Historic District.

Other than the transcript from the coroner's inquest, perhaps the most important sources of information regarding the tragedy are the people in Havre. The late Walter Mack and his wife, Jean, both remembered Reverend Christler, Anna Christler, and Margaret Carleton. They provided invaluable information to the author while researching this story. Walter's mother, although not Episcopalian, regularly attended Christler's services. Other Havre informants include Gary Wilson and and Robert Lucke.

White Hoods under the Big Sky
Montanans Embrace the Ku Klux Klan
by Anne Sturdevant

What could be more incongruous than Southern race hatred, peaked white hoods, and burning crosses thrown against a background of the snow-covered Rocky Mountains or the high-plains grasslands of eastern Montana? Admittedly white, federal-government treatment of Montana's Native Americans had set an ugly precedent. But what was the Ku Klux Klan doing in "the Treasure State" in the 1920s?

Answers to this question emerge from a post-World War I Montana society in almost complete disarray. Social, economic, ethnic, and political standards had been skewed by fast-moving technology and America's involvement in world affairs. Local banks had failed; dryland homesteading had become untenable; mining and timber jobs had evaporated. Into these troubled times rode the torch-carrying leaders of "the Realm of Montana," ready with answers, secrets, mystical rituals, a bevy of "K" labels, and Grand Dragon Lewis Terwilliger, a Livingston community leader.

The Klan's life in the state proved remarkably short. Nevertheless, Montana's KKK needs exposure—now more than ever—to bright sunlight, ridicule, and public censure.

–Dave Walter

Klansmen Stage Night Spectacle

Thousands of visitors to the Midland Empire Fair were treated tonight to a spectacle not advertised on the Governor's Day program. At 10:00 sharp, the city was aroused by a continuous bursting of air bombs over the high rimrocks that surround the northern part of the city. This was followed a little later by the bursting into flames of a cross nearly 50 feet in height, the "fiery cross of the K.K.K." As the cross blazed, lighting the entire top of the hills for miles around, hundreds of red flares were touched off. And, on the edge of the hills 300 yards above the city, marched hundreds of white-robed members of the

Ku Klux Klan rally and picnic on South Bridge, Billings, ca. 1925.
COURTESY WESTERN HERITAGE CENTER, BILLINGS, MONTANA

organization, carrying red and green flaming torches. . . .
According to officials of the Klan, the meeting held tonight
was a statewide gathering, nearly 2,000 members being
present.

Billings Gazette, September 21, 1923

Most Montanans are justly horrified when they learn that the Ku
Klux Klan (KKK) gained widespread popularity in the state during
the 1920s. In this current era of the Montana Militia, the Aryan Nations,
and the Freemen—all involving relatively small numbers of
participants—it seems illogical that the Klan once established chapters
from Plentywood to Hamilton and from Miles City to Thompson Falls.

Yet from 1923 to 1931, the KKK functioned as a vibrant political,
social, and fraternal organization under the Big Sky. The Realm of
Montana became a component in Nathan Bedford Forrest's astounding
1915 revival of the Ku Klux Klan. By the mid-1920s, the organization
boasted more than 5,000,000 registered members nationwide.
Membership was restricted to white Protestant males born in the
United States.

At its height in 1924, the Montana Klan boasted more than forty
Klaverns (chapters) and a dues-paying membership of almost 5,200
men. Since the state's population at the time was about 540,000, the
total KKK membership remained less than one percent of the
population.

However, the group's influence far exceeded its membership base.
In addition to the KKK proper, sympathizers could join: the Royal
Riders of the Red Robe, for foreign-born Klansmen; the Junior KKK
program, for boys under eighteen years of age; the Women of the Ku
Klux Klan, an auxiliary whose numbers frequently exceeded the
membership of the local chapter itself. The Klan also received silent
support from those Montanans who feared formal membership in such
a radical group—regardless of its famed secrecy.

On September 16, 1923, the national Imperial Wizard Hiram
Wesley Evans chartered the Invisible Realm of Montana. In theory the
Montana realm reflected its parent, headquartered in Atlanta, Georgia.
A full-page ad in the *Billings Gazette* (September 30, 1923), listed the
"cardinal principles" of the organization:

1. The Tenets of the Christian Religion.
2. Upholding the Constitution of the United States.

3. The Sovereignty of our States Rights.
4. The Separation of Church and State.
5. Religious Liberty.
6. Freedom of Speech and Press.
7. Compulsory Education in Free Public Schools.
8. Protection of our Pure Womanhood.
9. White Supremacy.
10. Limitation of Foreign Immigration.
11. Closer Relationship between Capital and American Labor.
12. Just Laws and Liberty.

Critics would find it difficult to argue in the abstract with these principles. In reality, however, the KKK advocated the suppression of Catholic schools; the elimination of "non-white immigrants," Jews, and Blacks from business and politics; and the severe restriction of immigration—in addition to its standard white-supremacy plank.

In truth, the Klan found itself caught in a paradox: While ostensibly supporting the Constitution and the Bill of Rights, it worked to target its four enemies: immigrants, Jews, Catholics, and Blacks. Further, in pursuit of its goals, the KKK easily justified violence— symbolized by its hoods and masks, swords, and burning crosses. In at least one case, that violence wrote an ugly chapter in the Montana chronicle.

The KKK sprouted and thrived in Montana during the 1920s because residents faced both a society in flux and an uncertain economy, and they succumbed to fear. That society was proportionately heavy in foreign-born residents, and it still suffered from the anti-German hysteria promoted during World War I. Further, the state's economy remained unstable—its mining and timber industries, in particular, suffered post-war busts. Through the 1910s, tens of thousands of foreign-born homesteaders had arrived to file on dryland farms. When the drought hit Montana's high plains (1917-1919), prairie society unraveled. For example, 435 banks operated in the state in 1921; by 1926, 220 of those institutions had failed.

Thousands of white Montanans, faced with this confusing situation, found the Ku Klux Klan ready to salve their wounds and to identify the supposed annihilators of their traditional lifestyle: immigrants, Jews, Catholics, and Blacks. The Klan proved particularly appealing because of its "secret" membership and covert activities— best represented by the hoods and the robes.

The organization masterfully built secrecy upon its special lexicon of terms, its mysterious rituals, and its use of violence. To a young, white Montana man who wanted to "belong" and needed to blame others for what he did not understand, the Invisible Empire offered an appealing solution. Nevertheless, the Montana KKK suffered some real problems when it tried to identify its targets within the state.

Despite the focus of the hate literature that poured out of the KKK national office in Atlanta, Georgia, Montanans found it difficult to generate a concerted hatred of Jews and Blacks—when so few Jews and Blacks resided in the state. Thus the Realm of Montana concentrated its hatred on the state's Catholics.

And there were plenty of Catholics here! A 1920 federal religious census noted that a full *65 percent* of Montanans who declared a religion were Catholic. Butte alone reported twenty-five thousand registered Catholics. The Realm of Montana's newsletter, the *Official Circular,* quoted Grand Dragon Lewis Terwilliger: "Butte is the worst place in the State of Montana, so far as alienism and Catholicism are concerned."

Throughout the Montana Realm's existence (1923-1931), Terwilliger led Montana Klansmen. He had arrived in the state from Michigan as a teacher in 1895 and served as a principal in Butte and Townsend. He then became the principal of Park County High School in Livingston (1903-1913), where he also started a real-estate/abstracting business and ran a 640-acre ranch outside town. Terwilliger was a strong Methodist, an avowed Republican, and a thirty-third-degree Mason. Residents attested to his popularity by electing him the mayor of Livingston for two terms (1919-1923).

Terwilliger had been a member of the national Ku Klux Klan since its revival in the mid-1910s. Delegates elected him the Grand Dragon of the Realm of Montana at their organizational convention in Livingston in 1923. As Grand Dragon, Terwilliger received an annual salary of $1,150—at a time when the average American wage was $680 a year, and the typical American farmer's wage was $275!

The Grand Dragon's salary derived from the dues of Montana Klansmen, $5 per year. Other KKK expenses included a $10 initiation fee, $5 for the hood and robe, and $1 a year for the national KKK publication, the *Kourier.* The Klan also performed the rituals expected of a fraternal organization: It collected special assessments to aid afflicted members; it buried its dead; it supported with donations those causes and organizations that it liked. The Montana KKK particularly liked the Salvation Army, the Methodist Church, the Protestant orphanage in Helena, the Deaconess Hospital in Havre, and Inter-Mountain Union College in Helena.

Also, *unlike* other fraternal organizations, the Klan publicly burned crosses in the dark of night—as a weapon of intimidation. For example, the *Laurel Outlook* noted (September 16, 1925):

> From out of the gloom, a flaming cross bloomed forth on top of Square Butte, four miles west of Laurel, on Thursday night! A Ku Klux Klan meeting was in process, at which it was estimated that 2,500 were in attendance and some 100 or more candidates were initiated. The customary white-robed figures, bearing torches, were to be seen moving about and, at one time, a number of bombs and sky rockets were set off. . . . Not since the days when the Indians held ceremonies on the Butte has there been the spectacle of burning fires and moving figures such as were seen Thursday night.

In addition to this type of dramatic intimidation, the Klan used outright threats in pursuit of its goals. One instance involved the Black wife of an Anaconda pastor. The *Anaconda Standard* reported (February 6, 1923):

> Mysterious letters, written over the signature of crossed bones and signed "Ku Klux," are spreading terror in Anaconda homes. . . . Mrs. M. A. Clements, the colored wife of the pastor of the African Methodist Episcopal Church, yesterday received the following anonymous letter, printed in pencil and enclosed in a pink envelope, ordering her to leave town: "Mrs. Clements: Your tongue has trapped you with your race and the white race. You had better leave town or we will tar and feather you. Beware.—Ku Klux."
> Anacondans are very much alarmed over the entire proceedings.

The most violent incident involving the Montana KKK occurred at Crow Agency, eleven miles southeast of Hardin. In late October 1926, a Black man named James Belden—mistakenly suspected of petty theft—had been told by a few local whites to "get out of town or suffer the consequences." Two years earlier, Belden had moved from Butte to Crow Agency, where he repaired shoes and did odd jobs around the community.

When Belden refused to abandon his home, the locals contacted Big Horn County Sheriff Robert P. Gilmore in Hardin. At the time, Gilmore was running for another term as sheriff in the upcoming November election; he was widely known as an official in Hardin's Klan #35. Gilmore promised that he "would rid the town of that nigger Belden."

On October 29, Gilmore and Undersheriff Andy L. Dornberger drove to Crow Agency on a "campaign trip." When the two lawmen approached Belden's shack, the Black man opened fire, killing Gilmore and wounding his deputy. Quickly lawmen, volunteers, and sightseers surrounded the cabin and began firing fusillades at Belden. The *Billings Gazette* estimated that, within an hour, more than two hundred men had encircled the shack.

In the exchange of gunfire, Belden also killed John MacLeod who, for four years, had served as a special officer for the Office of Indian Affairs on the Crow Reservation. MacLeod was attempting to skirt the shack to reach an adjacent barn, to set it afire. Shortly thereafter the barn was torched (*Billings Gazette*, October 30, 1926):

> A. C. Cole and John Lawrence, employees of the Big Horn Garage, risked death by throwing gasoline on the barn and setting it afire, after they had recovered MacLeod's apparently lifeless body. Indian youths had prepared arrows and flaming excelsior to fire the structure from behind beet wagons and the Catholic Church, when Cole and Lawrence accomplished the task.

After a short time, the burning barn ignited Belden's shack (*Hardin Tribune-Herald*, October 29, 1926).

> The building burned like tinder, and soon the flames forced the negro to come out. In the yard, he was riddled with bullets from upwards of a hundred guns. After he had been brought down, he fired three more shots as he lay on the ground. The crowd rushed up to him and picked up his body while he was still gasping. There was talk of a "neck tie party," but instead the crowd threw him into his cabin, where he soon was consumed by the flames.

Authorities filed no charges as a result of this two-hour confrontation. The next week hundreds of sympathizers—including "ten Crow Indian chiefs in full regalia"—attended the funerals of Gilmore and MacLeod in Hardin. Among the dignitaries at Gilmore's service appeared Lewis Terwilliger, the Grand Dragon of the Realm of Montana.

Most local Klan activity in Montana assumed a less physically violent character. For example, a visit to Montana by the Imperial Wizard Hiram Wesley Evans in August 1926 combined business with pleasure (*Livingston Enterprise*, August 6, 1926):

A state-wide meeting of the Montana Ku Klux Klan closed here tonight with a lecture by Dr. H. W. Evans, head of the national organization. It is said that many of the more important cities and towns of the state were represented. The Strand Theater was used for the day session. A parade of nearly 400 robed marchers passed through the streets of the city. This number included 50 to 60 women members of the auxiliary branch. It is estimated that upwards of 2,000 Livingston people assembled along the streets to witness the parade. Friday the members and their families will leave for a tour through Yellowstone National Park.

Evans also had made an earlier appearance in Montana. On November 15, 1924, he spoke in Billings at the Methodist Church and at the Coliseum Theater, to standing-room-only crowds. Evans addressed the issues of restricted immigration, racial purity, and political tactics.

In fact, Klan activity in Montana consistently displayed a strong political bent. The KKK routinely backed Republican candidates, particularly if they were Masons or held Klan membership. For example, in the 1924 race for Montana's U.S. Senate seat, incumbent Democrat Thomas J. Walsh encountered an unexpectedly tough opponent in Republican challenger Frank Linderman, the noted Montana author. A newspaperman and an insurance salesman, Linderman received enthusiastic Klan endorsements and substantial Klan financial support. This assistance proved revealing, as Terwilliger identified Linderman as "a present or former Klansman." Walsh barely survived with 52 percent of the total vote.

Terwilliger's *Official Circular* regularly previewed county and state elections and used a "secret code" to identify candidates both acceptable and unacceptable to the Klan. The code noted, for instance:

B. Branded by our Imperial Office as having an undesirable record in regard to Klan principles. They recommend that this candidate be defeated.
C. Considered a candidate of the A.C.M. [Anaconda Copper Mining] Company.
D. Dry [in favor of Prohibition].
F. Favorable to the Klan and Klan principles.
H. Wife is a Roman Catholic.
M. Mason.
O. Opposed to the Klan.
P. Protestant.
R. Roman Catholic.
U. Unworthy of the support of Klansmen, because he is opposed to our principles.
W. Wet [in favor of the repeal of Prohibition].
* Present or former Klansman.

KKK fervor built inexorably toward the 1928 presidential election, because it offered such a clear-cut choice between candidates. The Democrats nominated Al Smith, a Catholic urban dweller who favored the repeal of Prohibition. The Republicans, on the other hand, nominated "country boy" Herbert Hoover, a Protestant who favored strongly enforced Prohibition. During the summer of 1928, Lewis Terwilliger worked himself into a frenzy in his newsletters, rallying Montana Klansmen to work against Al Smith.

Hoover won the election with 58.2 percent of the national vote. He also carried Montana by about 34,000 votes (113,000 to 79,000). No one can say to what extent Klan work assisted Hoover in Montana, but Smith carried only Butte, Anaconda, and Glacier County.

Membership in the Realm of Montana declined after the 1928 election for several reasons. The strident nativism that had begun with World War I German-bashing finally ran its course. In addition to this waning hatred of immigrants, Montanan Klansmen had always found it difficult to focus on Jews and Blacks—regardless of the Klan's national policy—when the state offered so few of either minority.

Further, all fraternal organizations lost membership during the late 1920s. They became the victims of such other leisure-time

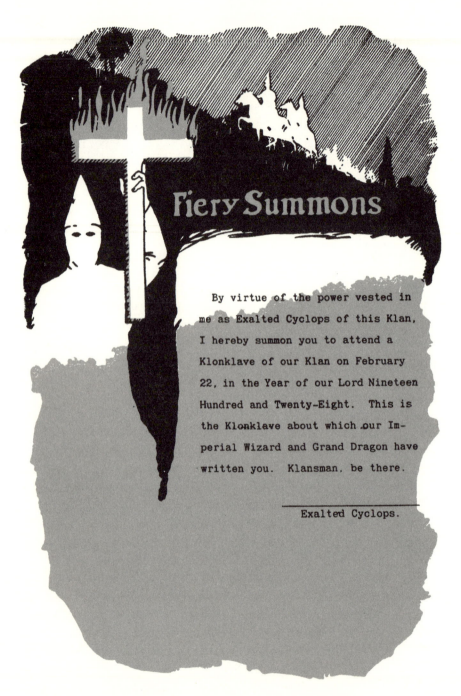

Fiery Summons

By virtue of the power vested in me as Exalted Cyclops of this Klan, I hereby summon you to attend a Klonklave of our Klan on February 22, in the Year of our Lord Nineteen Hundred and Twenty-Eight. This is the Klonklave about which our Imperial Wizard and Grand Dragon have written you. Klansman, be there.

_____

Exalted Cyclops.

Montana KKK ephemera from February 22, 1928.

attractions as talking movies, radio, sports, and automobile travel to nearby towns on improved roads. The young Montana workman suddenly faced either a Tuesday-evening Klan meeting at the local Klavern or a date with Sweet Nell at the Roxy Theater—and he opted for a talking movie and Nell.

Then, when adultery, drunkenness, and embezzlement scandals rocked the national KKK leadership, Klansmen who had joined to support "moral purity" abandoned the organization. Finally, as economic uncertainty and dislocation became truly severe in the early 1930s, the dues and costs of holding a KKK membership became luxuries to many Montana Klansmen.

So, in the early 1930s, the Montana Klan movement withered and died for lack of viable targets, for lack of enthusiasm, for lack of relative excitement. In 1931 the state's surviving membership—consolidated in "the Grand Klan of Montana"—numbered less than one hundred stalwarts.

In retrospect, if the Ku Klux Klan were to forge solid inroads in 1920s Montana, it needed to establish a beachhead in Butte—that bastion of Catholicism. Yet, throughout its existence (1923-1928), members of Butte's Kontinental Klan #30 lived in abject fear and proved wholly ineffective.

In response to reports that the KKK was recruiting in Butte, Silver Bow County Sheriff Larry Duggan said (*Butte Miner*, July 22, 1921), "My deputies have orders to shoot any Ku Kluxers on sight—shoot them down like wolves." Grand Dragon Lewis Terwilliger noted the dire situation in a 1924 letter to Butte's Exalted Cyclops Albert W. Jones: "I know that you are involved in the most difficult, the most dangerous situation in Montana. It is nothing short of a war zone."

In the face of Catholic opposition, Kontinental Klan #30 ran scared. For instance, its officials published their meeting announcements under spurious names, rather than identify themselves as Klansmen. For a time, the Butte Klan called itself "the Butte Men's Literary Society." It also hid behind the names "Protestant Men's Welfare Council" and "Krishna Improvement Association."

At one point, Exalted Cyclops Jones complained to Terwilliger that he thought Butte's Irish Catholic postmen were intercepting his KKK mail from the Atlanta headquarters. Before the Grand Dragon could reply, Jones seemingly solved his own problem. He informed Terwilliger that he had "changed his name to Knute Karl Knutson [KKK] and rented a new post-office box." Within weeks, however, Jones

Recruitment ad in the *Butte Miner*, July 16, 1921.

was forced to admit that the Irish Catholic postmen had figured out his ruse—and he still was receiving no official mail from Atlanta.

Ultimately the Ku Klux Klan sustained only a short, eight-year run in Montana. Its influence proved modest in Montana politics, less strong in the arena of social reform, and ultimately ineffective in targeting with violence its enemies: immigrants, Jews, Catholics, and Blacks.

Nevertheless, present-day Montanans can learn a lesson from the KKK's remarkable popularity in the state during the 1920s: Given the right set of circumstances, this type of despicable racism could again gain a foothold under the Big Sky. Constant vigilance and vocal opposition—the kind that recently fostered the "Not in Our Town!" response in Billings—are required to combat similarly covert radical cells.

The admonition of German anti-Nazi theologian Martin Niemoller speaks directly to the current situation in Montana and the Northwest:

> In Germany they came first for the Communists, and I didn't speak up because I wasn't a Communist. Then they came for the Jews, and I didn't speak up because I wasn't a Jew. Then they came for the trade unionists, and I didn't speak up because I wasn't a trade unionist. Then they came for the Catholics, and I didn't speak up because I was a Protestant. Then they came for me, and by that time no one was left to speak up.

~

Sources

The primary archival source for research in Montana's Ku Klux Klan movement is Manuscript Collection 236: Knights of the Ku Klux Klan—Kontinental Klan No. 30 (Butte, Montana) Records, 1916, 1921-1931, held by the Archives of the Cheney-Cowles Museum in Spokane, Washington. This collection, while focusing on the Butte Klan, includes important materials from the Realm of Montana and from the national organization. The collection's many publications of the KKK's own press in Atlanta, Georgia, are important to an understanding of the entire movement.

The Montana Historical Society Library/Archives holds the Cheney-Cowles collection on microfilm (MF 457); microfilm copies are also available at the Butte–Silver Bow Public Archives and the Butte Public Library. A thorough inventory accompanies this material, both in hard copy and on microfilm.

Two unpublished works provide the best overview of the KKK in Montana: Anne Sturdevant, "The Ku Klux Klan in Montana during the 1920s," Honors Paper, Carroll College, 1991; Christine K. Erickson, "The Boys in Butte: the Ku Klux Klan Confronts the Catholics, 1923-1929," M.A. thesis, University of Montana, 1991.

Basic volumes addressing the Klan's 1915-1932 movement include: David M. Chalmers, *Hooded Americanism: The History of the Ku Klux Klan*, 3rd ed. (Chapel Hill, N.C.: Duke University Press, 1987); Henry P. Fry, *The Modern Ku Klux Klan* (Boston: Small, Maynard and Company, 1922; reprinted—New York: Negro Universities Press, 1969); Kenneth T. Jackson, *The Ku Klux Klan in the City, 1915-1930* (New York: Oxford University Press, 1967); John M. Mecklin, *The Ku Klux Klan, A Study of the American Mind* (New York: Russell and Russell, 1963); Arnold S. Rice, *The Ku Klux Klan in American Politics* (Washington, D.C.: Public Affairs Press, 1962; reprinted—Brooklyn: MSG Haskell House, 1972); William L. Katz, *The Invisible Empire: The Ku Klux Klan Influence on History* (Seattle: Open Hand Publishers, 1994).

See also the following volumes: Shawn Lay, ed., *The Invisible Empire in the West: Toward a New Historical Appraisal of the Ku Klux Klan of the 1920s* (Urbana: University of Illinois, 1992); Nancy Maclean, *Behind the Mask of Chivalry: The Making of the Second Ku Klux Klan* (New York: Oxford University Press, 1994); Michael and Judy Ann Newton, *The Ku Klux Klan: An Encyclopedia* (New York: Garland, 1990); Richard K. Tucker, *The Dragon and the Cross: The Rise and Fall of the Ku Klux Klan in Middle America* (North Haven, Conn.: Shoe String Press, 1991).

Of particular interest to the Montana KKK experience are the following periodical pieces and theses: Robert Alan Goldberg, "Hooded Empire: the Ku Klux Klan in Colorado," Ph.D. dissertation, University of Wisconsin-Madison, 1977; Arthur M. Schlessinger, Jr., "Biography of a Nation of Joiners," *American Historical Review*, vol. 50 (1944), 1-25; Benjamin H. Avin, "The Ku Klux Klan, 1915-1925: A Study in Religious Intolerance," Ph.D. dissertation, Georgetown University, 1952; Robert Neymeyer, "The Ku Klux Klan of the 1920s in the Midwest and West: A Review Essay," *Annals of Iowa*, vol. 51, #6 (1992), 625-633; Michael Morris Jessup, "The Decline of the 1920's Ku Klux Klan: A Sociological Analysis," Ph.D. dissertation, Southern Illinois University-Carbondale, 1992.

See also the following periodical pieces: Jeff LaLande, "Beneath the Hooded Robe: Newspapermen, Local Politics, and the Ku Klux Klan in Jackson County, Oregon, 1921-1923," *Pacific Northwest Quarterly*, vol. 83, #2 (1992), 45-52; Leonard J. Moore, "Historical Interpretations of the 1920's Klan: the Traditional View and the Populist Revision," *Journal of Social History*, vol. 24, #2 (1990), 341-357; Kathleen M. Blee, "Women of the 1920s' Ku Klux Klan Movement," *Feminist Studies*, vol. 17, #1 (1991), 57-77; David A. Horowitz, "The Klansman as Outsider:

Ethnocultural Solidarity and Anti-elitism in the Oregon Ku Klux Klan of the 1920s," *Pacific Northwest Quarterly*, vol. 80, #1 (1989), 12-20; Horowitz, "Social Morality and Personal Revitalization: Oregon's Ku Klux Klan in the 1920s," *Oregon Historical Quarterly*, vol. 90, #4 (Winter, 1989), 365-384; Gerald Lynn Marriner, "Klan Politics in Colorado," *Journal of the West*, vol. 15, #1 (January 1976), 76-101.

Supplemental related material can be found in several oral-history interviews conducted by the Montana Historical Society's oral historian Laurie Mercier and held by the MHS Archives. See also: Craig Holstine, "Marching as to War: the Ku Klux Klan in Eastern Washington in the 1920s," paper presented at the Pacific Northwest Historical Conference, Helena, Montana, May 17, 1985.

One of the most fruitful sources for the continued study of the KKK in Montana would be the wealth of the state's daily and weekly newspapers. Largely untapped for KKK material, the 1920s microfilmed newspaper collection held by the Montana Historical Society Library will prove rich in KKK information.

"Keystone Cops" in Big Sky Country
The Harrison State Bank Robbery of 1930
by Dave Walter

Sometimes "jerks" identify themselves by their words. Sometimes they reveal their true characters with their actions. The young Ralph Harrington pursued "jerkdom" by both means—just to be sure. Despite his attempt at self-aggrandizement, however, Harrington needed help from Madison County Sheriff Frank Metzel to reach the "jerk" plateau.

The lawman, worried about reelection, conceived a bizarre plan to "handle" the scheduled robbery of the Harrison State Bank. Montana's 1860s vigilantes and 1870s Old West sheriffs might have proceeded this way—but, golly, this was 1930!

Not only did Metzel's scheme spin out of control, it escalated into a ridiculous case of mistaken identities, a high-speed car chase out the Pony Road, and a deadly gunfight between two lifelong friends. What in the world could have produced such grotesque events? Not surprisingly, the answers lie with our "jerk," Ralph Harrington.

NOT SINCE THE VIGILANTE DAYS 65 YEARS AGO HAS Madison County been as excited as it is over the bold robbery of the Harrison State Bank—in the face of a waiting posse of men who had been informed of the bandits' plans— and of the subsequent death of the county's beloved sheriff, Frank Metzel, grizzled pioneer peace officer. . . .

(Butte) Montana Standard, October 30, 1930

Young Ralph Harrington thought he'd finally caught the break he deserved. The Nebraskan had come to Montana as a kid and worked on ranches in the lower Madison Valley—around Three Forks and Harrison and Norris. In 1919 he and sixteen-year-old Marietta Sacry tricked her parents and slipped away to Bozeman to marry. By 1926 they had moved to Butte. Here Ralph worked as a miner, while trying to nail down a full-time job as a livestock inspector. At thirty-two years of age, his swagger and braggadocio offended some people, but impressed others.

Ralph Harrington's break seemed so bizarre that he took it as a "sign." Because of his part-time work as a stock inspector in 1930, he had taken to packing a pistol on his hip—even while walking the streets of Butte. One day in early October, two strangers approached him and asked him if he used that gun "for good or for evil?" Ralph was quick enough to reply, "I use it for whatever pays more."

Thus Ralph gained the confidence of two seasoned criminals: thirty-four-year-old Walter Varnes and fifty-five-year-old Whitey Jackson. Each had served prison sentences in other states—Varnes in California and Jackson in Ohio and Washington. They were, Harrington told Marietta, "a couple of real tough hombres" who had been living quietly in Butte for about six weeks. Prior to that time, they had engaged in nickel-and-dime crimes in the Libby-Eureka-Roosville area of northwestern Montana.

But Varnes and Jackson harbored big-time aspirations, and they needed someone familiar with southern Montana to pull them off. They would begin by robbing banks in Harrison and Wisdom.

Ralph perked right up when he heard the town of Harrison mentioned, because his uncle, Henry M. Rundell, was a director and a heavy stockholder in the Harrison State Bank. Immediately Ralph's supple mind took flight: If he could serve as the "undercover man" to prevent the robbery of the Harrison State Bank and force the capture of Varnes and Jackson, would not his goal of securing a full-time job as a Montana stock inspector be virtually assured? In addition, if the bank's directors would promise him a bounty for Varnes and Jackson—dead or alive—he might even make a tidy profit from his potentially dangerous role.

So, on Monday, October 20, 1930, Ralph drove his almost-new Willys-Knight, five-passenger coupe-sedan east out of Butte. Taking the oiled-gravel road over Pipestone Pass, he motored to the ranch of his aunt and uncle—Dollie and Henry Rundell—eight miles northwest of Harrison. After revealing the thieves' plan to the elderly Henry, the pair drove into the town of Harrison.

This community of two hundred residents, perched along the east side of Montana State Route 191 (Madison County Road 1) in the lower Madison Valley, relied on surrounding mining and livestock operations for its survival. To the west rose peaks of the Tobacco Root Mountains. Created as "Stringtown" along Willow Creek in the 1870s, the settlement suffered a fitful existence, even after the Northern Pacific Railroad ran a line through the town in 1890.

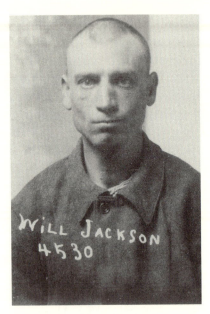

Will Jackson, ca. 1915.

Walter Varnes, April 14, 1932.

Only when the homestead boom of the 1910s brought a healthy wave of farmers to the valley was the town's future secured. A sign of its permanence was the establishment of the Harrison State Bank in 1915. By 1930 Harrison had survived Montana's agricultural recession of the 1920s and was digging in to weather the Great Depression.

Once in Harrison, Ralph told his tale to a second bank director, Samuel S. Young—the owner of the Harrison Mercantile Company—and to Harrison State Bank cashier James E. Kreigh. However, because no specific date had been fixed for the burglary, bankman Kreigh advised that the group resist the temptation to rush too hastily to local law-enforcement officials. To this Harrington agreed, asserting that, "as an undercover operative," he and the bank people "very likely could handle the situation themselves."

To conclude this meeting, Harrington proposed that the Harrison Bank's board of directors pay him $250 apiece for the capture of Varnes and Jackson, dead or alive. Rundell and Young informally agreed to the deal.

While Jim Kreigh pondered the veracity of Harrington's story, Varnes and Jackson decided that they would hit the Harrison bank at night—on Monday, October 27. To survey the Harrison layout, Harrington drove his coupe-sedan back to the Rundells' ranch on Wednesday, October 22, bringing Walt and Whitey with him. Early on Thursday morning, the yeggs ("criminals"; "dynamiters"; "safe-crackers") drove into Harrison and walked the town. Satisfied that the job was a cinch—*if* they could get into the bank's safes—the three plotters motored back over the Divide to Butte.

During their stay at the ranch, Harrington had been able to inform Mrs. Rundell that the heist definitely would occur on Monday evening, October 27. So she called Sam Young on Thursday morning, and the merchant immediately reported the news to Jim Kreigh.

This time Kreigh believed Harrington's warning. He telephoned his superiors, Karl Elling, the president of the "Elling banking chain" in Virginia City, and Fred W. Bleck, the head cashier at the Virginia City bank. (The "Elling bank chain" comprised the parent institution in the Madison County seat, the Southern Montana Bank in Ennis, the Harrison State Bank, and a share of the Morris State Bank in Pony.) He also called Madison County Sheriff Frank Metzel.

This sixty-eight-year-old lawman had built an enviable reputation in Madison County. As a child he had lived in Nevada City in 1863-1864, when the Vigilantes hanged Henry Plummer and other members of his gang of Innocents. After years of ranching in the upper Ruby Valley and one term in the state legislature, he was serving his third consecutive term as county sheriff.

In fact, in late October 1930, the Republican Metzel was campaigning hard for reelection. Although the (Virginia City) *Madisonian* called him (October 31, 1930) "the most popular officer this county has ever had," the incumbent was locked in a tight race with Democrat candidate James Emmett Womack for the office.

Sheriff Metzel covered the forty-five miles from Virginia City to Harrison in ninety minutes and immediately conferred with Jim Kreigh and Sam Young. Kreigh first aired his reservations about Ralph Harrington. But Metzel assured him that Harrington had been working undercover for the West Park Cattle Association and for Madison County Attorney Frank Blair on a cattle-stealing case—and Blair had vouched for his honesty.

Kreigh then diplomatically suggested that a crime of the magnitude of the Harrison bank robbery required outside law-enforcement assistance. In fact, he asked Sheriff Metzel to bring in Jere Murphy, the chief of police in Butte. Metzel, however, demurred. Savvy to the political realities of an election only ten days away, the sheriff declared (Montana Supreme Court *Docket #7031*, transcript page 269): "No sir. I just guess that I can take care of this situation myself."

Metzel further reasoned to Kreigh and Young (*Docket #7031*, page 417): "These men can't be picked up in Butte because we don't have anything on them. . . . What we could do is to let them go through with the job, and then we could capture them in the act."

Thus was hatched a scheme to foil the robbery of the Harrison State Bank—a scheme wholly in keeping with Madison County's self-reliant, vigilante tradition. Bank and law-enforcement authorities would assist the gang's burglary, rather than defensively protect the bank's cash and securities. (Metzel even knew a Butte operative named "Mike" whom he could plant in the bank as the cashier.) Then, in true Old West fashion, a posse would capture the thieves as they emerged from the bank. What could be simpler, or more effective?

Sheriff Metzel put his plan into action by deputizing Sam Young. He instructed Young to deputize at least three other townsmen to form a posse for the Monday night action. Over the next two days, Young recruited and briefed Harrison harness-maker Harley Fitzhugh; Fred W. Brownbeck, the town's blacksmith; and Jim "Babe" Nicholson, the Madison County road supervisor in Harrison.

On Friday, October 24, two important meetings occurred involving the edgy principals. In Virginia City, the Elling Bank's head cashier Fred Bleck conferred with president Karl Elling. Bleck complained that he opposed Sheriff Metzel's scheme to plant "Mike"—a man whom no one knew—in their Harrison bank during the robbery. When Elling solicited an alternative, Bleck replied (*Docket #7031*, page 270): "Well, there isn't anything to do except for *me* to go over there and go on in, if it has to be done."

Thus Fred Bleck secured the role of the Harrison Bank cashier for the Monday night event.

On that same Friday, Jim Kreigh and Sam Young drove over to Virginia City to consult with Sheriff Metzel. However, Metzel was unavailable, having motored down to Silver Star. Here he was scheduled to meet with Ralph Harrington, who would slip over from Butte, to discuss the "undercover operative's" role in the Harrison decoy.

So Kreigh and Young followed the sheriff into Silver Star. The four men sat down at the Barkell Springs facility and hashed through the details of the ambush: the timing; the lighting; the open safes; the positioning of deputies. Harrington volunteered that his "criminal partners" wanted to kidnap both cashier Kreigh and his young wife.

On Saturday and Sunday, members of the posse prepared for the Monday night confrontation. Road supervisor "Babe" Nicholson erected a bright porch light on the back of the Harrison Mercantile and mounted its switch beside one of the Merc's north-looking second-story windows. From this series of upstairs windows, one could look across the intervening vacant lot, directly at the south side of the bank building. The new light clearly illuminated the back door of the brick-veneer bank—much as the street lights located near the Merc and the dance hall lit up the bank's front door.

The other posse members cleaned and loaded their weapons. All relied on shotguns except Nicholson, who packed a .303 Savage rifle. In a gun battle at close range, a shotgun offered the inexperienced lawmen the best coverage.

In the meantime, endangered cashier Jim Kreigh informed bank director Sam Young that he was leaving town until this craziness was over. On Saturday night, the cashier and his wife quietly slipped out of Harrison and drove to the ranch of Clarence Bell on Antelope Creek, almost six miles west of town. Here they planned to hide out until at least the following Tuesday.

On Monday morning, October 27—the day of the anticipated

robbery—cashier Bleck stopped Sheriff Metzel on Virginia City's main street. He informed the lawman that he had volunteered to take Jim Kreigh's place in the Harrison bank that evening, so the sheriff could cancel his friend "Mike" from Butte. Bleck then drove to Harrison, arriving shortly after noon. Sheriff Metzel, accompanied by Undersheriff Claude O. Dale, reached Harrison by early afternoon.

Since Jim Kreigh was absent, assistant cashier T. E. Williams opened the bank at 9 A.M., worked the window during business hours, and closed it at 3 in the afternoon. Early in the afternoon, Bleck informed Williams that the robbery was expected that evening. He also inspected the bank's vault doors and its safes. Both safes relied on "three part" time locks and were considered "burglar proof."

Then, right at closing time, Bleck and Metzel met in the bank lobby and discussed their next move. The sheriff said (*Docket #7031*, pages 280-281), "Be sure you tell Mr. Williams not to put on them time locks."

Cashier Bleck responded, "Well, I am not handling this affair. I am not giving the orders. If you want to tell him, *you* tell him."

Whereupon the sheriff directed Williams to close and lock the two safes, to turn their combination dials, but to forget setting the time locks. The vault doors also could be locked and the combination-dials spun, because Bleck knew the combinations to all the vault and safe doors.

At 7 P.M., in the darkness of the early evening, Sheriff Metzel deployed his posse. To the upstairs window of the Harrison Garage he sent his undersheriff, Claude Dale. Although Dale could not see the front door of the bank from his perch, he commanded important coverage of the road in front of the bank.

Metzel assigned north-facing, second-story windows in the Harrison Mercantile building to the rest of his men: shotgun-toting harness-maker Harley Fitzhugh took the westernmost window; "Babe" Nicholson, armed with his .303 Savage, peered out of the middle window—within reach of his newly-installed back-porch light switch; the sheriff kept the eastern window for himself, because it afforded the clearest view of the bank's rear door, only about fifty-five feet away. Sam Young and blacksmith Fred Brownbeck also assumed spots on the second floor, although they were not assigned specific windows. Metzel, Young, Brownbeck, and Fitzhugh all carried shotguns, loaded with #00 buckshot or with #2 goose shot.

At about 9 P.M., the phone rang downstairs in the Mercantile. Sam

Young spoke briefly with Mrs. Rundell. She said that Harrington, Varnes, and Jackson had arrived at the ranch in midafternoon, had eaten supper with the Rundells, and had just left for Harrison. The tension spread among the men when Young reported this news to Sheriff Metzel.

Shortly Harrington's Willys-Knight rolled north on Harrison's main street. It paused in front of the bank and a dark figure jumped out, peeked through the partially closed blinds inside the bank's two front windows, and returned to the vehicle. The car proceeded to the north end of town, turned around, and extinguished its headlamps. It then glided back down the road and parked in the dark next to the Northern Pacific depot.

In the bank, cashier Bleck had spent several fitful hours. At 7 P.M. he had unlocked the front door, turned on the lights, opened the vault doors, and removed the loans ledger, on which to work during the evening. Time crept *very slowly*. Finally, at about 10:15, a tense Bleck heard a rattle at the front door. As he crossed toward the door, Harrington burst into the lobby and loudly ordered (*Docket #7031*, pages 247-250), "Get into the vault!"

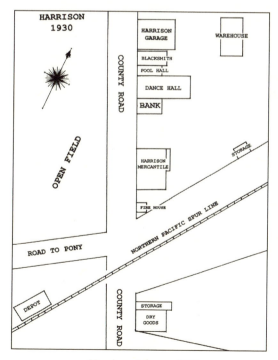

Harrison Schema, 1930.

A shaky Bleck asked, "Who are you?"

The intruder replied, "I am Harrington! Get in there right away and don't make any false moves. Do just as they tell you, for they are a couple of tough hombres!"

As Bleck entered the open vault, a second bandit—this one masked, wearing bib overalls, with a gray cap pulled down over his eyes, brandishing a pistol—rushed through the lobby and into the banking room. Whitey Jackson jammed his gun into Bleck's back and ordered, "Turn around and get that safe open or you will be singing with the angels."

A frightened Bleck fumbled with the combination dial, but finally opened the first safe. Jackson then commanded, "Now get out there and do the same to the other safe." The cashier quickly followed these orders.

With both safes wide open, Jackson began rifling their contents. He growled to Harrington, "Pull your damned gun, put that guy down on the floor, and keep him covered." To Bleck he said, "How much money is there in this bank?"

When Bleck answered, "About $2,000," Whitey raged: "Damn it! I thought this was a bank, not a damned chippy outfit! I have a damned good notion to plug you!"

Harrington averted violence by saying to Jackson, "Don't waste time. Get back over there and load up the money." It took the seasoned thief only two more minutes to gather up the bags of silver and currency, some Liberty Bonds, a bit of gold, and some securities. "Where is that damned Varnes?" he mumbled.

This was a good question. According to the plan, Walter Varnes was the designated lookout: He would enter the bank last and keep an eye on the street. With Harrington and Jackson almost finished inside, Walt had reached the front door—only to hear a shotgun explode within the Harrison Mercantile next door! A startled Varnes dashed south, into the safety of darkness near the depot.

While observing the robbery in progress, from the Merc's lightless middle room, Sam Young had grabbed "Babe" Nicholson's hammerless shotgun by mistake. Fumbling, he discharged the unfamiliar gun into the floor, thus frightening Varnes from the trap.

Loaded up with bags of loot, Whitey Jackson also heard the shotgun blast and tried to escape by the bank's back door. As Jackson emerged, crouching on the back stoop, Sheriff Metzel shouted to Nicholson: "Turn on the light now. . . . Turn on the damn light!" The new porch lamp poured bright light across the vacant lot and splashed it over the back of the bank. This sudden surprise drove Jackson back into the bank.

"The beef's on!" Whitey shouted as he ran through the bank to the front door. When Harrington tried to follow, the bandit yelled, "Get back in there and keep him covered!" He then backed cautiously out the front door and into the road, awash in yellow light from the bank's front windows and from the two nearby street lights.

When Jackson reached the middle of the road, he was greeted with a fusillade of shotgun fire from the Mercantile building and from the Harrison Garage. The robber dropped to his knees and cried, "I am done! I am through!" Believing that their quarry was wounded and trying to surrender, the possemen stopped shooting. As the shotgun-wielding men rushed into the street, Jackson crawled out of the pool of light, under a barbed-wire fence, and escaped into the blackness on the west side of the road.

Surprised possemen shot blindly into the empty field to the west. They then returned to the middle of the road to find the robber's cap, his blood-soaked pistol, three blood-splattered bags of silver coins, and some silver dollars pierced by shotgun pellets. (These artifacts currently comprise a display in the Thompson-Hickman Museum in Virginia City.) Somewhere from the ink-black field, they heard Varnes call out, "Did they get you, Whitey?"

While Sheriff Metzel frantically tried to deploy his troops in a search pattern, Varnes found Jackson in the pitch-dark pasture. He helped his wounded, bleeding cohort to crawl to the south, toward the depot. However, upon reaching Harrington's car, they found the ignition empty; Ralph had purposely pocketed the keys. So the fugitive pair disappeared again into the dark safety of the open field and began to work their way north, toward the Yellowstone Trail (a.k.a. U.S. Highway #10).

Undersheriff Dale ordered several of the posse to get their cars from the Harrison Garage and to train their headlamps into the escape field west of the county road. After about ten minutes, Metzel told "Babe" Nicholson and T. E. Williams to position Williams' car near the depot and to shine its lights on Harrington's car. The pair followed these directions, but, by that time, the bandits had come and gone. Metzel and his undersheriff then used the sheriff's car to patrol the streets of Harrison, looking for the crooks.

Suddenly a closed sedan, with two passengers, broke from a pocket of darkness under the cottonwood trees, north of the Harrison Garage. It roared through the crime scene in front of the bank, and it raced out the road to Pony. Believing they had flushed out the yeggs, Metzel and Dale fired their shotguns at the retreating auto, shattering its rear window, perforating its back end, and creating a slow leak in one rear tire.

The lawmen followed the car a short way up the Pony Road, but then returned to Harrison to secure a more powerful vehicle. This time Sheriff Metzel hopped into cashier Bleck's Chrysler coupe and the pair sped west, into the darkness. Undersheriff Dale—who harbored doubts about Metzel's identification of the suspect car—took a couple of possemen and drove the eight miles north to cover the Leib Corner intersection of the Harrison Road and the Yellowstone Trail.

Dale's doubts were well-founded. The occupants of the closed sedan were not the bank robbers, but two teenage boys: sixteen-year-old Buddy Young, the son of Mercantile owner Sam Young, and his seventeen-year-old friend Harold Marshall. Buddy had heard his father discuss the ambush plan at the supper table on Monday evening, and he concluded that he and his best friend Harold should witness the event. So Buddy had driven the family Buick out to pick up Harold, and they had returned to Harrison to park in the dark, up the road from the bank.

From this vantage point, the boys observed the shootout and the escape of Varnes and Jackson. But, when the posse began sweeping the area, they panicked. All Buddy could think was to escape from the hunters. So he started the car, roared down the road, and turned at the Pony intersection.

The shotgun blast that shattered their rear window terrified the boys even more. As they sped west, the pair was convinced that they were being chased by the bank robbers. Nevertheless, when the lights chasing them disappeared, the boys quickly changed the flat rear tire on the powerful car. At the Johnson Road "T," Buddy Young swung north, crossed Antelope Creek, and pulled into the front yard of rancher Clarence Bell. He parked the Buick under a row of cottonwood trees, near a line of sheds. The house was well-lit because, coincidentally, this was the refuge where Jim Kreigh and his wife had been hiding out for two days.

The boys rushed up on the porch and blurted out their predicament. Forty-three-year-old Clarence Bell armed the boys and took down his own pump shotgun. He ordered Jim Kreigh to take the women and children upstairs and to keep the lights out on the second floor. Buddy, Harold, and Clarence then sequestered themselves behind some lilac bushes near the front porch and awaited the robbers' automobile.

Sheriff Metzel and Fred Bleck picked up the escaping car's tracks on the Pony Road and followed them through the Johnson Road "T," right into the front yard of Clarence Bell. Metzel recognized "the robbers'" sedan as the one he had fired at in town. He searched it and then, finding it empty, climbed the front-porch steps with Bleck.

Crouched in the bushes, what Bell and the boys saw was a dark coupe pull into the yard and park near the tool shed. In the shadowy night, two men ("the robbers") packing shotguns then approached the pellet-riddled Buick and searched it. Briskly they climbed the porch steps and were silhouetted against the light from within the house.

Just as Fred Bleck pounded on the front door, Frank Metzel heard some rustling in the bushes. He turned and discharged two shotgun blasts into the darkness. Clarence Bell returned the fire. His shotgun pattern caught Metzel flush in the chest and dropped him on the porch. A single #6 pellet tore into Bleck's neck.

Only when Fred knelt beside the sheriff and Clarence emerged from the pitch-black night did the men recognize their ghastly mistake. Ironically, Clarence Bell and Frank Metzel had been the closest of friends for thirty years.

Despite his wound, Fred helped Clarence load Frank Metzel into Bleck's car and the trio sped off toward Whitehall. However, the sheriff died en route—before they could reach the office of Dr. L. R. Packard. The physician was able to remove the single pellet of #6 shot from Bleck's neck.

Almost immediately on Monday night, Madison County authorities were overwhelmed with offers of assistance from law-enforcement officers across Montana. As soon as word of the robbery and the fatal shooting had been telephoned to Butte, Chief Jere Murphy deployed a shotgun squad to set a roadblock on the Yellowstone Trail at Pipestone Pass, in case the yeggs had stolen a car and were attempting to reach Butte. Gallatin County lawmen established another roadblock on the Yellowstone Trail near Bozeman, to catch the thieves if they were trying to journey east.

By Tuesday morning, more than two hundred Madison County friends of Sheriff Metzel were combing the roads and fields of the lower Madison and Jefferson Valleys. Within the day, the search extended to a twelve-county area. Despite what the (Butte) *Montana Standard* called "the largest manhunt in the history of Montana," no conclusive trace of either Varnes or the wounded Jackson was uncovered during the next month.

Undersheriff Dale was the most successful. He discovered the tracks of two men who had walked the Northern Pacific right-of-way north from Harrison, toward Sappington. And indeed, these tracks belonged to the felons.

Varnes had helped the bleeding Jackson stumble the ten miles to the Northern Pacific mainline near Sappington—lugging the bank loot with them. Here the pair caught a westbound freight over the Divide into Butte. En route they encountered no lawmen, despite the authorities' contention that the two were (*Bozeman Daily Chronicle*, October 29, 1930) "big-time outlaws, of the type who would hasten to the cover afforded by a larger city [i.e., Butte]."

By dawn on Tuesday, Varnes was driving his auto toward Spokane. Jackson, after recuperating for three days, followed Walt west in his own vehicle. The two robbers would reunite in Spokane a week later to split up the booty.

Despite Whitey Jackson's angry complaint to Fred Bleck that he was running "a chippy outfit," the loot from the 1930 Harrison Bank robbery was respectable. The two thieves carted off a total of $6,348: $2,048 in currency, coins, and bank notes; $4,300 in Liberty Bonds of various denominations. Jackson had backed out of the bank with $853.24 in "hard money" or silver coins, but he had dropped $692.24 of it in the middle of the road when possemen shot him. Neither the "hard money" balance of $161, nor the $1,877 in currency, nor the $4,300 in negotiable bonds was ever recovered.

For that matter, Montana authorities never caught Whitey Jackson. Most lawmen figured that the felon reached Canada and disappeared there.

However, the Spokane police did arrest Walter Varnes in July 1931 and did return him to Virginia City. Madison County Attorney Frank Blair prosecuted Varnes in November 1931, on the charge of first-degree burglary. This trial ended in a hung jury—primarily because Ralph Harrington refused to return from Los Angeles to testify against Varnes unless Blair paid him inflated witness money.

Retried in March 1932, Walt Varnes was found guilty by a jury of the burglary of the Harrison State Bank. The judge sentenced him to three years in the Deer Lodge State Prison. He was paroled on October 13, 1933.

In Varnes' second trial, Harrington did appear as a state's witness, and his testimony swung the decision against the bandit. In an interview in the (Virginia City) *Madisonian* (April 1, 1932), Ralph maintained:

My motives in helping to plan the robbery and in aiding the officers did not involve a money reward. Just to help to effect the capture of the robbers was, in itself, sufficient reward, since I thought it would assist me in obtaining a [stock-inspector's] position I wanted.

The selfless "undercover agent" failed to inform the interviewer about his deal with the Harrison Bank directors to pay a bounty of $250 on each thief. He also forgot to mention that the same bank directors had provided him with $50 in "expense money" on October 24, *or* that he subsequently had written two letters to them demanding additional expense funds. And, last, he neglected to reveal that those directors had made the final payment of $320.64 on his Willys-Knight coupe-sedan to the Commercial Credit Company in Butte.

In the end, one can argue that Sheriff Metzel paid the ultimate price for his headstrong, election-campaign decision to "take care of this situation myself." Unfortunately, the law officer's actions involved Clarence Bell. Authorities did not charge the rancher with any crime. However, locals still say that Bell never really recovered from the shooting of his lifelong friend on that fateful October night.

Sheriff Metzel is culpable in the case of the Harrison State Bank robbery of 1930—whether or not he believed that he was acting legitimately in the tradition of the Vigilantes of Madison County. The role played by Ralph Harrington involves, clearly, a more convoluted, duplicitous story.

~

Sources

Montana State Prison records (Manuscript Collection 197), held by the Montana Historical Society Archives in Helena, offer some basic information on the felons Walter Varnes and "Whitey" Jackson. *Bulletin #597,* issued by the secretary of the Montana Bankers Association in November, 1930, proved useful in identifying the "official" version of the incident, as well as in describing the stolen property.

Two volumes of local history, compiled by the Madison County History Association, are helpful in providing background details on some of the major players in the Harrison episode: *Madison County: Pioneer Trails and Trials, 1863-1920* (Great Falls: Blue Print and Letter Company, 1976); *Madison County: the*

Progressive Years, 1920-1950 (Butte: Artcraft Printers, 1982). Interestingly, neither volume discusses the Harrison State Bank robbery.

Area newspapers from 1930 to 1932—while sometimes presenting misinformation—are rich sources of detailed information on the robbery and the shooting of Sheriff Metzel. Particularly the (Virginia City) *Madisonian,* the (Butte) *Montana Standard,* and the *Helena Daily Independent* covered the debacle and its aftermath with concern and editorial comment. Perhaps just as important, these papers convey a strong feeling of the times.

Ultimately, however, the most generous source on the topic of the Harrison State Bank robbery is the Montana Supreme Court case *Docket #7031: Harrison State Bank v. United States Fidelity and Guaranty Company and National Surety Company* [94 Montana 100]. The thick case file from this case, held by the Montana Historical Society Library/Archives on microfiche, provides the Supreme Court decision (April 13, 1933), as well as transcripts of the two earlier, lower-court trials. All of the major players in the Harrison events—save Sheriff Frank Metzel and bank-robber Whitey Jackson—appear in these court proceedings and provide exceptional detail about the incident.

Finally, retired Montana district judge Lester H. Loble's writings (held by the Montana Historical Society Archives) were instructive in providing an attorney's perspective on the crimes and the ensuing lawsuits. Loble represented the Harrison State Bank in its unsuccessful attempt to recover its losses from the two insurance companies.

The Naked Truth about Jacob Thorkelson
Seaman, Physician, Congressman, Nazi Sympathizer
by Jon Axline

In the twentieth century, Montana has sent some truly outstanding politicians to Washington, D.C.: Thomas H. Carter, Jeannette Rankin, Burton K. Wheeler, Thomas J. Walsh, Mike Mansfield, Lee Metcalf. To a state sporting such a sparse population, these leaders brought recognition, honor, and respectability.

In contrast, Montana also sent Jacob Thorkelson. The most imaginative fiction writer could not have created "Thorky," as he was known to his few intimates. Prior to joining the U.S. House of Representatives in 1939, Thorkelson had led a swashbuckling life as a seaman, a physician, a small-businessman, the proprietor of a nudist colony (in Butte, at six thousand feet!), and an unremarkable Republican politician.

Once in the House, Thorkelson started ideologically as an arch-conservative and then drifted to the right! His colleagues finally could abide his bizarre rhetoric no longer and denied him the privilege of placing his remarks in the Congressional Record. *Then, on the eve of World War II, German Chancellor Adolf Hitler invited "Thorky" to Berlin for an audience. "Jerkdom" thy name is Thorkelson.*

–Dave Walter

Webster's New Universal Unabridged Dictionary defines "enigma" as "a perplexing, baffling, or seemingly inexplicable matter or person." Dictionary compilers could have illustrated this entry with a portrait of Dr. Jacob Thorkelson of Montana, and no one in the state would have argued. For few Montana politicians have proven as diverse, as compelling, as obscure, or as puzzling as the Butte physician.

Seaman, physician, storyteller, nudist, club-joiner, and knee-jerk fascist—this remarkable fellow had led an exuberant life and had never hesitated to voice his opinions. In 1939 Thorkelson was described by a critic: "[It is] as if he were invented by Joseph Conrad—crinkled eyelids, raw beef-colored complexion, enormous chest, fists like capstans,

. . . [with] a heavy Scandinavian accent." A female supporter lauded him in 1938 as the "Last of the Vikings,"

> an emphatically . . . forthright and downright person. He is frequently blunt, sometimes brusque, but at all times terrifically honest. After talking with him, you go away feeling you have met a "he-man." He has strong convictions, exhaustless initiative, and unlimited courage. He is anything but a pussy-foot. Physically he is rugged. Abstinence from liquors and devotion to regular exercise have preserved in him a reservoir of energy found only in men twenty years younger. [At the time, Thorkelson was sixty-eight years old.]

Jacob Thorkelson was known to his friends as "Tork" or "Thorky." In today's political parlance, he might be called a "super-patriot," or a "militiaman," or a "posse comitatus" member. He regularly displayed some distinctly unsavory ethnic, racial, and political prejudices while serving as Montana's representative to Congress (1939-1941). By the end of his first (and only) term, the congressman had been vilified by the national press, virtually ostracized by his colleagues, and labeled "a glaring embarrassment" by the citizens of Montana.

The Thorkelson controversy continues. Did "Tork" actually believe the propaganda he spread on behalf of the country's home-grown fascist groups? Or was he simply their unwitting dupe in those last days before United States entry into World War II (1941-1945)? The man remains an enigma. If he were bright enough to become a physician, graduating with honors, could he also be the oblivious pawn of the political right?

Jacob Thorkelson was born in Egersund, Norway, in 1876. At age fifteen he left home for a life at sea, eventually commanding some of America's last commercial sailing vessels. He later claimed that he once had lived on "boiled seaboots and flying fish caught with the ship's bucket, while becalmed in the South Atlantic." He also boasted that, while a seaman, he had enjoyed an audience with the Pope and had "broken bread with the Hidden Buddha in the Temples of Tibet."

At the outbreak of the Spanish-American War (1898), Thorkelson enlisted in the U.S. Navy. He most distinguished himself during Admiral George Dewey's homecoming celebration in Washington, D.C. On this occasion, Thorkelson loudly harangued his Virginian crew because they refused to salute the tomb of Union General Ulysses S.

Jacob Thorkelson.

PHOTO FROM *MONTANA: ITS STORY AND BIOGRAPHY*, EDITED BY TOM STOUT
(CHICAGO: AMERICAN HISTORICAL SOCIETY, 1921)

Grant. Although sources conflict, Thorkelson became a naturalized U.S. citizen sometime between 1900 and 1906.

Perhaps because of an intestinal problem that he suffered while at sea (perchance from eating the boiled sea boots?), Jacob enrolled in the University of Maryland's College of Physicians and Surgeons in 1907. After graduating with honors from that institution in 1911, he became a professor of anatomy at the school. In 1913, at the age of thirty-seven, the physician migrated to Montana.

He first settled in Dillon, opened a private practice, and served as the Beaverhead County physician. In 1918 he removed to Anaconda. Here, in addition to his own practice, he became the chief surgeon at the nearby Warm Springs State Hospital. An inveterate "joiner," Jacob belonged to at least thirteen civic and professional clubs. These included the Masons, the Odd Fellows, the Elks, the American Medical Association, and the Explorers Club of New York.

In 1920 Thorkelson relocated his practice in Butte. This move provided him the opportunity to indulge some of his other interests. In 1930 he and former creamery manager Fred Ackerman established the Butte Neon Outdoor Advertising Company. By 1938 this business employed fifteen people. Thorkelson became the company's president, and Ackerman served as its general manager.

In 1933 "Thorky" and Ackerman established a nudist colony on the Butte Flats. They purchased an existing house and remodeled it into a clinic. They surrounded the building with a park, which they landscaped for nude sunbathing.

The idea for the nudist camp was derived from a fad then sweeping Germany. Called "Naked Clubs," these groups first appeared in the 1920s, as a way of maintaining one's spiritual and physical health by getting close to nature. Although the clubs were the subject of much titillating speculation in the American press, a number of nudist camps subsequently appeared in this country, based on the German model.

Thorkelson was a practitioner of this "back to nature" philosophy. He later defended it by stating, "I have advocated fresh air and sunshine for many cases, because leading progressive doctors today recognize that fresh air and sunshine frequently can do much more than can pills or the operating table."

Unlike directors of the German clubs, however, Thorkelson and Ackerman separated the sexes into designated sunbathing areas. In Butte, the sexes (as far as such reports can be trusted) were not allowed to commingle. The camp operated for only two years (1933-1935).

Then the clinic burned down, under mysterious circumstances. Today the site of the Butte Flats camp still exists—as a small wrecking yard, enclosed by the trees and shrubs planted by Thorkelson and Ackerman to protect Butte nudists from curious eyes.

Thorkelson's arrival in Butte—Montana's "Mining City"—also signaled his entry into state Republican politics. Evidence suggests that he did not support Republican President Herbert Hoover (1929-1933) or his virtual "do-nothing policies," practiced in the early years of the Great Depression (1929-1939). Indeed, he championed Democrat President Franklin Delano Roosevelt (FDR; 1933-1945), *until* the President moved to "pack" the Supreme Court in 1937.

Jacob Thorkelson claimed that he was a liberal. However, he was, in fact, an ultra-conservative—one who believed in a decidedly literal interpretation of the first twelve amendments to the Constitution. He was also a rabid isolationist, an anticommunist, and an anti-Semite. In 1938 he became a pawn in the battle between two Butte Democrats: U.S. Senator Burton K. Wheeler and freshman Congressman Jerry O'Connell.

An outspoken radical-liberal, O'Connell had split with Wheeler over the 1937 "court packing" issue. He chastised the senator for criticizing President Roosevelt's plan to appoint additional judges to the Supreme Court—judges who would support FDR's New Deal programs. O'Connell threatened that he, with the President's assistance, would take Wheeler's Senate seat from him in the 1940 election.

In retaliation, an angry Wheeler fired up his Montana political machine to ensure that O'Connell was not re-elected to Congress in 1938. The Wheeler camp threw its support to the Republican Thorkelson—like Wheeler, an avowed isolationist. "Thorky" further believed that the United States could be revitalized by means of Constitutional reform and the wholesale "house-cleaning" of the federal government, rather than through the New Deal.

Wheeler likely backed the sixty-two-year-old Thorkelson because the Republican supported Dr. Francis Townsend's old-age pension bill. The two Montanans also shared some of the same anti-interventionist principles promoted by the America First Committee. Most important, Thorkelson was the ideological opposite of the radical O'Connell. The Wheeler forces wisely enlisted Butte radio entrepreneur Ed Craney to run "Thorky's" campaign.

The 1938 House race between O'Connell and Thorkelson was particularly bitter. Although the tenets of O'Connell's platform are somewhat difficult to determine, no such problem exists with Jacob Thorkelson's beliefs. He presented himself as a self-made country doctor who was worried about America's downward political, economic, and moral spiral. Like many of the radio demagogues of today, he used the medium to prey on the emotions of prospective voters.

As a staunch isolationist, "Tork" was against any entangling alliances between the U.S. and either Great Britain or France. The country, he proclaimed, was overly dependent on foreign imports—especially those from British territories. Further, he believed that New Deal social-welfare programs were increasingly forcing American farmers and factory workers to depend on the federal government. This dependance, a strident Thorkelson preached, made Americans more vulnerable to communism.

During the campaign, the candidate gave numerous public speeches and radio talks addressing the sad state of the Constitution. He was a loud and boisterous supporter of "American-style democracy," and he claimed direct political kinship with John Adams and Thomas Jefferson. Thorkelson honestly believed that many of the country's problems could be traced to the Seventeenth Amendment. This amendment established the *popular* election of U.S. senators, rather than election by a state's legislators. Ironically, the corrupt 1899 election of Montanan William A. Clark to the U.S. Senate initially had propelled the passage of the Seventeenth Amendment.

As the election approached, radio-man Craney produced a series of broadcasts over Butte's KGIR station. These presentations aired, through link-ups, all across Montana's Western Congressional District. In these programs, Thorkelson blasted most of the amendments to the Constitution. He called them "unnecessary wastes of time which did nothing but confuse Americans and lure them into a false sense of security."

The Republican said that the country would be best served by fostering a second American Revolution—one that would return it to the course set by the Founding Fathers. The real problem, he maintained, was not with President Roosevelt, but with the corrupt "yes men" and "racketeers" rife in the federal bureaucracy. Not surprisingly, "Thorky" also blamed many of the nation's problems on those "hyphenated" Americans (particularly Jews) who had immigrated to the United States after the Nazis took power in Germany in 1933.

Although Thorkelson wanted to conduct a "clean" campaign, his

Democrat opponent initiated the fine art of mud-slinging. Jerry O'Connell ridiculed Thorkelson's heavy Norwegian accent, questioned his citizenship, and cast aspersions on the Republican's medical ability. Thorkelson's dedication to nudism also became prime fodder for the incumbent's attack. O'Connell bragged that the election contest really pitted the Democrats' "NEW Deal" against Thorkelson's "NUDE Deal."

So, perhaps at the recommendation of Ed Craney, Thorkelson began to attack O'Connell's character, his abuse of Congressional privilege, and his receding hairline. He derided the incumbent's young age (twenty-nine years), his lack of experience, and his service in the Communist-backed "Abraham Lincoln Brigade" at the beginning of the Spanish Civil War (1936). He also accused O'Connell of cavorting with "bored and pampered, pink [i.e., Communist] movie stars."

Thorkelson charged that O'Connell had filled the Butte office of the Federal Works Projects Administration (WPA) with his supporters— and that he had suggested to others in the office that they should vote for him if they wished to keep their jobs after the election. "Thorky" even condoned the composition and distribution of a little ditty called "Jerry the Bald," in reference to the incumbent's lack of hair.

In November 1938, Thorkelson was elected to the U.S. House of Representatives by a significant margin over O'Connell (49,253 to 41,319). His next two years in Congress would feature exceptionally wordy inserts in the *Congressional Record*. Many of these diatribes railed against Congress and Jews; others advocated strong Constitutional reform.

Although Thorkelson was consistently vigorous in his condemnation of the New Deal and of FDR's foreign policy, little evidence suggests that he was much concerned with Montana's interests. Within months of his election, he managed to alienate both his Congressional colleagues and many of his Western District constituents. Specifically they were irked by his feverish preaching and by his public association with the more reactionary elements of the America First Committee and of other isolationist groups then active in the United States.

Unlike other freshmen Congressmen, Thorkelson was not content to "keep [his] mouth shut, learn the ropes, do jobs for [his] constituents, and let nature take its course." Within days of his inauguration (January 1939), "Thorky" began inserting voluminous extensions of his remarks into the *Congressional Record*.

By mid-July, he had placed twenty-two speeches into the *Record*.

Not surprisingly, most of these pieces dealt with the unconstitutionality of the U.S. Constitution, problems with the gold standard, the dire threat of foreign imports, and what he believed was America's "drift to dictatorship."

All too soon, Representative Thorkelson's bombastic condemnations of the New Deal and the Constitution assumed a darker and a more frightening tone. In an insert to the *Record* on May 1, 1939, Thorkelson asked for one minute to address the House on the issue of Native American civil rights. Instead, he launched into an extended harangue on the threat of the "Invisible Government"—a secret cabal of men "who are willing to sacrifice peace to satisfy an insane desire for power by the control of our Nation's monetary wealth."

According to Thorkelson, the "Invisible Government" was composed of Jews, most of whom had immigrated to this country after Hitler seized power in Germany. Further, he contended that most of these Jews were communists. The "Invisible Government," he concluded, represented an even graver threat to the United States than did the Nazis.

> I do not believe that the so-called "Hebrew purge" in Germany is a cause for war. As a matter of fact, it is none of our business. I question the truthfulness of many of the statements published in our newspapers, for I find upon investigation that German-Hebrews are in a better position in Germany than many of our people in the United States. Furthermore, I do not believe that we should meddle in German affairs or in the disposition of her citizens. We have plenty to do at home, and we should evict aliens instead of receiving them with open arms, as we are now doing. . . . I am firmly convinced that Hebrews with German citizenship prefer to remain in Germany.

Thorkelson's "facts" were derived from Nazi-German newspapers that American fascist organizations fed to him. Based on these same sources, the Congressman demanded that the U.S. government stop using motion pictures to distribute information because, he said, these studios were controlled by the "Invisible Government."

Throughout the month of May, Thorkelson contributed weekly inserts to the *Congressional Record* condemning the Jewish-backed "Invisible Government." At the same time, his congressional colleagues and his Montana constituents increased their attacks on him. "Thorky" soon believed that he had become the victim of vicious propaganda engineered by the Roosevelt administration and by the "Invisible Government." Nevertheless, he continued his verbal assault on "the true enemies of the American Way of Life."

In *Record* remarks, Thorkelson referred to Jewish immigrants as the "rot and filth of the alleys and byways of Europe." He complained that U.S. immigration laws were a "deliberate attempt by which international money-mad fanatics expect to take charge of the United States, so that it may be converted into a home for themselves and their strange un-American cults."

Finally, he threatened a "day of reckoning, a day of liquidation [when] the people should mark those who have been instrumental in sending our nation and our people on the road to poverty and destruction." He predicted that the revolution would occur sometime during 1940.

The Congressman never did believe that Nazi Germany was a threat to the U.S.—because "our political philosophies are so dissimilar, [so] why worry about it." Besides, he reasoned, Europe had nothing we could possibly want.

This significant, strident change in "Tork's" rhetoric makes it likely that his early floor speeches and *Record* inserts had drawn the attention of some of the country's ultraconservative isolationist groups. For the remainder of his term in office, Thorkelson's name was inextricably linked with organizations like the America First Committee, the Christian Front, the Knights of the White Camellia, Fritz Kuhn's German-American Bund, and William Dudley Pelley's Silver Shirts.

One man from this clique, retired Major General George Van Horne Moseley, publicly advocated the use of U.S. military force to round up American liberals, communists, and Jews. He explained that these people had infiltrated and now controlled the federal government. Moseley, whom Thorkelson considered "a patriot," was the source of the Congressman's call for a revolution against the New Deal. To demonstrate his support, "Thorky" sat next to the general while Moseley was interrogated by Martin Dies' House Un-American Activities Committee, then investigating subversives in the U.S. government.

Neither Thorkelson's association with these isolationist fringe groups, nor his use of the *Congressional Record* to promote their agenda, escaped notice in Washington, D.C. and Montana. In late June 1939,

House Majority Leader Sam Rayburn (D-Texas), Jewish Congressman Adolf J. Sabath (D-Illinois), and other House members attempted to prevent Thorkelson from placing any additional inserts in the *Record*.

Rayburn contended that Thorkelson was attempting to inflame racial prejudice and intolerance in America, at a time when it was necessary for the country to present a united front to serious overseas threats. Indeed, Rayburn pointedly asked Thorkelson if he were really defending the Constitution by promoting dissension in the U.S. By June 28, Rayburn had garnered sufficient support in the House to temporarily deny Thorkelson access to the *Record*.

In response, Thorkelson accused every ranking Jewish member of the House of Representatives of being a communist or an operative engaged in "un-American activities." When Rayburn questioned him on this point, Thorkelson replied that it was none of the Majority Leader's business what he believed.

When asked by another representative if it were his intention to spread racial prejudice, Thorkelson again responded that that was none of the colleague's business. Representative Sabath concluded the exchange by calling Thorkelson's material "highly obnoxious and bigoted [in] nature. . . ."; he demanded an apology from the Montanan. "Thorky" refused, stating that his material comprised nothing but the Constitutional facts.

Many journalists found Thorkelson's public statements repugnant and bizarre. Nevertheless, they considered him a decent human being at heart—one who naively was being fed highly selective information by several fringe isolationist groups. Both the inflammatory nature of the material presented by Thorkelson in Congress and his inarticulate responses to questions and to criticism bears out this analysis.

The writer Bruce Catton—who thought Thorkelson was a "swell" person—defended him by saying, "The lunatic fringe deluges him with phone calls, letters, and personal appearances, and he is getting shoved over into the camp which blames everything on the radical—and then assumes that all the radicals are Jews." Catton concluded his appraisal of Thorkelson by urging him to get back on track before the physician irrevocably ruined his political career.

The editor of the *Great Falls Tribune*, however, was neither so kind nor so forgiving. The newspaper regularly published editorials about Thorkelson, labeling him an "intolerant fanatic." Many of these pieces cited the embarrassment suffered by Montana citizens and by the state's Republican Party because of Thorkelson's actions.

The *Tribune* never did take Thorkelson seriously. In an editorial entitled "Why Not Run Thorky for President?" the editor stated that the Congressman

> . . . started erupting Constitutional decisions the minute he struck Washington and has never ceased since that eventful day. . . . Everything in Washington is unconstitutional—the President, the popularly-elected Senate, the Supreme Court, and parts of the Constitution itself. . . .The least that the Montana Republicans could do now that they have presented this thundering statesman to the nation is to nominate him for the Presidency, . . . [although] we would hate to be deprived of [his] astute counsel. . . .

Through 1939, Thorkelson's remarks earned him regular, unflattering publicity in the national press. Yet it took an incident in October of that year to generate the most controversy. On October 13, "Thorky" placed in the *Congressional Record* a letter purportedly written by Colonel Edward House in 1919, twenty years earlier. House—at that time, President Woodrow Wilson's aide to British Prime Minister David Lloyd George—proposed a plan for the peaceful reunification of the American colonies with Great Britain.

Thorkelson presented the "House letter" as proof that the two nations long had been plotting a liaison that would compromise U.S. sovereignty. He charged that the current Roosevelt administration was in collusion with British authorities, and he accused FDR of deliberately trying to provoke war with the Axis powers. When asked by Representative Robert E. Thomason (D-Texas) if Colonel House had actually signed the letter, Thorkelson stated that he did not know.

Congressional staff members soon discovered that the "Colonel House letter" was a fake, written as a joke in 1920 by an Irish-American. An embarrassed Representative Thorkelson withdrew the letter from the *Record*. Yet, even in defeat, he defensively maintained that "had [Colonel House] been seized by a desire to write Mr. Lloyd George, this letter express[ed] what he would have said."

Before the letter had been withdrawn, however, Representative John Martin (D-Colorado) demanded that the House permanently revoke Thorkelson's privilege to insert material into the *Congressional Record*. In reply, Thorkelson asked the House not to condemn him because ". . . the majority of the House had been condemning the

American people for the last seven years."

The "House letter" incident provoked almost universal censure of Thorkelson. *Time* magazine claimed that the doctor's already low popularity in Congress hit rock bottom with the letter's publication.

At a press conference held shortly after the Montanan withdrew the letter, *Time* reported that ". . . the Butte doctor said that he had the 'Colonel House letter' printed to find out whether it was true. He then reverted to his regular theme . . ." of attacking the communists and Jews. The *Nation* also dismissed him—not as a true fascist, but, instead, as a "true-blown representative of Thorkelsonianism." The *Great Falls Tribune* called the "Colonel House letter" Thorkelson's "weirdest effort to receive publicity."

For the rest of his term (to January 1941), Thorkelson continued to attack the communists, the Jews, the constitutionality of the federal government, and the nation's policies involving the Axis powers. For example, he criticized the Federal Bureau of Investigation's (FBI) scrutiny of the German-American Bund and of the Silver Shirts.

"Thorky" publicly supported the formation of the German-Italian-Japanese alliance in 1940—stating that it would control the destiny of Europe, Asia, and parts of Africa. He also condemned the Anti-Nazi League (ANL) as a Jewish organization. And he questioned why the ANL always hid behind the Catholics and the Protestants in the United States, instead of openly taking their own stand.

In June 1940, Hans Thomsen of the German Embassy in the United States informed his superiors in Berlin that Adolf Hitler had granted Thorkelson an interview. Thomsen stated that a transcript of that interview would be published in the June 22 *Congressional Record*. Apparently, however, Montana's representative retained enough good sense to turn down *Der Führer's* offer.

In the midst of all this adverse publicity, his plummeting support in Montana, and the numerous death threats made against him, Thorkelson declared his bid for reelection to the House in 1940.

Just after this announcement, Representative Sabath called Thorkelson a "tool of designing men" who were trying to inflame the American people against the Jews, the Catholics, and the Blacks. He also accused the Butte doctor of sponsoring reprints of his *Congressional Record* remarks for the benefit of "certain subversive organizations." In truth, "Thorky" had only authorized the reprint of his remarks for William Dudley Pelley's Silver Shirts—although he then complained that the cover of the group's thick pamphlet was too reminiscent of a cheap Western novel.

Sabath's remarks were delivered just prior to the House's adjournment for spring break, on May 8, 1940. Although Thorkelson rarely spoke on the floor of the House, he curiously chose this time to defend himself against Sabath's remarks.

To an audience of only eight representatives, "Tork" responded to Sabath. The *Great Falls Tribune* called the defense a "rambling and virulent" outburst in which Thorkelson made a "disgusting exhibition of himself." Truth must have supported the *Tribune's* statement, because the House adjourned in the middle of the Congressman's speech. Thorkelson returned to Montana shortly thereafter. Fellow Republicans gave him the cold shoulder at their state convention in Kalispell, by pointedly failing to invite him to speak to the assembly.

To no one's surprise, Thorkelson did not win the 1940 Republican primary—being beaten by Jeannette Rankin. Nevertheless he maintained his political ambitions and his unconventional perspective concerning the Constitution. He ran for the U.S. Senate in 1942 and for the governor's office in 1944, losing both primary elections by significant margins.

Through this 1940-1945 period, "Thorky" continued to lecture Montanans on the Constitution and on the communist threat posed by the Democratic Party. Although he pledged his support for the U.S. war effort after the Japanese attack on Pearl Harbor (1941), Thorkelson clearly remained uneasy about the war in Europe and about the U.S. alliance with the Soviets.

On November 18, 1945, Jacob Thorkelson died of a heart attack that he had suffered three days earlier in Butte. And even in death, he remains an enigma. His skills as a seaman and as a physician—indeed his prowess as Montana's most prominent nudist (apologies to John Colter)—are indisputable. However, his opinions about the U.S. Constitution were naive, and his choice of Washington associates was politically short-sighted, even foolish.

It is difficult to determine if "Thorky" actually believed the gibberish that he presented in the *Congressional Record*. Time after time, he was unable to respond to questions about those insertions. Congressman Thorkelson probably was neither a true fascist nor a Nazi, but he was definitely clueless. "Montana's most prominent enigma"—one hell of an epitaph.

Sources

For the most part, Jacob Thorkelson himself (posthumously, of course) provided the best source of information for this chapter. The papers of Ed Craney, "Thorky's" campaign manager, contain personal information provided by Thorkelson to Craney in 1938. These files contain extensive information about his life, his political beliefs, and, more subtly, how he was able to win the election. The Ed Craney papers (Manuscript Collection 122: the Edmund B. Craney Collection) are housed at the Montana Historical Society in Helena. See there also complementary documents in: Manuscript Collection 182: the Barclay Craighead Papers.

Other resource materials include articles in national news magazines—such as *The Nation, Time,* and *Newsweek*—and frequent editorials in the *Great Falls Tribune.* (Thorkelson is rarely mentioned in his hometown newspaper, the [Butte] *Montana Standard.*) However, perhaps the best source of "Thorkelsoniana" is contained in his frequent inserts in the *Congressional Record* (Washington, D.C.: General Printing Office, 1939-1941).

Finally, the genesis of this chapter was a 1991 Montana Department of Transportation road-reconstruction project. Part of the project required an inventory of all the historical sites along Butte's Holmes Avenue. In this process, it was observed that Thorkelson's old nudist camp was located close enough to Holmes Avenue to be considered eligible for the National Register of Historic Places. From that small spark, Thorkelson's "jerk" nomination ultimately results.

Author Biographies

Jon Axline earned an M.A. in American history from Montana State University in Bozeman in 1985. After working several years in museums and for a cultural resource firm, he took a position (1990) as the historian for the Montana Department of Transportation in Helena. Jon is currently the manager of the department's highway historical-marker program and supervises its historic-roads-and-bridges program. He is a co-author of all three volumes of the Helena local-history series, *More from the Quarries of Last Chance Gulch* (1995, 1996, 1998). Jon's work for the department led him to the nudist-camp site of Jacob Thorkelson, outside Butte. His other contributions to this volume address Calamity Jane Canary, Butte's Ed Morrissey, and the Reverend Leonard Christler.

Salina Davis is a native of Spokane, Washington. After graduating from high school in Spokane, she enrolled at Carroll College in Helena, Montana. In 1997 Salina received dual B.A.s in history and psychology from Carroll, where she first researched and wrote the tale of "Montana's First Unabomber." Salina currently is pursuing her M.A. in public and U.S. history at Washington State University in Pullman. In search of a thesis topic, she is seeking someone—anyone—as intriguing as Ike Gravelle.

Jodie Foley was born and raised in Missoula. She attended the University of Montana, studying at the undergraduate and the graduate levels, from 1983 to 1990. Jodie left Missoula in 1990 to fill an opening with the Montana Historical Society Archives in Helena. In 1993 she was promoted to her current position of Archivist/Oral Historian. Jodie is the co-author of *Speaking of Montana: A Guide to the Oral History Collection of the Montana Historical Society* (1997). Her piece on Mary Gleim stems from graduate research she conducted on historical prostitution in Missoula.

Lyndel Meikle is a Montana native and National Park Service ranger. She generally concentrates her research on the history of Grant-Kohrs Ranch National Historic Site in Deer Lodge, Montana, where she has worked since 1976. Lyndel's discovery and editing of the memoirs of John Francis Grant, published as *Very Close to Trouble* (1996), have added new dimension to the history of Montana's territorial days. She also has written a weekly newspaper column, "Back at the Ranch," since 1982. Lyndel's topics—Crow Indian agents, timber depredations, Montana's 1889 Constitutional Convention, and the Deer Lodge valley "smoke wars"—have provided an enjoyable diversion from her primary focus on the West's frontier cattle era.

Anne Sturdevant was born in Illinois and moved with her family to Great Falls, Montana, at the age of two. She graduated from C. M. Russell High in 1987 and from Carroll College in Helena in 1991. The following year Anne began graduate studies at Washington State University in Pullman, where she also earned a Washington State teaching certificate. She has been teaching on the high-school level in Vancouver, Washington, since 1996, and accepting summer teaching positions overseas. Anne developed her interest in the Montana Ku Klux Klan while working with Dr. Robert Swartout at Carroll. She will expand that material into an M.A. thesis under Dr. Leroy Ashby at Washington State in 2000.

Dave Walter graduated from Wesleyan University (Connecticut) in 1965 and spent ten years working with Montana historian K. Ross Toole at the University of Montana in Missoula. He joined the staff of the Montana Historical Society in Helena in 1979, where he currently serves as the Research Historian. Since 1983 Dave has contributed a regular Montana-history column to *Montana Magazine,* and he is the author of several books, including *Today Then* (1992) and *Montana Campfire Tales* (1997). Dave's work on Montana's endless supply of "jerks"—including Sir St. George Gore, the Carlin hunting party, and the Harrison Bank robbery participants—represents a lifelong commitment.

INDEX

Page references in *italics* indicate photographs.
Page references in **bold** refer to a table.

Browning, Captain George Leslie
  Browning, 32
Buffalo Girls (McMurtry), 50
Bureau of Indian Affairs (BIA), 25
Burns, C. P. "Bobby," 92–95, 96
Butte copper mines, 116–117
Butte Daily Bulletin, 135, 136,
  138, 140, 141, 142–143
Butte Daily Miner, 67, 125, 134,
  140, 171
Butte Daily Post, 125
Butte Neon Outdoor Advertising
  Company, 194
Butte Police Department. *See*
  Morrissey, Ed
Butte Reveille, 125
Byrne, Nora, 134, 135

C

"Calamity Jane." *See* Canary,
  Martha
*Calamity Jane: A Study in
  Historical Criticism* (Sollid), 51
California and Oregon Trail, The
  (Parkman), 9
Callaway, James E., 68, 69
Canary, Martha "Calamity Jane,"
  50–61
  as alcoholic, 51, 53, 55, 57, 59,
    60
  appearance of, 52–53, 56–57,
    58
  Bill Hickok and, 55–56, 60
  "Black Hills Florence
    Nightingale," 54
  careers of, 53–54
  children of, 55, 59
  death of, 56, 60
  fund for, 59
  as heroine, 52, 53, 56
  jail time of, 60
  Jane Hickok McCormick hoax,
    55

  marital status, 55
  as prostitute, 52, 53, 54
  rejection of, 59
  as sideshow attraction, 56–57
  as vigilante, 54–55
Carleton, Frank, 146, 147, 148–
  149, 151, 156, 157, 158–159
Carleton, Margaret Davenport
  Lotz, 144, 145–147, 148, 149,
  150, 151, 155, 159, 160
Carlin hunting party in the
  Lochsa, 72–84
  Abraham Lincoln Artman
    "Abe" Himmelwright, 74,
    75, 77, 78, 81, *82*, 83
  Ben Keeley, 75, 76, 77, 78, *82*
  camps, 75, *77*, 78
  George Colgate, 74, 75, 76, 77,
    78, 79–80, 81, 83
  Jerry Johnson, 75, 76, 77, 78,
    79, 83
  John Harvey Pierce, 74, 76, 77,
    78, *82*, 83
  Lolo Trail's ruggedness, 73, 75,
    76
  Martin P. Spencer, 74, 76, 77,
    78, 81, *82*, 83
  rescue, 80–81
  weather and, 75–77, 78, 79, 80
  William Edward "Will" Carlin,
    73–74, 76, 77, 78, 79, 80, *82*,
    83
  William H. Wright, 80, 81, 83
  William P. Carlin, 73, 80–81
Carr, William, 31
Carter, Thomas H., 43, 63–64
Catholics hatred by Ku Klux
  Klan, 165
cattle rustling, 30–31, 100–101
Catton, Bruce, 200
Chapman, Father Charles, 149,
  151, 152
Chatillon, Henry, 9, 10, 13

E

economy
greed, 118, 121, 123, 125–126,
128, 129
uncertainty and Ku Klux Klan,
164, 171
Egan, Lieutenant James "Teddy,"
52
"Eighth Baronet of Manor Gore."
See Gore, Sir St. George
Elling, Karl, 179, 181
Elliott, Lieutenant Charles P., 80,
83
Evans, Hiram Wesley (Imperial
Wizard), 163, 168

F

Faber, Bishop William, 147–148,
157, 158
Fee, Charles, 102
Fitzhugh, Harley, 180, 182
foreign-born issues, 64–66
Forest Reserve Act (1891), 44
Forrest, Nathan Bedford, 163
Fort Gore, 14, 15, 16
Fort Union, 15–16, 17
Foss, Carl Foss, 144, 148, 152,
154, 155
"Freemen," 1, 2
Free Timber Act (1878), 39, 41,
42
"French Emma," 95
Front Street in Missoula, 87, *88*
Frost, George W., 26, **31**, 32
Fulton, Charles W., 46

G

Gillmore, Robert P., 167, 168
Gleim, John Edgar, 86–87
Gleim, Mary Gleeson, 85–98
alcoholism of, 88, 90
C. P. "Bobby" Burns' attempted
murder by, 92–95, 96

death of, 96–97
enemies of, 88–89, 90–91, 92–
94, 95, 96
Front Street in Missoula, 87,
88
John Edgar Gleim and, 86–87
madams in history, 85, 86, 97
marriage of, 86–87
Patrick Mason and, 92, 93, 94
prostitution in history, 85–86,
97
rage of, 88, 89, 90, 92, 95, 96
trials, 93–96
wealth of, 86–87, 88, *89*, 96–97
William Reed and, 92, 94
goods never delivered fraud,
28, 30
Gore, Sir St. George "Slob
Hunter," 7–23, *12*
American Fur Company
(AFC), 8, 9, 10, 13, 15, 16,
17, 18, 19
Black Hills expedition, 20–21
burning surplus goods, 18–19
cost of expeditions, 22
Crows and, 14, 15, 17
eating habits of, 13, 14–15
food supply depletion by, 15,
17
Fort Gore, 14, 15, 16
Fort Union, 15–16, 17
Great Plains tours, 8–17
Henry Chatillon and, 9, 10, 13
Hidatsas and, 21–22
hunting hounds, 11, 20, 21, 22
hunting of, 13, 14, 15, 16, *16*,
20, 22
James Kipp and, 15, 17, 18, 19
Jim Bridger "Old Gabe" and,
10, 13, 14, 15, 19, 20, 21
luxuries of, 10–13, 14
retribution, 20–22
selling surplus goods, 17–18

Toole, Joseph K., 41–42, 69–70, 102, 105, 112–113, 123
Toole, K. Ross, 4
Torpey, Joe, 136, 141
Townley, Charles, 55
Turner, Robert T., 4

U
"Unabomber, The" (Ted Kaczynski), 1, 2, 99, 100. *See also* Gravelle, Ike
Uno's burial, 15

V
Varnes, Walter, 177, *178*, 179, 184, 185, 187, 188
Vaughn, Alfred, 17
Villard, Henry, 40
voters' intimidation by police, 135–136
vote-selling, 65

W
Walker, I. N., 60
Walker, L. A., 62
Wallace, William, Jr., 108, 109, 110
Walsh, Thomas J., 153, 168
"War of the Copper Kings," 43
Warren, Charles, 65–66
Warren, Otey Yancy, 125
Washington Post, 1, 25
Washoe Smelter, 119, 121
Weiss, Charles, 136, 139
Wentworth-Fitzwilliam, Sir William Thomas Spencer "Lord Fitzwilliam," 9, 10, 11, 13
Western News (Libby), 125
Weston, Rusty, Jr., 1, 2
Wheeler, Burton K., 195
White, Stewart Edward, 145

Whitehill, Henry, 69
Whitten, Harvey, 101–102, 103, 113, 115
Williams, A. E., 155
Williams, T. E., 185
Wittenberg, David, 139–140
Womack, James Emmett, 180
women's issues, 64, 65, 68–70
Wood, Joseph K., 93
Workingman's Party, 66–67
Wright, James, 26, **31**, 32
Wright, William H., 80, 81, 83

Y
Young, Buddy, 186
Young, Samuel S., 179, 180, 181, 182, 183, 184